Essential Test Tips Video from Trivium Test Prep

Dear Customer,

Thank you for purchasing from Trivium Test Prep! Whether you're looking to join the military, get into college, or advance your career, we're honored to be a part of your journey.

To show our appreciation (and to help you relieve a little of that test-prep stress), we're offering a **FREE *Property Casualty Essential Test Tips* Video** by Trivium Test Prep. Our video includes 35 test preparation strategies that will help keep you calm and collected before and during your big exam. All we ask is that you email us your feedback and describe your experience with our product. Amazing, awful, or just so-so: we want to hear what you have to say!

To receive your **FREE *Property Casualty Essential Test Tips* Video**, please email us at 5star@ triviumtestprep.com. Include "Free 5 Star" in the subject line and the following information in your email:

1. The title of the product you purchased.
2. Your rating from 1 – 5 (with 5 being the best).
3. Your feedback about the product, including how our materials helped you meet your goals and ways in which we can improve our products.
4. Your full name and shipping address so we can send your **FREE *Property Casualty Essential Test Tips* Video**.

If you have any questions or concerns please feel free to contact us directly at 5star@triviumtestprep.com.

Thank you, and good luck with your studies!

Property and Casualty Study Guide and Practice Test Book for the Insurance Licensure Exam [5th Edition]

B. Hettinger

ISBN-13: 9781637985106

Table of Contents

1. Insurance Basics

Basic Definitions

Insurance is an agreement between two parties to provide a predetermined financial benefit for a specified loss, injury, or illness. It offers financial protection for individuals and businesses by reducing or eliminating the risks associated with unexpected events. Insurance is a type of **indemnification**, meaning one party pays for the losses incurred by another party.

An insurance **policy** outlines the agreement's terms, conditions, and scope of coverage. Several distinct sections lay out the details of a policy's coverage:

- **Declarations** define who is insured, the risks that are covered, liability limits, and the length of the policy.
- **Definitions** define the terms used in the policy.
- **Insuring agreements** contain details of the coverage.
- **Endorsements** and **riders** codify changes to the policy.
- **Conditions** list qualifications that must be met for insurance claims to be paid.
- **Exclusions** detail what is NOT covered on the insurance policy.

The person or entity covered by the policy is the **insured**, and the **insurer** is the company that agrees to make the payment. The **policyholder** is financially responsible for the policy and must pay any **premiums**—regular payments that are required to keep the policy in force. Policyholders must also monitor the policy expiration date and inform their insurers of any changes in circumstances that would impact the policy, such as income adjustments and the number of household members who should be covered.

A **claim** is an official request to an insurance provider to fulfill coverage in accordance with the terms outlined in the policy. After a claim is filed, the insurer will determine if a payment will be made based on the terms of the policy.

Quick Review Questions

1) What is the benefit of purchasing an insurance policy?

2) What is indemnification?

Understanding Risk

Risk, Perils, and Hazards

A **risk** is the possibility that something unexpected will cause a financial burden on the insured. The direct cause of the unexpected financial burden is called a **peril**. For example, if an athlete sustains a broken leg while skiing, the broken leg is considered the peril; the sport—skiing—is considered the risk. In property terms, the possibility that a covered item (e.g., a house or business) would be affected by severe weather is considered the risk; the severe weather event is the peril. For example, if hail damages a home's roof, causing a leak, the chance that the weather event will affect the roof is the risk; the hail is the peril.

There are two types of risks: pure and speculative. **Pure risks** *can* be covered by insurance because they involve the likelihood of a future loss beyond the control of the individual or organization facing the risks. Examples of pure risks include

- fire,
- theft,
- sickness, and
- death.

> **Did You Know?**
>
> The higher the risk of an event, the higher the premium the person will pay for insurance coverage. On the other hand, if an insurer perceives a low risk for the occurrence of a particular peril, the premium will be lower.

Speculative risks *cannot* be covered by insurance because they are conscious choices that involve the possibility of a loss *or* a profit and are not necessarily uncontrollable. Speculative risks include

- investing in stocks,
- developing real estate, and
- trading cryptocurrency.

In insurance, a **hazard** is a situation or condition that could cause a dangerous event with an accompanying financial cost to take place. There are three types of insurance hazards: physical hazards moral hazards, and morale hazards.

- **Physical** hazards relate to a policyholder's behaviors or physical characteristics/conditions about the covered item that could contribute to peril. Examples of physical hazards include broken railings on stairs or rotting boards on a building's deck.
- **Moral hazards** are conscious behaviors wherein parties assume additional risk-taking based on the knowledge that they will be financially protected—or even stand to earn money—from the consequences of the risk. Deliberately allowing a business's smoke alarm system to fall into disrepair in the hopes that the building will catch fire is an example of a moral hazard.
- **Morale hazards** describe attitudes of carelessness or indifference that can result in a perilous event; however, the indifference is not geared toward intentionally trying to claim money, which differentiates it from moral hazards. An example of a morale hazard is disregarding inspection notices for the building's HVAC or not paying for snow removal.

Quick Review Questions

3) What are physical hazards in terms of property and casualty insurance?

4) What is the difference between moral hazards and morale hazards?

5) What is the difference between risk and peril?

How Insurers Manage Risk

Minimizing risk is the primary focus of the insurance industry. One method of doing this is known as **homogenous risk**, or **risk pooling**, which spreads the risk among a large number of similar policyholders. Business insurance companies, for example, will often calculate premiums based on the percentage of a given group of individuals encountering a routine hazard. The rationale is that the higher costs associated with fire damage on the plan will be offset by the lower costs associated with those businesses who are careful with their sprinkler systems. Other ways in which insurers help manage risk are described in Table 1.1.

Table 1.1. Risk Management Solutions

Solution	Description
Exposure avoidance	ceasing the activities that could cause harm (e.g., storing flammable supplies in a shed away from other buildings)
Loss prevention/reduction	making efforts to minimize a risk (e.g., installing new smoke detectors in each hallway)
Sharing	assuming financial costs between two or more parties in order to lift the burden of responsibility from a sole individual (e.g., purchasing debt repayment insurance in case business is interrupted and the insured cannot repay the loan)
Contractual transfer	transferring repair costs from the insured to the insurer (excluding deductibles and premiums)
Retention/acceptance	acknowledging that some risks are inevitable and making insurance decisions on that knowledge (e.g., a business owners plan that has a high deductible but is less expensive)

Helpful Hint

The acronym STARR is used to remember the five basic ways to manage risk: sharing, transfer, avoidance, reduction, and retention.

Insurance companies use the law of large numbers to make predictions about the amounts paid to policyholders and the frequency at which policyholders are paid. According to the **law of large numbers**, the anticipated value of claims mirrors the average of a large set of data points and that the addition of data points narrows any difference in the anticipated value of claims.

Insurable interest motivates someone to buy insurance and is the foundation of all insurance policies. An **insurable interest** is an investment in something (or someone) wherein damage, destruction (or injury or death) would result in financial loss or hardship; insurable interests generally exist between family members and business partners. A policyholder must have an insurable interest in the property or person to be covered in order for the contract to be valid. Insurable interest policies should be designed to prevent any moral hazards—incentives for the policyholder to cause (or allow) a loss to happen. For example, in many situations, a spouse would no longer be able to rely on the insured partner's income should the insured partner pass away unexpectedly. Spouses therefore have an insurable interest in their partners because of the financial hardship they would endure (e.g., mortgages, child support) should their partners die.

Insurable risks are those over which an individual typically has some degree of control and which pose a potential financial threat—but one not so great that the cost of insurance premiums would outweigh the benefits. In contrast, **uninsurable risks** are those which are too large or too small to justify the cost of insurance. Similarly, **uninsurable perils** are those which an insurance company deems have too great a likelihood to warrant coverage and/or those in which the factors leading to the peril are beyond the control of the insured party. Examples of uninsurable perils in life and health insurance often include catastrophes, pandemic-related illnesses, and those related to political upheaval or terrorism.

For a risk to be insurable, it must involve the potential for a **measurable loss**. If a loss is not measurable, it is impossible to determine how much coverage a policyholder needs or how much the policy should cost. For example, an insurance company will look at various bills (e.g., mortgage, childcare) to determine how shared expenses would affect a spouse whose partner passes away, and the insurance company will base the policy on that information.

In order for a risk to be insurable, it must meet three critical conditions:

1. **The loss must be certain.**
    - This means that the insurance company must be able to predict the likelihood and amount of a claim.
    - If there is too much uncertainty, the risk is considered uninsurable.
2. **The loss must be accidental.**
    - This means that the insured did not deliberately cause the loss to happen.
    - If the loss is deliberately caused, it is uninsurable.
    - For that reason, cases of arson or death by suicide are typically not covered under an insurance policy.

3. **The loss must be significant.**

- The amount of the loss must be large enough to be financially worthwhile to pay for insurance premiums to protect against the loss.

Did You Know?

Economic hardship is a financial situation that makes it difficult to cover basic living expenses; it is caused by a variety of factors (e.g., job loss, unexpected medical bills). Insurable risk and economic hardship are two distinct concepts: insurable risk is typically covered by insurance; economic hardship is not.

Quick Review Questions

6) What is the purpose of the acronym STARR?

7) Who is typically the beneficiary of a life insurance policy?

8) How does risk pooling protect an insurance company?

9) Name the three critical characteristics of an insurable risk.

10) How does purchasing a life insurance policy help the policyholder?

11) What is meant by the term uninsurable perils?

Limiting Insurer Liability

Limits of liability are just one way through which insurance companies limit their financial liabilities. **Limits of liability** define the maximum dollar amount an insurer will pay out, depending on the unique details of the policy. A business owner's policy's limits of liability allow insureds to understand the range of protection they can expect to help them meet financial obligations. Once the limits of liability are clear, the policyholder must choose an appropriate amount of coverage, usually at least 80 percent of the value of business buildings.

If an insured risk occurs, the insurer's **indemnity**, or responsibility for payment, is limited to the actual loss or damage incurred. This means that the amount paid out in benefits cannot exceed the value of the loss or damage suffered by an individual policyholder. This part of the indemnity principle also applies to group policies, where it limits payouts and ensures that funds are available to cover legitimate claims.

Subrogation is a common right that insurance companies have to recoup the costs of a claim from a third party; doing this helps maintain the policyholder's premium levels by putting the financial burden on the party determined to be at fault for the peril. For example, if a policyholder's home is damaged by a car that crashed into it, the policyholder's insurance company will work with the insurance company of the party at fault (the driver of the car) to ensure that reimbursement is made to the policy owned by the insured homeowner.

> **Helpful Hint**
>
> Not all plans offer subrogation rights; those that do may have different rules and regulations. Before entering into any contract, individuals should carefully review their provider's policies on subrogation.

When filing a claim, the policyholder is responsible for a specific dollar amount of expenses before the insurance company will pay any covered losses; this is called a **deductible**. The deductible reduces the amount insurance companies need to pay out when processing a claim from a policyholder. Generally speaking, the lower the deductible, the higher the policy premium.

In addition to deductibles, many health insurance policies have coinsurance, which is a form of shared risk.

Coinsurance is the percentage—usually fixed—that an insurance policy requires the policyholder to pay toward a service. The service can be covered by the plan or may be limited to a specific type. Coinsurance is paid after the deductible has been met.

Furthermore, some policies require an **elimination period**—a specified number of days that must pass before the insured is eligible for policy benefits. The elimination period usually begins at the onset of disability or illness, on the date of admittance to a hospital or institution, or at any other qualifying moment defined by the policy.

Quick Review Questions

12) What does the limit of liability clause define?

13) What, if any, are the limits to indemnity?

14) What term describes the legal right of insurance companies to pursue a third party for reimbursement?

15) What is the purpose of coinsurance?

Types of Insurance

A variety of insurance policies exist to help protect people from the risks associated with the many areas that make up everyday life, such as health, property, and business. Different policies are designed to cover different types of losses. Table 1.2. describes some of the most common forms of insurance policies available.

Table 1.2. The Various Types of Insurance

Insurance Type	Protected Losses
Property insurance	• damage to buildings • damage to property stored within buildings • damage to outdoor structures

Table 1.2. The Various Types of Insurance	
Insurance Type	**Protected Losses**
	• damage to plants or driveways
Casualty insurance	• accidents or injuries to people caused by a property owner's negligence • theft of items from a policyholder's property
Health insurance	• illness • accident • disability
Life insurance	• death • disability
Automobile insurance	• repairs to a vehicle • medical care for people riding in an insured vehicle
Credit life insurance	• payment of a debt in case of insolvency or death

An **annuity** is a financial asset backed by an insurance company that allows the participating individual to receive steady income throughout the duration of the annuity's contract. The policyholder submits a lump sum or periodic payments toward the annuity; in turn, the insurer backing the annuity submits regular payouts to the policyholder throughout the course of the policyholder's life and beyond. Annuities are designed to outlive the policyholder and are therefore attractive options for people who seek to supplement their income, boost their Social Security and retirement, and provide for their loved ones after their death.

Quick Review Questions

16) How do casualty and property insurance differ?

17) What is the purpose of credit life insurance?

18) How does an annuity differ from life insurance?

Types of Insurers

Main Types of US Insurers

There are three main types of insurers in the United States:

- **Commercial insurers** are mainly for-profit companies that provide life, home, auto, or any other type of insurance that pays out claims upon the occurrence of certain conditions.
- **Non-commercial insurers** provide services funded by donations or grants, often as part of nonprofit organizations.
- **US government-sponsored programs** include services such as flood coverage, Medicare, veterans' benefits, and Social Security.

There are many types of commercial insurance companies:

- **Stock insurers**, also known as **stock insurance companies**, are owned by their investors.
    - The investors receive profits generated through premiums and investments in the stock market.
    - They often generate more profit than traditional insurance companies.
    - The earnings from their assets are used to pay policy dividends in cash or stock to shareholders or to fund reserve requirements mandated by regulators.
    - **Dividends** are earnings that a company distributes to its eligible shareholders.
- A **participating company** divides profits and risks among a network of companies through a process called **sharing**.
- A **nonparticipating policy** is a type of life insurance policy in which the insurer will pay out any cumulative dividends to its stockholders rather than back to the individual policyholder.
    - This policy provides consistent premium payments and a guaranteed death benefit.
    - It has no cash value or loan provision, a low probability of an increase in premiums, and no surrender fees or penalties.

There are also several types of non-commercial, or nonprofit insurers:

- **Mutual insurers** are organizations owned by their policyholders.
    - They function as cooperatives.
    - Their structures are similar to those of nonprofit organizations.
    - They operate according to the principle of mutuality: insurance is provided based on members pooling and managing risks together and sharing all profits.
- **Reciprocal insurers** pool money and resources together.
    - Reciprocal insurers share risk.
    - The risk is spread among policyholders rather than to the organization itself.
- **Fraternal insurers** serve members with similar interests or beliefs.
    - They provide members with quality financial services and life insurance products.

Did You Know?

Excess and surplus lines insurance (E&S) is highly specialized and provides coverage that more common insurance products decline to cover (e.g., hazardous materials, art, classic cars). It offers a viable option for those who are otherwise unable to obtain such coverage.

- Many fraternal insurers offer multiple resources and services to help support customers' changing needs.
- They offer comprehensive coverage at more affordable rates than other insurers.

Quick Review Questions

19) Who owns stock insurance companies?

20) To whom does a nonparticipating policy provide cumulative dividends?

21) How is risk spread with reciprocal insurers?

22) How do fraternal insurers support a customer's changing needs?

Reinsurers

There are a few ways in which insurance companies reduce the impact of risk on their profit margins.

> **Helpful Hint**
>
> Facultative reinsurance applies to a single risk or, in some cases, a specified bundle of risks. Treaty reinsurance takes on all risks from the ceding company.

Reinsurers are companies that provide risk-sharing services to other insurers; in other words, they are insurance companies for insurance companies. Their purpose is to spread out and mitigate the financial risks taken on by primary insurance providers. In exchange for a portion of the premiums collected by insurers, reinsurers offer protection against potential losses caused by catastrophic events. By reducing the primary insurer's required capital reserves, reinsurance allows the primary insurer to control spending, protect its balance sheets, and safely underwrite more policies.

Some types of reinsurance allow insurers to transfer specific risks or portions of them to another insurer through a contract between the two insurance companies:

- **Facultative reinsurance** lets insurers apply reinsurance to individual policies.
- **Treaty reinsurance** establishes a framework between the original insurer and one or more other insurers to share risks associated with a policy.
    - This arrangement is initiated due to high sales volumes or more extensive types of risk that an insurer may not feel comfortable accepting on its own.
    - Treaty reinsurance benefits both the **ceding company** (the original insurer) and the reinsurer itself by providing portfolio diversity and spreading potentially higher levels of insured risk across multiple companies.
    - By utilizing treaty reinsurance to spread out risk, insurers can guarantee improved security for policyholders and maintain solvency for all entities involved in the agreement.

Quick Review Questions

23) How do reinsurers benefit primary insurers?

24) How do facultative reinsurance and treaty reinsurance differ?

Risk-Retention Groups and Self-Insurers

Risk-retention groups (RRGs) are liability insurance providers that are owned by their members—typically employers who share similar risk exposures. Instead of purchasing traditional commercial insurance from outside insurers, the members contribute to a shared pool to be used to pay claims experienced by any member.

Self-insurers are individuals or organizations that assume full financial responsibility for risks associated with their activities rather than transferring that risk to insurance companies. They provide this form of insurance by pooling funds to cover potential losses, which typically require reserves of cash and investment assets. Self-insurers often supplement these funds with **stop-loss reinsurance policies** that cover specific losses that may arise. Self-insuring is beneficial when the costs from a claim or series of claims are more predictable and manageable over time. It also helps organizations provide customized coverage with cost savings compared to traditional insurers.

Quick Review Questions

25) Why would a company choose to participate in an RRG rather than purchase a traditional insurance policy?

26) What is a stop-loss reinsurance policy?

Domicile and Authorization

Insurance domicile, also known as the home state of an insurance company, describes the specific laws and regulations governing an insurance company's activities while doing business in that state. Generally, these rules dictate the type of business an insurer can conduct and in which states it is allowed to operate. According to US insurance law, there are three types of insurance domiciles:

- **Domestic insurers** are insurance companies that hold licenses to conduct insurance business within the borders of specified states.
- **Foreign Insurers** are insurance companies that are based in different states from the ones in which the policyholders to whom they sell reside.

- **Alien Insurers** are insurance companies that are based outside the US and are soliciting insurance business from within the US.

Authorized (admitted) insurance companies have received permission from the state government to conduct business in that state. Furthermore, authorized organizations must conform to all applicable laws, regulations, and guidelines imposed by their coverage areas.

Unauthorized (non-admitted) insurance companies do not meet the criteria established by governing bodies, such as the Department of Insurance; as a result, they can potentially expose customers to higher levels of financial risk due to their lack of oversight.

> **Did You Know?**
>
> Alien insurers must be licensed to do business within the United States.

Quick Review Questions

27) What is the difference between a foreign insurer and an alien insurer?

28) Why are admitted insurance companies considered to be more reliable in terms of the protection they provide for their policyholders?

Insurance Professionals

Licensed **insurance agents** typically sell insurance on behalf of just one insurance company and usually specialize in specific insurance types (e.g., life or health). Many agents will also choose to diversify the products they sell; however, they must do so with the same insurance company to which they are appointed. In some cases, agents can represent more than one issuer. (This is described in more detail in Table 1.3.) Only officially appointed insurance agents have the power to **bind** the policy coverage—to confirm in writing that a policy will be issued—and make the policy take effect.

Insurance producers hold the required licenses and are responsible for selling, soliciting, and negotiating insurance services on behalf of different insurance companies. Producers can offer more complex policy options than agents.

Insurance brokers act as intermediaries between insurance buyers and insurers. They offer advice, manage risks, facilitate transactions, research products, and negotiate with insurers to obtain the most favorable prices and coverages for clients.

Whereas producers, agents, and brokers help clients get the best policies for their needs, **insurance solicitors** work on behalf of insurance agents by gathering leads for potential applicants. Insurance solicitors are prohibited from selling insurance products; however, they must still take the licensure exam and hold a valid license.

> **Did You Know?**
>
> Insurance consultants are professionals who advise companies and individuals on optimal approaches to risk management. They develop plans to minimize costs, identify areas for improvement, increase the efficiency of claims processes, and review existing policies for accuracy.

Quick Review Questions

29) How do insurance producers differ from insurance agents?

30) What is the benefit of using insurance brokers?

31) What does it mean to bind an insurance policy?

Types of Distribution

There are many ways through which insurance companies can connect with customers and develop individualized insurance policies for them. Traditionally, companies have used brick-and-mortar offices to connect with potential clients, but with the rise of e-commerce and digital marketing, the insurance industry has evolved to make the most of these new platforms.

Agencies

Insurance companies traditionally use **agencies** comprised of licensed agents who represent the insurance company associated with the agency. Agents have expertise about policies, coverage, and exclusions in order to help clients purchase the best policies for their needs. By using agencies, the burden of distributing insurance products can move from the company to these agents who can customize policies to best serve their customers. The personalized service and relationship-building carried out by agents encourages repeat business for the agencies in the long run. Insurance companies therefore benefit from the agency model since direct marketing and sales force budgets are not required.

Table 1.3. The Types of Insurance Agents

Agent Type	Description
Captive agent	• only represents one company • incentivized to promote the products of that company • allows the company to control the ways in which its products are presented
Independent agent	• represents more than one insurer • allows more flexibility about what is offered to the client • allows easy price comparisons
Managing general agent (MGA)	• provides specialized assistance to companies in underwriting, issuing policies, and customer service • saves companies time and money on administrative costs

Quick Review Questions

32) Which type of agents can ONLY offer the products of the companies they represent?

33) Whom do independent agents represent?

34) What cost-saving benefit does the agency distribution model offer?

Technology and Insurance Marketing

Whereas the previously mentioned professionals present products directly to clients, insurance companies also use impersonal methods to connect with potential clients:

- **Mass marketing** typically employs advertising via digital, broadcast, and/or print media, which allows companies to offer information about their products to large groups of people.
- **Direct marketing** reaches more focused groups of potential customers by directly engaging them via emails, phone calls, direct mail, or internet ads.
- **Franchise marketing** involves an insurance company partnering with a familiar retail brand that promotes the insurance products through its pre-existing distribution channels.
  - In most cases, insurance companies pay fees to the retailer for each policy sold to their customers.
  - This system provides both parties with mutual benefits—increased earnings and customer retention—thus proving a worthwhile investment in marketing strategy.

Direct-writing companies—those that offer services directly to the client—often use these types of impersonal marketing strategies to attract clients. They dispense with agents in favor of customer service representatives at a call center who underwrite and administer their policies. Direct-writing companies represent an opportunity for insurance carriers to control their operations, reduce costs, and more effectively create coverage for consumers from any market segment. Direct-writing companies (e.g., GEICO and Allstate) use either mass or direct marketing to promote and distribute their products.

Quick Review Questions

35) Which kind of marketing uses an unrelated company's contacts to promote the insurance company's products?

36) How does direct marketing differ from mass marketing?

37) Why might an insurance company use a direct-writing company?

Chapter Review

Table 1.4. Chapter 1 Review: Insurance Basics	
General Insurance Concepts	
People	• *insured*: the person who is covered by a policy; usually the policyholder • *insurer*: the company who provides the policy • *underwriter:* the person who researches the potential insured and creates the policy, factoring in things like medical conditions, credit rating, and reputation
Concepts	• *policy*: a contract between the company and the insured that defines how much the insured will pay when loss occurs, and how much and when benefits will be paid • *premium:* money paid to the company by the insured to purchase the policy, usually monthly; may be in one lump sum • *loss*: reduction of the value of an asset; could include death, accident, illness, or other required services for which the policy is contracted to pay • *claim*: a demand for payment made by the insured to the company in order to pay for a service or some other provision promised by the policy
Risk	
Definition of risk	• the possibility that a loss will occur • may include risk of unemployment, death, illness, disability, destruction of property; includes common risks (e.g., needing to see the doctor) and more rare risks (e.g., accidental death)
Types of risks	• *pure risks:* when there is only a chance of a loss (e.g., with an accident) • *speculative risks:* when there is a chance of either a loss or a gain, and since a person willingly gambles with the risk, the person is uninsurable • NOTE: Insurance generally only takes on pure risks.

Factors that give rise to risk	• *peril:* the direct cause of an unexpected financial burden
	• *hazard:* any factor that gives rise to a peril
	    • *physical hazards:* those that arise from material, structural, or operational factors (e.g., broken steps)
	    • *moral hazards:* those that arise from people's habits and values (e.g., choosing to smoke even though it is known to be bad for health)

Table 1.4. Chapter 1 Review: Insurance Basics	
General Insurance Concepts	
	• *morale hazards:* those that arise out of carelessness or responsibility (e.g., failing to check the safety of a facility)
STARR method for managing risk	• The acronym *STARR:* • *sharing*: assuming financial costs between two or more parties in order to lift the burden of responsibility from a sole individual (e.g., purchasing debt repayment insurance in case business is interrupted and the insured cannot repay the loan) • *transfer*: transferring risks to an insurance company so that individuals can recoup their money after losses (e.g., taking out a policy that pays to rebuild a house after a fire) • *avoidance:* avoiding activities that could result in losses (e.g., not letting children deep fry a turkey by themselves) • *reduction:* reducing the likelihood that risks could occur (e.g., installing smoke detectors in kitchens) • *retention:* accepting the risk and choosing to retain it
Law of large numbers	• Insurance companies have data about large numbers of people who undertake similar risks so that they can predict the likelihood of losses, which is why they are willing to take on other people's risks.
Insurable interest	• a person's legitimate interest in the preservation of property or life • required for a life insurance policy to be effective (e.g., the loss of a person whose loved ones will suffer financially after the loss) • not required for a policy that covers property since the financial loss is clear after a loss occurs
Insurable risks	• large numbers of similar policyholders • measurable loss • losses that must be certain • economic hardship • the exclusion of catastrophic perils

ANSWER KEY

1. The benefit of purchasing an insurance policy is that it offers financial protection for individuals and businesses by reducing or eliminating the risks associated with unexpected events.

2. In insurance, the term *indemnification* refers to one party (the insurer) reimbursing the policyholder (the insured) for financial losses.

3. Physical hazards relate to a policyholder's behaviors that could contribute to a peril. An example includes allowing a sidewalk to crumble, resulting in a visitor accidentally tripping and spraining her ankle.

4. Moral hazards are conscious and intentional behaviors wherein the insured party assumes additional risk-taking, knowing that the insurance plan provides financial protection from those consequences. On the other hand, morale hazards describe attitudes of carelessness or indifference that can result in a perilous event; however, the indifference is not geared toward intentionally trying to claim money, which differentiates it from moral hazards.

5. A risk is the possibility that an unexpected even can occur and lead to a financial burden; a peril is the direct cause of the unexpected financial burden.

6. The acronym *STARR* is used by insurance professionals to remember the five ways to manage risk: sharing, transfer, avoidance, reduction, and retention.

7. The most likely beneficiaries of a life insurance policy are family members or business partners.

8. Risk pooling, also known as homogenous risk, is a method used by insurance companies to spread the risk among a large number of similar policyholders. This can include calculating premiums on the basis of total medical costs for a group of individuals, with the thought that the higher costs associated with less healthy individuals on the plan will be offset by the lower costs associated with the healthier individuals on the plan.

9. The three critical characteristics of an insurable risk are that the loss must be measurable, accidental, and significant.

10. A life insurance policy creates an insurable interest in the insured person's life, meaning that if something should happen to the person who is insured, the insurance company will help cover the negative financial effects caused by that person's death or disability.

11. An uninsurable peril is a peril—the direct cause of the unexpected financial burden—that an insurance company determines has too great a likelihood to warrant coverage and/or includes factors that are beyond the control of the insured party, such as terrorism or a pandemic illness.

12. The limit of liability clause defines the maximum dollar amount a policy will pay.

13. Indemnity—the insurance company's responsibility to pay for a loss—is limited to the actual loss or damage incurred. In other words, the amount of benefits paid cannot exceed the value of the loss or damage suffered by the individual policyholder.

14. The term *subrogation* describes an insurance company's legal right to pursue a third party for reimbursement.

15. Coinsurance—a percentage of the full cost of covered service that is paid by the policyholder after the deductible is met—is designed to relieve the policyholder from the burden of having to pay the full amount of a costly medical bill.

16. Casualty insurance protects property owners from liability for negligence if someone is hurt on or something is stolen from their property. Property insurance protects the policyholder from the unexpected expenses related to damage to physical structures owned by the policyholder and the property stored within those structures.

17. Credit life insurance is designed to pay off a financial obligation in the event of the death or insolvency of the policyholder.

18. An annuity provides a steady stream of income to the policyholder throughout the duration of the policyholder's life and to beneficiaries after the policyholder's death. (Life insurance is only paid out to beneficiaries upon the death of the policyholder.)

19. Stock insurance companies are owned by their investors.

20. The insurer of a nonparticipating life insurance policy pays out cumulative dividends to its stockholders instead of to its individual policyholders.

21. With reciprocal insurers, risk is spread among policyholders rather than to the insuring organization.

22. Fraternal insurers offer comprehensive coverage at more affordable rates than other insurers in order to support their customers' changing needs.

23. Reinsurers protect primary insurers from potential losses that could result from catastrophic events—they are insurance for insurance companies. Reinsurers mitigate the financial risks taken on by primary insurers by helping them spread the risks out in exchange for a portion of the premiums that the primary insurers collect. By doing this, the primary insurer can control spending, protect its balance sheets, and safely underwrite more policies.

24. Facultative reinsurance applies to a single risk or, in some cases, a specified bundle of risks; treaty reinsurance takes on all risks from the ceding company.

25. Some companies choose to become members of risk-retention groups (RRGs) because they cut down on premium costs by having members who share similar risk exposures contribute to a shared pool that is used to pay claims.

26. A stop-loss reinsurance policy is a separate insurance policy wherein a second company covers a specific, predictable loss that a self-insurer is likely to encounter.

27. A foreign insurer is an insurance company that is located in a state that is different from the one in which its policyholders reside. An alien insurer is an insurance company that is not based in the US but solicits insurance business from within the US.

28. Since admitted (i.e., authorized) insurance companies are regulated by state laws, the protection they offer their policyholders is considered to be more reliable.

29. While insurance producers and insurance agents are both licensed to sell insurance products, insurance producers may sell complex insurance options on behalf of different insurance companies whereas insurance agents typically specialize in a particular type of insurance and usually sell for just one insurance company.

30. As intermediaries between insurance buyers and insurance companies, insurance brokers can offer advice, manage risks, facilitate transactions, research products, and negotiate with insurers to obtain the most favorable prices and coverages for clients.

31. To bind an insurance policy means to provide written confirmation that coverage is in place, even if the policy has not yet been issued by the insurer. Only an officially appointed representative has the authority to bind a policy.

32. Captive agents can only offer the products of the companies they represent.

33. Independent agents represent any insurance company by whom they have been officially appointed.

34. Due to the personalized service and relationship-building offered by the agency distribution model, insurance companies avoid having to create direct marketing and sales force budgets.

35. Franchise marketing is a technique wherein an insurance company partners with a familiar retail brand in order to promote insurance products through the partnering retail brand's pre-existing distribution channels.

36. Direct marketing emphasizes reaching a specific, focused group of potential customers; mass marketing emphasizes reaching a large audience—regardless of focus.

37. Direct-writing companies use customer service representatives to underwrite and administer an insurance company's policies; for the insurance company, this results in reduced costs, improved control of operations, and more effective coverage for consumers from any market segment.

2. Insurance Contracts

The Legal Purpose of an Insurance Contract

The legal purpose of a contract is to formalize a business relationship between two or more parties. Contracts outline each party's rights, responsibilities, and obligations. Like other contracts, insurance contracts are legally binding.

There are four important elements of a contract, and a judge will consider all of them when determining whether or not a contract existed between parties. The four elements of a contract are as follows:

1. **offer and acceptance:** The parties to the contract make a written promise to do something or stop doing something in the future, and they sign their names to accept the contract. (E.g., The insured person signs the insurance policy.)
2. **consideration:** This is the value that each party gets from the contract. (E.g., An insurance company offers to provide auto collision coverage, and the driver agrees to the price of the premiums.)
3. **legal purpose:** Contracts must be legally enforceable under the law. (E.g., An agreement with a drug dealer is not a legal contract because buying and selling drugs is illegal.)
4. **competent parties:** Contract law states that only competent parties may enter into legal contracts. (E.g., A 16-year-old driver cannot obtain her own auto coverage because minors are not considered competent to make financial decisions.)

There are four other common terms in an insurance contract that are important:

- **representations:** factual statements that receiving parties can rely on that influence them to enter into a contract (e.g., statements about the value of vehicles that the company will insure)
- **warranties:** promises to indemnify receiving parties if the representations turn out to be false (e.g., an insurance company warranting that an insurance contract is legally enforceable)
- **concealment:** failing to disclose information (intentionally or not) that is pertinent to the terms of the contract or would affect the other party's financial consideration to enter into the contract
- **binders:** temporary insurance contracts that provide insurance until the permanent policy is in force

Did You Know?

A person with cognitive function loss (e.g., dementia) does not have the mental capacity to understand or enter into a contract; therefore, the contract may be voided unless someone who has the legal authority to care for that person has also signed it.

Quick Review Questions

1) In order to get a lower rate, a homeowner insurance applicant intentionally tells the insurer that her home is 1,300 square feet when it is actually 2,300 square feet. Which element of a contract applies to this misinformation?

2) Which document could a homebuyer bring to the closing if he has not yet received the official policy?

3) What is it called when an auto body shop tells a car owner that it is an official vendor for the insured's auto insurance carrier?

Insurance Policy Structure

Insurance policies have seven distinct parts. These components of an insurance policy, and their definitions, are as follows:

1. "Declarations": The declarations "declare" the information in your policy in a one-page summary. It is the first page of a policy, and it includes information such as

- the policy number,
- effective dates,
- the agent's name and contact information,
- the names of the insureds,
- coverages and limits,
- property covered,
- deductibles, and
- premiums.

2. "Definitions": The definitions clarify what the terms mean in an insurance policy. The definition of a term could become an important factor in the event of a claim or lawsuit regarding what the policy intends to cover or exclude.

Did You Know?

Insurance companies often define concepts differently than how they are used in other contexts. For that reason, it is important to check the "Definitions" portion of an insurance policy to ensure that the coverage is completely clear.

3. "Insuring Agreement": This is part of an insurance policy that outlines the exact circumstance of when the policy will provide coverage in exchange for the premium payments. The agreement may state broad terms and then narrow the coverage by listing conditions or exclusions.

4. "Endorsements": Endorsements amend the terms of an insurance policy and will state what is or is not covered and to what degree. Insurance carriers may charge extra premiums for endorsements.

5. "Additional Coverage": Coverage can be added to a basic policy by adding an endorsement. Endorsements may cover additional insureds or additional property. Policies may state a maximum limit of coverage for the endorsement.

6. "Conditions": Insurers place certain conditions on when they will act or fulfill their promise to pay a claim. If the conditions are not met, the carrier does not have to pay the claim.

7. "Exclusions and Policy Limits": Insurance policies state what they will cover, and exclusions state what they will not cover. For example, a home policy may cover water damage from a sink that overflows but not water damage that backs up through sewers or drains. Policy limits refer to the maximum amounts particular coverages will pay for losses.

Quick Review Questions

4) Which part of the policy tells the insured what their deductibles are?

5) Where in the policy would the homeowner look to find out what replacement cost coverage means?

6) Which component of the insurance policy states that the insured must notify the insurer if a loss is experienced?

7) Which component of a commercial property policy outlines named perils versus open perils?

The Insured

The **insured** is a business or person who is covered by a personal or commercial insurance contract. Insurance policies may cover more than one person.

Policies have a **first named insured** who is listed first and is the owner of the policy. This person is entitled to all of the coverage and benefits of the policy, is responsible for premiums, and will receive any refunds. In the event of a cancellation, the insurance company will notify the first named insured.

Policies may also cover an **additional insured** which can be a person or organization covered by the plan. Although additional insureds are not owners of the policy, they are entitled to receive certain benefits and some amount of coverage under the policy. The policy lists additional insureds in the policy declarations or by endorsement.

> **Did You Know?**
>
> The insured person may or may not be named on the policy. Property and casualty insurance coverage may simply apply to a covered location or structure rather than a specific person.

In the "Duties After Loss" portion of an insurance policy, the named insured must perform certain duties as listed in the policy. These include

- notifying the insurer of a loss,
- notifying the police if a crime was committed,
- protecting the property from further damage,
- preparing an inventory of damaged property,
- keeping an accurate record of expenses, and
- cooperating with the investigation of a claim.

Quick Review Questions

8) A homeowner has both a first and second mortgage on her home, and both lenders asked to be added to the homeowner's insurance policy. Would the first mortgagee be the first named insured?

9) If a home insurance policy states that it covers all individuals living in the household, would a foster child be covered under the policy?

Provisions and Clauses in an Insurance Contract

There are many common provisions and clauses found in an insurance contract. Homeowners policies may have many or all of them, and it is important for policy owners to review them carefully:

- **assignment:** Assignment refers to transferring the right of ownership, including all benefits, rights, and liabilities of an insurance contract to another person.
- **appraisal:** An appraisal is a provision in the "Loss Settlement" portion that refers to a written assessment of the replacement value of certain described property. Appraisals are generally provided by professionals, such as jewelers or antiques experts.
- **arbitration:** Arbitration is a process that involves an independent third party helping to decide a case between the insured and the insurance company: both parties present their cases, the arbitrator reviews the facts, and then the arbitrator decides in favor of one of the parties.
- **other insurance:** An other insurance clause is a provision that states which insurance policies covers what and the extent of each's indemnity when more than one insurance policy covers a loss.
- **pro rata:** A pro rata clause pertains to situations where more than one insurer protects an insured and states each party's percentage of liability.
- **notice of claim:** A notice of claim provision requires an insured to notify the insurer as soon as possible after becoming aware of a loss.
- **proof of loss:** A proof of loss is a legal document that describes the property that has been damaged or stolen and the value of that property.
- **cancellation and nonrenewal:** A cancellation clause describes the circumstances, such as nonpayment of premiums or insurance fraud, where an insurer may cancel an insurance contract. A nonrenewal clause is a clause that states the insurer has the right to not renew an insurance contract at the end of the policy term.
- **mortgagee rights:** A mortgagee clause grants protection to a mortgage company that has a financial interest in the property and is named as an additional insured on the policy.
- **loss settlement:** A loss settlement clause describes how an insurer determines how much money it is required to pay an insured for a loss.
- **policy territory:** The policy territory describes the geographical areas where insurance coverage applies. (This is especially helpful for homeowners policies.)

- **severability of interests:** A severability clause refers to the fact that the insurance coverage applies to all insureds as if they each had their own policies.
- **indemnification:** An indemnification clause is a promise by an insurer to pay for an insured's loss.

Quick Review Questions

10) Which type of documentation would a jeweler need to present to the claims adjuster to prove the value of a stolen necklace?

11) The insured owes $200,000 to a lender on a building that was destroyed by a fire. The lender is listed as an additional insured on the policy. Who will be compensated for the loss: the insured or the lender?

12) What is it called when an insured immediately contacts the insurance company after returning from vacation to learn that her home has been burglarized?

13) If an insurance company paid less than the insured felt a destroyed item was worth, which provision would apply to settle the dispute and prevent a lawsuit?

Underwriting

The purpose of the underwriting process is for an insurer to assess the amount of risk being insured. The information underwriters gather is used to determine whether applicants are eligible for certain types of policies and how much the applicants' premiums will be. Underwriters use data and information from various sources including

- application information,
- motor vehicle reports,
- licensed drivers in the household,
- licensed drivers who drive for a company,
- credit reports,
- interviews,
- property inspections,
- claims histories,
- insurance histories, and
- public records (including social media).

Did You Know?

Before the 1970s, creditors offered applicants credit largely based on subjective information from landlords, employers, banks, and credit card companies. The lack of standardization created unfairness, and there was no way for individuals to correct inaccurate information on their credit reports.

Insurance companies rely on the accuracy of the information on an application. If a prospect lies or materially misrepresents information on the application, it is considered insurance fraud, which is illegal. Most insurance companies have special investigation departments that help the company identify suspicious claims. Underwriters must apply the same standards to all applicants. In property and casualty insurance, underwriters are not allowed to discriminate based on a person's race, color, gender, age, or the location of the property. Underwriters must also exclude any information they cannot independently verify.

Did You Know?

If an insurer discovers an applicant made an error on an insurance application, the insurer could decline the application, even if the incorrect information was accidentally given.

If the insurer discovers a misrepresentation after the policy was issued—even if an underwriter approved the application—the company could deny the claim. In this case, the insured would have to pay for the loss themselves. Also, under the cancellation provision, an insurance company would be able to cancel the policy before the end of its term. In addition, if an insurance company paid a claim and later discovered the policyholder misrepresented information on the application, the insurance company could file a lawsuit to recoup their payment.

Quick Review Questions

14) If an underwriter discovers that two teen drivers are not mentioned in a recent auto insurance application, what decision could the insurer legally make?

15) Could an insurance company decline a claim for fire damage if it discovers that the policyholder misrepresented the age of the building's fire suppression system?

Federal Regulations

The Fair Credit Reporting Act (FCRA)

The Fair Credit Reporting Act (FCRA; Public Law No. 91-508) was passed into law in 1970 to ensure that credit reports shown by credit reporting agencies are accurate, fair, and protect the privacy of people's personal information. To protect consumers, the law restricts the way credit reporting agencies can gather, access, utilize, and share credit and personal information.

A **credit report** includes the following:

- a rating of creditworthiness
- a description of credit standing and capacity
- statements of personal character, reputation, personal characteristics, and lifestyle

No person or organization can access someone's credit report without a permissible reason, such as offering credit, issuing an insurance policy, or renting a dwelling. Companies are mandated to follow certain procedures in handling consumer reports:

- giving consumers their credit scores
- informing consumers if they are denied an application for credit, insurance, or employment based on something in their credit report
- allowing consumers to request and access the information in their credit files

- requiring written consent for employers to obtain applicants' credit reports
- devising a process for consumers to dispute the information in their credit files
- allowing consumers to put a freeze on their credit reports
- allowing consumers to opt out of prescreened credit offers

There is a difference between consumer reports and **investigative consumer reports** which reflect information about a consumer's character, personal characteristics, reputation, and lifestyle. Investigative reports are commonly used by employers to assess a person's character.

Insurance companies are not allowed to disclose personal information to nonaffiliated, third-party individuals or organizations unless they meet the following conditions:

- They must have a permissible purpose (e.g., underwriting).
- They must obtain the consumer's permission to get medical information.
- They must provide notice if they increase rates, deny, or terminate a policy based on a consumer report.

Quick Review Questions

16) Is it legal for an insurance company to increase an individual's rate for auto insurance based on a consumer report that shows a low credit score?

17) What is the purpose of FCRA?

The Gramm-Leach-Bliley Act (GLBA) and Other Legislation

The official name of the **Gramm-Leach-Bliley Act (GLBA)** is the Financial Services Modernization Act; it was enacted in 1999. The act allows banks to sell insurance as long as it is not their primary activity. GLBA repeals parts of the Glass-Steagall Act (1933) which prevented commercial banks from offering financial services, such as insurance and investments, as part of their normal operations.

The GLBA also sets rules for protecting consumer data and ensuring consumer privacy. The law requires property and casualty producers to explain their practices to customers related to information sharing and to guard their personally identifiable information. According to the act, property and casualty agents must

- explain privacy practices,
- give consumers a chance to opt out of having their information shared,
- ensure personally identifiable information is secure, and
- restrict information they share with third parties.

Under the **National Association of Registered Agents and Brokers Reform Act (NARAB II)**, created in 2015 as part of GLBA, the **National Association of Registered Agents and Brokers (NARAB)** was established. Its purpose is to simplify and streamline the producer licensing process. Essentially, once brokers or agents get licensed in their home states, they can legally sell in other states; however, the Act stipulates that brokers and agents must become members of NARAB and pay each state's fees. Also, NARAB lays out the procedures for disciplining insurance producers.

Quick Review Questions

18) For what purpose did Congress enact GLBA?

19) Under GLBA, property and casualty agents are legally required to do which THREE things?

The Terrorism Risk Insurance Act (TRIA)

Before the attacks on the World Trade Center and the Pentagon on September 11, 2001, insurers lacked data to estimate future terrorism losses. Back then, insurers included terrorism coverage on commercial insurance policies at no charge; however, after the attacks, commercial insurers started charging exorbitant rates for terrorism coverage, and some did not offer coverage at all.

> **Did You Know?**
>
> The TRIA has been renewed in 2005, 2007, 2015, and 2019. The current law expires in 2027.

In 2002, the federal government enacted the **Terrorism Risk Insurance Act (TRIA)** in order to help businesses manage this risk. Under TRIA, the federal government shares in financial losses with commercial property and casualty insurers when terrorism is the cause of the loss. TRIA requires insurers to offer terrorism coverage to commercial customers, although customers are not required to purchase it.

The TRIA law, which applies to foreign and domestic terrorism acts, defines terrorism as "any acts that are dangerous to human life in violation of the law and are intended to intimidate or coerce a population, influence governmental policy, or affect the conduct of a government."

In 2015, the federal government updated TRIA by enacting the **Terrorism Risk Insurance Program Reauthorization Act**. This Act changed the coverage as well as the amounts and percentages the federal government pays. The following changes are included:

- decreasing the federal share of compensation by 1 percent each year, beginning at 85 percent, until the percentage is reduced to 80 percent
- increasing the trigger for aggregate losses by $20 million each calendar year until it reaches $200 million (up from $100 million)
- raising the aggregate retention amount by $2 billion each calendar year until it reaches $37.5 billion (up from $27.5 billion with the figure subject to future revisions)

Quick Review Questions

20) Why is terrorism insurance coverage viewed differently now than it was before the attacks on September 11, 2001?

21) Does the definition of TRIA apply to attacks by citizens of the United States, all other countries, or both?

Chapter Review

Table 2.1. Chapter 2 Review: Insurance Contracts and Laws	
Contract Law	
Parts of a contract	• *agreement:* insuring agreement • *consideration:* payment of premiums by insured, payment of claims by insurer • *competent parties:* all signatories; must be of sound mind, free from the influence of substances, and of legal majority • *legal purpose:* the contract only applies to legal activities
Legal definitions	• *representations:* material in the application that is believed to be true; not guaranteed • *misrepresentations:* factually-incorrect statements that may or may not lead the insurer to invalidate the contract • *material misrepresentation:* an inaccurate statement that is so significant that discovering it is false would require the underwriter to change the policy premiums or even cancel the policy • *warranty:* an absolutely true statement upon which the insurance policy relies to be valid • *concealment:* the intentional withholding of information that is critical in making a decision about issuing a policy
Binders	• temporary agreements between the producer and insured that are in place until the official policy is received • expire once the official policy is in force
Policy Components	
Parts of an insurance policy	• *"Declarations":* a page listing all of the important details of a policy (e.g., the insured's name, contact info, coverage, and premiums) • *"Definitions":* the portion that explains how the insurer understands the concepts in the document • *"Insuring Agreement":* the agreement between the insured and the insurer about what each will provide • *"Additional Coverage":* items that are covered without the payment of additional premiums

Table 2.1. Chapter 2 Review: Insurance Contracts and Laws	
Contract Law	
	• *"Conditions":* explanations of procedures and rules each party must follow • *"Endorsements":* printed additions that change the policy's original coverage • *"Policy Limits":* the maximum amounts of coverage included in the policy
Policyholder and Insurer	
Facts about the insured	• *insured:* anyone covered under the policy (may or may not be named) • *named insured:* the person or people whose name(s) is/are listed on the declarations page • *first named insured:* the person whose name appears first on the declarations page • *additional insureds:* other people who may be on the declarations page (such as a spouse or mortgage company)
Duties of the insured in case of loss	• Protect the property. • Make an inventory of damaged or lost property. • Cooperate with insurer in case of a loss. • Call the police if a theft occurred. • Send the insurer a sworn proof of loss within a certain timeframe.
Common Provisions	
Provisions common to property and casualty policies	• *appraisal:* official documents used to prove the value of a lost or damaged item • *arbitration:* the right to have a neutral third party resolve a dispute • *cancellation:* the right of the insurer or insured to end coverage before the policy's expiration date • *loss settlement:* (re: professional liability policies), the requirement that the provider must obtain the insured's permission to settle a claim • *mortgagee clause:* the understanding that if a lender is listed as an additional insured on a property policy, the outstanding loans must be paid before the insured receives any claims payments

Table 2.1. Chapter 2 Review: Insurance Contracts and Laws	
Contract Law	
	• *nonrenewal:* termination of a policy at its expiration date without offering new or continuing coverage • *notice of claim:* document from the policyholder to the insurer explaining when, how, and where a possible loss occurred • *other insurance:* defines which company will pay first if more than one company has insured a potential loss • *pro rata:* provision that explains which percentage of loss will be paid by whom if more than one company is insuring the property • *proof of loss:* sworn statement made by the insured to accompany any claims
Sources Needed for Underwriting	
Information sources	• application form • records from Department of Motor Vehicles • credit report • interviews with friends, employers, and neighbors • property inspection • insurance history
Federal Legislation	
Fair Credit Reporting Act (FCRA)	• overseen by the Federal Trade Commission (FTC) • protects consumers from inaccurate, out of date, or subjective credit information • protects consumer privacy
Gramm-Leach-Bliley Act (GLBA)	• prevents companies from disclosing private information to a nonaffiliated third party • allows customers to opt out of having their information shared • requires companies to ask clients before sharing their information • requires companies to provide clients with a privacy policy explanation once per year
National Association of Registered Agents and Brokers Reform Act (NARAB)	• created in 2015 as part of GLBA

Table 2.1. Chapter 2 Review: Insurance Contracts and Laws	
Contract Law	
	• simplifies and streamlines the licensing process for producers, allowing them to be licensed in more than one state • lays out the procedure for disciplining insurance producers
Terrorism Risk Insurance Act (TRIA)	• temporary act • shares losses from terrorist acts between insurers and US government • requires insurers to meet deductibles before the government helps • requires insurers to offer coverage to clients, which clients may reject.

Answer Key

1. This is concealment. The owner is concealing the true size of the home in order to avoid a higher premium.

2. A binder is a temporary insurance contract until the permanent one is in place.

3. This is representation. The worker at the body shop is representing to the car owner that the shop is an official vendor.

4. The declarations page provides a summary of the policy, including its deductibles.

5. The definitions are listed at the beginning of the policy so that insureds, claims adjusters, attorneys, and judges understand the insurance company's intent about what is and is not covered.

6. The conditions portion of an insurance policy describes what an insured must do in order for the insurance company to pay a claim.

7. The insuring agreement outlines the exact circumstances under which the policy will pay a claim.

8. No, the first and second mortgagees would be additional insureds, because only the homeowner stated on the policy is the first named insured.

9. Yes, because the insurance policy covers all individuals living in the named insured's home regardless of whether the individual is directly related to the named insured or not.

10. The appraisal can attest in writing to an item's value.

11. Since the insured owes the lender money, the insured would have to satisfy his loan before the insurance company would pay the insured anything.

12. By making the phone call to the insurance company, the insured has filed a notice of claim.

13. The insured has the right to have a dispute settled by an arbitrator.

14. The insurance company can decline the application, ask for further explanation, or cancel the policy.

15. Misrepresentation is a legal reason to decline a claim.

16. Insurance companies use consumer reports to underwrite policies, and they can increase rates based on any information they find there.

17. The Fair Credit Reporting Act (FCRA) allows individuals a chance to correct false information on their credit reports, and it standardizes the way consumer reporting agencies gather, access, utilize, and share information.

18. The passage of the Gramm-Leach-Bliley Act (GLBA) permitted banks to sell insurance as long as it is not their primary activity.

19. Under the Gramm-Leach-Bliley Act (GLBA), insurers must 1) restrict the types of information they share with third parties; 2) keep the information secure; and 3) explain their privacy practices to clients.

20. Before the attacks on September 11, 2001, terrorism losses were rare, and insurers lacked data to estimate future terrorism losses.

21. The Terrorism Risk Insurance Act (TRIA) applies to all acts of terrorism, both domestic and foreign.

3. Personal Dwelling Policies

Dwelling Policy Basics

Dwelling Property Coverage

Dwelling insurance provides basic coverage in most situations for rental properties or other dwellings that are not used as primary residences. In some instances, homeowners are unable to obtain homeowners policies, so they purchase a dwelling policy instead in order to provide basic coverage against loss. The following situations are appropriate for dwelling policies:

- owner-occupied, tenant-occupied, or both
- buildings with up to four residential units
- buildings with up to five roomers or boarders
- properties in the process of being constructed
- mobile homes secured to the ground with a permanent foundation
- seasonal dwellings that are vacant for three or more months per year

A dwelling policy typically covers the dwelling itself, including any structures that are attached and detached from it. Detached structures are buildings or features that are permanent but do not form part of the main dwelling (e.g., a separate garage, shed, pool, or fence). There is also coverage provided for personal property and fair rental value.

Insurance policies provide protection against **perils**, or exposures that open up the possibility of the property being damaged. Examples of perils typically covered by dwelling insurance include

- fire,
- lightning,
- wind,
- internal explosion,
- vehicles,
- aircraft, and
- smoke.

Some examples of exclusions include wear and tear, neglect, movement of the earth, and some types of water damage.

The consumer may choose from several endorsements to dwelling policies to cover businesses that may be in operation on the site. **Endorsements** are amendments that can be made to a policy without the need to renew the policy. They include changes, additions, and removals to policy coverage. When deciding to purchase additional coverage, there are several factors to consider:

- the type of business to be covered
- how much protection is needed for business equipment on and off premises
- whether or not public access is needed
- whether the business is mainly conducted from the dwelling versus a detached structure on the property

Loss of income, liability, and medical payments are not covered by endorsements on a dwelling policy.

Helpful Hint

Mobile and manufactured homes typically do not qualify for traditional homeowners insurance policies because they are not built to withstand harsh weather and are not permanently installed. Instead, they are covered under HO-7 policies, which are designed for these types of dwellings.

Quick Review Questions

1) What is a detached structure?

2) Who is typically eligible to obtain a dwelling policy?

Dwelling Coverage Forms

The types of coverage in dwelling and homeowner policies are defined by the **Insurance Services Office, Inc. (ISO)**. The ISO created the dwelling policy to provide coverage for a dwelling and, if needed, liability and/or the contents of the dwelling. The ISO classifies the type of insurance as a **DP (dwelling policy)** with a corresponding number, such as DP-1, DP-2 and DP-3.

Helpful Hint

The DP-1 is referred to as a "basic" policy (DP-1: Basic Form); the DP-2 is a "broad" policy (DP-2: Broad Form); the DP-3 is a "special" policy (DP-3: Special Form).

DP-1: Basic Form

The DP-1: Basic Form provides the most limited coverage and is therefore the least expensive. It has no minimum coverage. This policy provides coverage on a **named peril** basis, which means that in order to provide coverage, the loss must be caused by a peril that is specifically listed in the policy. Some examples of named perils include wind, hail, fire, explosion smoke, and lightning. There are three coverage forms for the DP-1:

- the **Basic Form**
- the **Option 1 Form**
- the **Option 2 Form**

Coverage for the Option 1 and Option 2 Forms must be purchased to supplement the most basic coverage. To ensure each individual risk has the coverage needed, it is important to review the list of named perils prior to selecting a policy.

The following are named perils in the Basic Form of DP policies:

- **fire:** Fire damage to the structures or personal property is covered.
- **lightning:** lightning damage to the dwelling, other structures, or personal property is covered.
- **internal explosion:** explosions inside the covered dwelling, another structure located on the same property, or in a structure containing covered personal property are covered.

Option 1 includes the following **extended coverage perils:**

- **windstorm or hail:** This coverage protects against damage caused by rain, snow, sleet, sand, or dust to the exterior of the building unless the direct force of the wind or hail causes an opening in that structure through which the rain, snow, sleet, sand, or dust can enter and destroy personal property.
- **explosion:** This coverage protects against explosion damage to the exterior of the building.
- **riot or civil commotion:** Most policies differentiate between rioting, civil commotion, or damage from insurrections or rebellions.
- **aircraft:** This peril includes damage caused by self-propelled missiles and spacecraft.
- **vehicles:** Damage caused by the property owner or a resident of the property is not covered. Vehicle damage to fences, driveways, and walks is also not included in this coverage.
- **smoke:** This peril includes damage that is sudden, accidental, and not caused over time, such as with the continuous usage of a fireplace.
- **volcanic eruption:** The damage is covered solely if it is caused by the volcanic eruption itself and not by an earthquake, land shock waves, or tremors.

Option 2 of the DP-1 includes all of the basic and extended perils along with coverage for **vandalism and malicious mischief** by pilferage, theft, burglary or larceny, or to property on the described location if the dwelling has been vacant for more than sixty consecutive days immediately before the loss. Coverage for vandalism and malicious mischief does not include loss to glass or safety glazing material constituting a part of the building other than glass building blocks.

Quick Review Questions

3) Which types of perils are covered under a DP-1: Basic Form?

4) How are the named perils similar on the DP-1: Basic Form?

DP-2: Broad Form

The DP-2: Broad Form covers losses on a named peril basis as well; however, it also provides coverage for additional perils which are not named in the basic policy. Perils listed on the DP-2: Broad Form include the following:

- **damage by burglars:** Coverage for this peril includes damage caused by the burglar to the premises; it does not provide coverage for the property taken.

- **falling objects:** In order to have coverage to contents inside the dwelling, the falling object must cause damage to the roof or outside walls of the dwelling. Coverage for this peril is for the items damaged by the falling object.
- **weight of snow, sleet, or ice:** Coverage for this peril pertains to a building or contents inside a building when damaged by the weight of snow, sleet, or ice, but does not include coverage for the loss to an awning, fence, patio, pavement, pool, foundation, retaining wall, bulkhead, pier, wharf, or dock.
- **accidental discharge or overflow of water or steam:** This peril refers to damage from plumbing; however, there are exclusions and not all losses may be covered. First, the cause and origin of the water must be confirmed to ensure coverage. The tear-out cost to access the part of the building where the repair is necessary may also be covered. The following exclusions may apply:
  - repeated seepage or leakage over a period of time
  - vacancy in the home for more than sixty consecutive days immediately before the loss
  - damage caused by or resulting from freezing except as provided by another peril insured against freezing
  - damage on the described location caused by accidental discharge or overflow which occurs off the insured location (e.g., a backup of a sewer line
- **sudden and accidental bulging, burning, cracking, or tearing apart:** This peril is covered as it relates to HVAC systems, fire sprinkler systems, or hot water heaters. The loss must be sudden and accidental.

Did You Know?

Coverages generally apply to random, sudden losses; gradual losses tend to be excluded from coverage.

- **freezing:** This peril applies to the freezing of plumbing, HVAC systems, fire-protective sprinkler systems, or household appliances ONLY if care was used to maintain heat in the building or the water supply was shut off and drained.
- **sudden and accidental damage from artificially generated electrical current:** Power surges caused by the electrical company can cause damage to the dwelling or contents, and coverage for this peril would apply; however, some carriers may limit or exclude damage to tubes, transistors, and other components inside electronics if the artificially generated current caused the surge.
- **lawns, trees, shrubs, and plants:** There is a list of named perils specific to the coverage of lawns, trees, shrubs, and plants. Wind and hail are not on the list. There is also a limit for the coverage of 5 percent of the Coverage A limit or $500 per any one tree, shrub, or plant. The property cannot be grown for commercial purposes.
- **breakage of glass:** This peril is broader and provides more coverage based on how the glass was broken; however, losses are mostly excluded if the structure has been vacant for more than sixty consecutive days prior to the loss, unless the loss itself was caused by movement of the earth.

- **collapse:** A collapse means an abrupt falling down or caving in which results in the building not being safe to occupy. In order to be covered, the collapse must meet one of the following conditions:
  - The collapse was caused by one of the perils named on the policy.
  - While decay is normally an excluded peril, if it is hidden from view and causes the collapse, there is a possibility for coverage to apply.
  - The weight of contents, equipment, animals, or people can cause the collapse and coverage would be provided.
  - If the weight of rain on a roof causes the collapse of the roof, there is a possibility for coverage to apply.
  - If defective materials or methods in construction, remodeling, or renovation cause the collapse, there is a possibility for coverage to apply.

Helpful Hint:

A building that is in danger of falling or caving—but has not yet collapsed—does not meet the definition of collapse, even if it shows evidence of cracking, sagging, settling, etc.

Quick Review Questions

5) Name an example of an accidental discharge of water that would be covered under the DP-2: Broad Form?

6) What must the named insured do in order to avoid a coverage issue when dealing with a frozen pipe loss?

7) The peril of collapse can include several situations; what are some examples of these?

DP-3: Special Form

The DP-3: Special Form provides the broadest coverage of the three dwelling policies and is therefore the most expensive. The DP-3: Special Form is an **open peril** policy, which means that all perils to the building are covered unless explicitly excluded from the policy.

Common exclusions on the DP-3: Special Form include some types of losses such as ordinance or law, flooding, movement of the earth, or war.

Table 3.1. Types of Dwelling Coverage Forms

Policy	Covered Perils	Exclusions
DP-1: Basic Form	named perils only	anything that is not a named peril

Table 3.1. Types of Dwelling Coverage Forms		
Policy	**Covered Perils**	**Exclusions**
DP-2: Broad Form	named perils only with expanded coverage from the DP-1	anything that is not a named peril
DP-3: Special Form	all perils	any perils specifically named on the exclusions list

Quick Review Questions

8. What does an open peril policy cover?

9. Which types of losses are commonly excluded on a DP-3: Special Form?

Types of Property Coverages

Property Coverage Overview

There are several types of property coverages in a policy. They include the following:

- Coverage A - Dwelling
- Coverage B - Other Structures
- Coverage C - Personal Property or Contents
- Coverage D - Fair Rental Value
- Coverage E - Additional Living Expenses
- Coverage F - Other Coverages

Helpful Hint:

To have full coverage, the policyholder must first ensure that all of the property's features are named in the policy, and then the policyholder must ensure that all anticipated perils are fully covered. If both coverages are not in place, the insurer will not payout on a claim.

Coverages A through D are considered the basic four types of coverage found in all DP forms. Every policy has coverages and exclusions. In addition, property owners can select the amount of their deductible, as well as their limits. They can also select whether to receive payments on an actual cash-value basis (i.e., what the item is worth at the time of the loss) or as the replacement cost required to purchase a new item.

Table 3.2. Property Coverages for Dwelling Policies				
	Damage Type	**DP-1**	**DP-2**	**DP-3**
A - Dwelling	direct	X	X	X
B - Other Structures on the Property	direct	X	X	X
C - Personal Property	direct	X	X	X
D - Fair Rental Value	indirect	X	X	X
E - Living Expenses	indirect	additional endorsement	X	X

As with all insurance policies, the cost of the premium depends on the deductible, the payout of the policy, and its limits of liability. In cases where a mortgage company is involved, the property owner will need to ensure there is enough coverage, or else the mortgage company may refuse to lend them money for the purchase of the property. The agent will walk the consumer through all of the policy options to ensure that all coverages, policy limits, deductibles, and loss settlements are clear and fit the client's needs.

In order to understand the policy's coverage, it is important to differentiate types of potential damage to the property. First, **direct damage** means the peril directly impacts the dwelling or property belonging to the insured. For example, during a strong wind storm, several shingles blew off the roof, allowing water to seep into the home, causing **indirect** water damage to ceilings. Because the wind caused minor physical (direct) damage to the roof, the missing shingles allowed rain to flow through the roof and damage the interior of the home. Thus, the wind indirectly damaged the building's ceiling. For example, an owner purchased a policy that includes protection against the weight of snow, sleet, or ice. After an ice storm, the house's roof and the diving board for the pool were damaged, so the owner filed a claim. Because both the building and the pool were listed on the policy's declarations page, the policyholder expects the company to pay for repairs to both features; however, she did not realize that snow, sleet, and ice damage coverage does not apply to swimming pools, so that claim was rejected.

Quick Review Questions

10) What is the difference between direct and indirect damage?

11) Which of the coverages are part of all dwelling policies?

Coverage A - Dwelling

Coverage A - Dwelling applies to the dwelling itself, which includes any room or addition under the same roof line or somehow attached to the main structure. In order to be considered a dwelling, the structure must be utilized principally for dwelling purposes. In other words, it must have a place to cook a meal, use a bathroom, and sleep.

Coverage A also covers materials and supplies located on or next to the described location intended for the construction or repair of those structures at the location. Lastly, it covers building equipment and outdoor equipment used to service the described location.

> **Helpful Hint**
>
> Like all dwelling and homeowner policies, Coverage A does not cover the actual land underneath the dwelling.

The following possible structures are considered part of Coverage A:

- house
- attached garage
- attached in-law suite
- screened-in porch

For example, the location in a policy's declarations has a house with an attached garage, a shed, and a pool. The policy limit under Coverage A is $250,000, and the deductible is $1,000:

- $\textit{Covered damage in the garage and kitchen} = \$25{,}000.$
- $\textit{Covered damage to the shed} = \$1{,}200.$
- $\textit{Covered damage to the pool} = \$18{,}000.$
- $\textit{The total damage}: = \$44{,}200.$

Based on the information provided, the payout would occur as follows under Coverage A - Dwelling:

- The house with the attached garage is the only structure covered under Coverage A - Dwelling.
- The insurer would only make payment for the damage to the house and the attached garage, which totaled $25,000—less the $1,000 deductible—for a payable amount of $24,000.
- In this example there is no implication that coverage does not exist for the shed or pool damage; payment for those losses would fall under Coverage B - Other Structures.

Quick Review Questions

12) Which type of structure would fall under Coverage A?

13) Does Coverage A include construction materials?

Coverage B - Other Structures

Coverage B - Other Structures protects other structures on the property separated from the dwelling by clear space. Examples include pools, fences, sheds, or barns. In order for these structures to be protected under Coverage B, they must be permanently installed to the ground. A plastic shed that is placed on the grass without any type of permanent anchoring would not be protected under this coverage but could potentially have coverage under **Coverage C - Personal Property**, which will be discussed in the next section.

There is no coverage for anything considered an "other" structure if it is rented or held for rental to anyone who is not a tenant of the dwelling unless it is being used as a private garage. In other words, if the dwelling is rented to one person and the detached garage is rented to a completely different person, what the garage in question is used for needs to be established in order to determine if Coverage B applies. If it is used as a private garage for a vehicle, it would be covered.

If something that is considered another structure is used wholly or partly for commercial, manufacturing, or farming purposes, there would be no coverage under Coverage B, unless

- the commercial, manufacturing, or farming property (equipment) is solely owned by the named insured or their tenant; and
- the property does not include gaseous or liquid fuel other than fuel in a permanently installed fuel tank of a vehicle or craft that is parked or stored in the structure.

The limit of liability for Coverage B - Other Structures is 10 percent of the Coverage A - Dwelling policy limit.

> **Did You Know?**
>
> Grave markers, including mausoleums, are not covered under Coverage B - Other Structures.

Returning to the previous example, the location in the policy declarations has a house with an attached garage, a shed, and a pool. The policy limit under Coverage A is $250,000, and the deductible is $1,000:

- $\textit{Covered damage in the garage and kitchen} = \$25{,}000.$
- $\textit{Covered damage to the shed} = \$1{,}200.$
- $\textit{Covered damage to the pool} = \$18{,}000.$
- $\textit{Total damage} = \$44{,}200.$

Based on the information provided, the payout would occur as follows under Coverage B - Other Structures:

- The house with the attached garage is covered under Coverage A, and the policy already paid out $24,000 toward repairing the house and the garage.
- Since the shed and the pool are not attached to the house, they are covered under Coverage B - Other Structures.
- The insurer would only pay for the damage to the shed and pool which totaled $19,200 less the $1,000.00 deductible for a payable amount of $18,200.00.

Quick Review Questions

14) Name three examples of properties covered by Coverage B - Other Structures.

15) The insured rents his detached garage to a neighbor, who uses it to run his auto repair business. Is there coverage for this detached structure under Coverage B - Other Structures?

Coverage C - Personal Property

Coverage C - Personal Property covers contents that do not form part of the dwelling or other structures. In other words, these are contents that are not permanently attached to the buildings. Also, the personal property should usually be found on that dwelling or property and should be owned or used by the named insured's family members who reside on that property. There is an additional endorsement for coverage of property owned by a guest or household employees while on the described location.

> **Helpful Hint**
>
> Several exclusions exist under Coverage C and include manuscripts, passports, currency, animals, fish, hovercrafts, motor vehicles, most watercraft, data, and credit cards.

If the insured purchases another property and is in the process of moving his personal property from one home to the other, Coverage C does allow for coverage with certain stipulations included in the policy language.

It is important to confirm that the policy actually provides coverage for personal property and what the limits are. The premium amount is proportionate to the amount of coverage selected by the owner.

For example, a policyholder suffers a covered loss to some of her personal property in the insured dwelling. The policy limit for Coverage C is $150,000, and the deductible is $1,000. There is no damage to anything under Coverages A or B. The following Coverage C items were damaged:

- motorcycle: $1,500
- books and magazines: $500
- two chairs: $3,000
- toys: $875
- gold coins: $2,000
  - The total loss is $7,875.
  - The total loss minus the value of the motorcycle and coins is $3,500.
  - **The amount of loss covered is $3,375.**

Because the motorcycle and gold coins are both listed in the policy exclusions, no payment can be made for either. The loss of the books, magazines, chairs, and toys totals $4,375 less the $1,000 deductible for a settlement of $3,375. If the insured does not pay an extra premium for the replacement cost coverage of personal property, there may be a deduction for depreciation.

Quick Review Questions

16) Would the DP-3 provide coverage for the dashboard stereo, tires, and music CDs in the insured's vehicle?

17) The insured had a house fire which destroyed $500 in cash sitting on the dining room table, as well as his model airplane and two of the dining room chairs. Which item(s) would DP-3 cover for the damage caused by fire?

Coverage D - Fair Rental Value

Coverage D - Fair Rental Value, also known as **FRV**, provides protection in case the owner or the resident has to move out of the property while repairs are being made. The FRV is determined by an in-depth market evaluation of the rental value of the home. This analysis includes the type and size of the home, the number of rooms/bathrooms, and the location.

In order for this coverage to apply, the loss must be covered by a peril insured under the policy; expenses that do not continue while the home is unfit to inhabit must be deducted. The payment can be claimed for the shortest amount of time it takes to repair or rebuild the described location that is rented or held for rental.

If the home is habitable but a civil authority prohibits people from staying in the home as a result of direct damage to a neighboring location by a covered peril, this coverage will provide the fair rental value for up to two weeks.

The periods of time referenced above are not limited by the expiration of the policy, which means the coverage can continue after the policy coverage dates expire until the two deadlines above are met.

For example, if a tornado causes the roof of a home to blow off, the home would most likely be considered uninhabitable until a new roof is constructed and any ensuing interior damage is repaired so that the home can once again be occupied. The insured can submit a claim for the loss of rent while the repairs are underway.

> **Helpful Hint**
>
> This coverage does not apply if a lease agreement is cancelled.

Quick Review Questions

18) A dwelling was destroyed due to flooding and the tenant had to move elsewhere. Would the insured have coverage for the loss of rent while the dwelling is rebuilt?

19) Can Coverage D - Fair Rental Value continue after the policy expiration date?

Coverage E - Additional Living Expenses

Coverage E - Additional Living Expenses pays additional expenses that the insured may encounter if the dwelling is rendered uninhabitable and the insured has to move out while repairs are underway. For example, if the insured has to board his pet, pay additional gas and tolls to get to work, or pay to do laundry, these expenses may be covered.

This coverage is only available for DP-2: Broad Form and DP-3: Special Form, and a proper investigation and review of each policy is important to ensure that the appropriate payments are made. The coverage is indirect and as such can only be triggered when the policy covers a direct damage claim under coverages A, B, or C.

There is also coverage for up to two weeks should civil authorities require the owner to leave the residence as a result of direct, covered damage to a neighboring location. The periods of time mentioned above are not limited by the expiration of the policy, but no coverage is provided if a lease or agreement is cancelled.

For example, a dwelling is uninhabitable for thirty days in order to repair damage from a covered loss. The only place the insured can stay for thirty days is a hotel with a microwave and a small fridge. The insured are eating restaurant food

> **Helpful Hint**
>
> Coverage E payments will be made for the shortest time required to either repair or replace the dwelling or for the shortest time required for the household to permanently relocate elsewhere if they decide to do so.

for three meals a day for most of the month. Table 3.3. shows their normal expenses prior to the loss and their current expenses.

Table 3.3. Additional Expenses

Expense Type	Normal Expense	Incurred While at Hotel	Additional Info
Hotel stay 30 days	$0	$3,850	They are still paying their mortgage on the dwelling.
Utilities	$600	$0	The hotel has no utility charges.
Groceries for month	$900	$200	They bought snacks and drinks for their hotel stay.
Restaurants	$400	$2,700	The hotel only has a small fridge and microwave.
Vehicle miles	$120	$230	The hotel is farther away from their jobs than their insured dwelling.
Total	**$2,020**	**$6,980**	**$4,960 over and above normal expenses**

In Table 3.3., the insured's normal expenses during a thirty-day period are $2,020; however, due to having to move out of their home during repairs, their monthly expenses for a thirty-day period increased to $6,980. As such, they are claiming $4,960 in additional living expenses to maintain a normal standard of living.

Quick Review Questions

20) If a hurricane causes an insured and her family's home to become uninhabitable, would Coverage E - Additional Living Expenses help cover the cost for food and shelter until the home can be habitable?

21) For how long are coverage E payments made?

Other Coverages

All three dwelling policies—DP-1, DP-2, and DP-3—have a section in the policy for "other coverages." As with the other coverages in a dwelling policy, The DP-2 and DP-3 have additional protection that the DP-1 does not. Each of the coverages outlined below can be found on all three policies:

Other Structures

Under the DP-1, this coverage allows up to 10 percent of the Coverage A limit to be used for payment of covered damage to other structures; however, the amount paid is then deducted from the total Coverage A payment limit. In the DP-2 and DP-3, the amount paid does not reduce the Coverage A limit and is considered additional insurance.

Debris Removal

This coverage applies to the removal of debris from the property, as long as the debris was caused by an insured cause of loss. The limit for this coverage is dependent on the coverage that is being utilized for that particular portion of the loss. For example, if the estimate is written to replace the roof of the dwelling, the debris removal of the original roof materials would be paid for under the limit for Coverage A.

Improvements, Alterations and Additions

The DP-1 and DP-2 provide coverage for any improvements, alterations, or additions made to that part of the described location only used and paid for by the tenant. The limit available is 10 percent of the Coverage C limit for personal property. This makes sense since their policy would not have any need for Coverage A or B due to the property being owned by someone else.

In principle, the tenant would only need coverage for the dwelling's contents, or Coverage C. The only difference between the DP-1 and the DP-2 for this coverage is that the amount paid for the loss reduces the limit for Coverage C from the DP-1, while on the DP-2, that 10 percent is an additional amount of insurance.

For example, if the limit for Coverage C is $100,000, the DP-1 and DP-2 provide coverage of 10 percent, or $10,000. Under the DP-1, the $100,000 limit is reduced by $10,000 if the full 10 percent is paid for the claim for improvements or alterations and additions, whereas the DP-2 allows the full $100,000 limit under Coverage C plus an additional $10,000 for those same repairs.

Worldwide Coverage

The DP-1, DP-2, and DP-3 provide up to 10 percent of the Coverage C limit to pay for covered damage to the insured's personal property while it is anywhere in the world. The property of guests and household employees is not included in this coverage under the DP-1, and none of the three policies cover rowboats or canoes. The payment made under this coverage reduces the amount of the Coverage C limit under all three policies.

Reasonable Repairs

Sometimes referred to as temporary repairs, this coverage allows the owner of the damaged property to be reimbursed for the cost of any repairs made solely to protect the property against further damage.

All three dwelling policies offer this coverage for damage to property that is caused by an insured peril, and it does not increase the limit that applies to the covered property.

For example, if a wind storm causes roof shingles to fly off, exposing the interior of the home to leaks, this coverage will allow for payment so the insured can have the roof tarped until permanent repairs can be made.

Property Removed

All three dwelling policies offer coverage for the property against direct loss from any cause while it is being removed from the premises to protect it from an insured peril. The coverage does not change the limit of liability that applies to that particular coverage. The DP-1 offers coverage for no more than five days, while the DP-2 and DP-3 offer it for no more than thirty days.

Fire Department Service Charge

The three policies provide coverage up to $500 for any fire department charges incurred when they are called out to save or protect covered property from a covered peril. If the peril is not covered (e.g., the need to save a dog who fell into a well), the incurred charges from the fire department are not covered either.

Ordinance and Law

This coverage protects against loss from the repair or replacement of items that need to be brought up to code or that must be demolished because of a local law. The limits to payment would be 10 percent of the total Coverage A limit and 10 percent of the Coverage B limit. The owner may use all or part of that 10 percent limit to remove debris associated with the code-enforced repair or demo.

The ordinance and law (O&L) coverage does not include any loss of value due to the requirements of any ordinance or law, and it does not cover any costs to comply with any O&L which requires the testing, cleanup, monitoring, and so forth of pollutants. Finally, the coverage is considered additional insurance; as such, it is above and beyond the policy limit under the coverage from which it is being paid.

Did You Know?

If the property is located within the limits of a city or municipality, the fire department charges should be covered by the property taxes paid on that property.

Quick Review Questions

22) Can the insured claim any out-of-pocket expenses for the removal of tree debris?

23) Will the coverage for debris removal allow for the removal of shed debris from the Coverage B policy limit?

24) The insured moved his expensive art to a storage unit away from the path of a hurricane for three days in order to protect it. Would there be coverage for the artwork should the hurricane's path change?

25) How much coverage does the insured have for his contents while away from the home in a different country?

Exclusions

Dwelling policies have a section with a list of perils that are excluded from coverage, and these losses are excluded even if a covered peril caused the initial loss. The exclusions are described below.

Ordinance or Law

This coverage varies depending on what the cause of the damage was. For example, if a tornado caused damage to the electrical panel of the home, there would be coverage for the repair of the electrical panel because tornadoes are a covered peril. While performing covered repairs, the electrician discovered that the wiring needed to be brought up to code. In this case, the O&L coverage described above under "Other Coverages" would pay for the code upgrade.

In contrast, a home is having electrical problems, and the insured makes repairs but does not bring the panel up to code. A few days later, the electrical panel in the home catches fire. Since the cause of the damage is due to not bringing the panel up to code, the repair cost would not be covered.

Movement of the Earth

All three policies exclude damage caused by any kind of movement of the earth, including earthquakes, landslides, sinkholes, or other types of movement of the earth from sinking, rising, shifting, human or animal force, or acts of nature. If a direct loss by fire or explosion ensues from any movement of the earth, only the damage caused by that fire or explosion is covered. The DP-3 also adds protection from damage caused by movement of the earth due to naturally or artificially created loss, on or off the described location, caused by or resulting from rain or snow.

Water Damage

This is a very broad peril. Any time water is involved in a loss, a very thorough investigation needs to take place to determine the cause and origin of the water. Some types of water losses that are excluded include flooding, water that backs up from a sewer system, and water that is below or above the surface of the ground and seeps in through a building, sidewalk, or foundation. As with the example above, if a fire or explosion causes ensuing damage, coverage would apply to that ensuing damage only.

Power Failure

Power failure which takes place off the residence premises is covered as long as it triggers peril coverage that is covered on the property.

Neglect

Coverage could be excluded if the insured fails to use all reasonable means to protect the property from damage either during or after the event that caused the loss.

War

Any damage caused by an act of war, including undeclared war—rebellion or otherwise—will be excluded from coverage. This includes damage caused by destruction, seizure, or use for military purposes.

Nuclear Hazard

This refers the insured to the "Conditions" section of the policy where the term *nuclear hazard* is defined as any nuclear reaction or radioactive contamination, whether controlled or not, however it is caused. It further states that a loss caused by a nuclear hazard will not be considered a loss caused by fire, explosion, or smoke. A loss caused by a nuclear hazard and resulting in fire will be considered for coverage.

Intentional Loss

Any loss caused intentionally by an insured or additional insured is excluded from coverage.

> **Helpful Hint**
>
> Even if the insured did not commit the loss, or if the insured was unaware of the intent of another resident on the property to commit a loss, the insured may still be excluded from coverage for the loss.

Governmental Action

Should any government authority cause any destruction or damage during the confiscation or seizure of property described under Coverages A, B or C, the damage would be excluded. The exclusion does not apply if the acts are ordered or taken at the time of a fire in order to prevent its spread, but only if the fire is covered under the policy and there are no other exclusions.

DP-3: Special Form Exclusions

The DP-3 further adds exclusions for Coverages A and B caused by losses from—but not limited to—faulty planning, zoning, design, workmanship, construction, materials used in repair, and maintenance.

Quick Review Questions

26) Would the insured have coverage for damage caused by a rotting tree he was repeatedly warned about by his landscaper?

27) Can an insurer deny a claim for intentional damage caused by the insured's son?

28) Is there coverage under the DP-3 if an appliance causes damage to flooring due to a maintenance or wear-and-tear issue?

29) If rioters break the insured's windows, would the claim be denied due to the exclusion of war?

Conditions in Dwelling Policy Forms

Dwelling policies include the conditions described below.

Policy Period

The policy for which the insured is paying a premium only applies to losses that occur during that policy's period.

Insurable Interest and Limit of Liability

Even if more than one person owns the property and therefore has an insurable interest in it, the policy will only provide coverage up to and no greater than the interest of the person insured under the policy at the time of the loss and no more than the policy's limits of liability.

Concealment or Fraud

Coverage for a loss can be affected and possibly denied if one or more persons insured under the policy are found to have intentionally concealed or misrepresented facts or circumstances, engaged in fraudulent conduct, or made any false statements relating to insurance before, during, or after a loss.

Duties After Loss

In case of a covered loss, the insured or their representative must comply with the following duties; otherwise, the loss could be excluded:

- Give prompt notice about the claim.
- Protect the property from further damage.
- Cooperate with the insurer during the investigation of the claim.
- Prepare an inventory of personal property per the policy guidelines.
- Provide the insurer with any records or documents requested.
- Submit to an examination under oath if requested by the insurer.
- Submit within sixty days of the date of the insurer's request the following documents: signed proof of loss with the time of the loss; the insured's interest in the affected property; other insurance which may apply to the loss; changes in title, occupancy or ownership; specifications of damaged buildings and detailed estimates; inventories of personal property, receipts for any additional living expenses.

Helpful Hint

In order to qualify for coverage, the insured must complete ALL of the required steps on time in order to receive payment for a loss.

Loss Settlement

Under the DP-1, losses are settled at actual cash value, which means there could be a deduction for depreciation based on the age and condition of the property being estimated. The payment cannot be more than the amount required to repair or replace the damaged property.

Under the DP-2 and DP-3 policies, personal property, awnings, carpet, appliances, antennas, and outdoor equipment will be settled at actual cash value. For property covered under Coverages A or B, the loss will be settled at replacement cost, with some stipulations, depending on whether at the time of the loss the amount of insurance on the damaged building is 80 percent or more of the full replacement cost of the building just prior to the loss.

Loss to a Pair or Set

If there is a loss to an item that is part of a pair or set, the insurer may elect to repair or replace it to restore the pair or set to its pre-loss value, or the insurer may pay the difference between the actual cash value of the property before and after the loss.

Glass Replacement

On the DP-1, broken glass caused by a covered peril will be paid for on a replacement basis with safety glazing materials when required by ordinance or law. This condition does not appear in the DP-2 or DP-3 policies.

> **Did You Know?**
>
> Many insurances policies cover replacing a set if it is impossible to find a replacement that will fit perfectly with the remaining piece(s). Insurance policies should be checked to see if an entire set can be replaced.

Appraisal

If the insurer and the insured cannot agree on an amount for the loss, either party may demand an appraisal for the loss. This is for the amount of the loss and is unrelated to any disagreement on whether a loss is covered or not. Each party will select a different appraiser, after which both appraisers will choose an umpire. Each party will pay their own appraiser's fees and each will share the expenses of the umpire equally.

Other Insurance and Service Agreement

If property covered under the insured's policy is also covered by a different policy, the insured's policy will pay for the proportion of the loss caused by the covered peril under that policy with the limit of liability of that policy. If the insured has a service agreement for the damaged property, the dwelling policy will be in excess over any amounts payable under the service agreement. Examples include home warranties and service plans.

Subrogation

Should the insurer have an opportunity to recover any payments made for a claim from an at-fault party, the insured must sign and deliver all related papers and cooperate with the insurer's efforts to recoup the loss.

Suit Against the Insurer

No legal action can be brought against the insurer unless there has been full compliance with all the terms of the policy and the action is brought on within two years after the date of the loss.

Insurer's Option to Repair or Replace

If the insurer gives the insured written notice within thirty days after receipt of the sworn proof of loss, the insurer may replace or repair the damaged property with material or property of like, kind, and quality.

Loss Payment

All losses will be adjusted with the insured, and payments will be made to the insured and/or any person named on the policy or legally entitled to receive payment. The loss will be payable within sixty days after receipt of the proof of loss and an agreement has been reached with the insured, when there is a final judgment, or if there is a filing of an appraisal award with the insurer.

Abandonment of Property

The insurer will not need to accept or be responsible for any property abandoned by the insured.

Mortgage Clause

If there is a mortgage on the insured dwelling and the damage is to the dwelling or another structure on the property, the insurer has certain stipulations which must be followed in order to protect all involved parties.

For example, the name of the mortgage company may be required to be named on any payments. If the insurer denies the insured's claim, the denial may not apply to the mortgage company if the claim is valid and additional stipulations in this section of the policy are followed. If the insurer decides to cancel or not renew the policy, they have ten days to notify the mortgage company before the date of cancellation; otherwise nonrenewal takes effect.

No Benefit to Bailee

No coverage will apply to any person or organization holding, storing, or moving property for a fee. If there is a loss, the payment will be made to the owner of the property, not the company moving it.

Cancellation

The insured may cancel the policy at any time by letting the insurer know—in writing—the requested date of cancellation. The insurer may also cancel the policy but only for certain reasons, such as nonpayment of premiums or if the dwelling has changed substantially since the policy's inception. If the policy has already been in effect for one year or more, the insurer may cancel in writing at least thirty days prior to the cancellation date.

Nonrenewal

If the insurer chooses not to renew the policy, the insured must be informed in writing at least thirty days prior to the expiration date.

Liberalization Clause

This clause explains the insurer's responsibility and what premium change, if any, will take effect when there is a change in the policy which broadens or restricts coverage under the policy's current edition.

Waiver or Change of Policy Provisions

Changes in a policy can be made by attaching an endorsement, but the changes must be made in writing by the insurer in order for them to be valid.

Assignment

Assignment or transfer of the ownership of a policy will not be valid unless the insurer gives written consent.

Death

If the named insured dies, the policy insures their legal representative, but only for property covered under the policy at the time of death.

> **Helpful Hint**
>
> Whenever an insurer makes changes to a policy, the law requires that these be done in writing.

Nuclear Hazard Clause

This condition explains that any loss caused by a nuclear hazard will not be considered a loss caused by fire, explosion, or smoke.

Recovered Property

If the property the insurer paid for is recovered, the insured has the opportunity to keep it in exchange for the reimbursement of the claim payment made by the insurer.

Volcanic Eruption Period

This condition explains that one or more eruptions within seventy-two hours will be considered as one loss; therefore one claim and one deductible will apply.

Loss Payable Clause

If the declarations page of the policy lists a loss payee (person) for certain property, that person is then considered insured under the policy for that specific property.

Adjustments to Coverage Limits

On the DP-3 only, this condition states that the limits of liability for Coverages A, B, C, and D represent the maximum limit of liability, but adjustments can be made at the renewal date time. It then specifies what percentage of change can be made under specific coverages.

Quick Review Questions

30) Can the insured file suit on a claim three years after the date of the loss?

31) How long does the insurer have to advise the mortgage company of a policy cancellation or nonrenewal?

32) How is property covered when an insured passes away?

33) How many of the "Duties After Loss" must an insured comply with should a loss occur?

34) Can the insured assign the ownership of a policy to a family member?

Dwelling Policy Endorsements

As discussed throughout this chapter, a dwelling policy provides many different types of coverage to protect property from loss; however, there are some perils that are excluded. Endorsements can be added to policies to provide supplemental coverage for additional perils. In some states where certain perils are common, insurers may be required by law to offer endorsements to cover damage not typically covered by the dwelling policy. This section describes some endorsements that are important in fully protecting a home and personal property from loss.

Automatic Increase in Insurance

This endorsement protects the owner of the property should there be a sudden change in costs for materials or labor to repair or replace covered damaged property in cases of inflation.

Dwelling Under Construction

A dwelling policy will provide coverage unless the home is vacant for more than sixty days, at which point it is considered to be at higher risk of theft, vandalism, or storm-related damage. This endorsement adds protection from theft or covered damage to the dwelling or the materials being used for the construction.

Sinkhole Collapse

The dwelling policy does not cover any type of movement of the earth (e.g., sinkhole or mudslide); however, there are some states where these are common and required to be added to a policy. This coverage helps to repair the home and the foundation or to stabilize the ground if the home begins to collapse into a sinkhole.

Condo Owners

This endorsement covers any covered costs associated with the owner's unit which are not covered under the condominium's policy (e.g., the loss assessment). In this case, the insurance would reimburse the unit owner in whole or in part for the owner's portion of the condominium association's deductible.

Water Backup and Sump Pump Overflow

A dwelling policy provides coverage for different types of water damage; however, it does not provide coverage for damage caused by a backup of water or sewage from drains, sump pumps, or sewage pipes. This endorsement can add coverage for those perils at a low cost.

Broad Theft Coverage

This endorsement offers off-premises coverage to the dwelling owner for property that is owned or used by the insured in the described location when the owner is away from the described premises.

Did You Know?

Broad theft coverage can be applied to all personal property with all risk coverage.

Limited Theft Coverage

This endorsement protects landlords when the insured dwelling is tenant-occupied. Coverage is limited to property used or owned by the landlord and the landlord's partner.

Quick Review Questions

35) Are endorsements free?

36) Can the insured have coverage for sinkhole damage?

37) What does the endorsement for owners of condominiums cover?

38) What does an endorsement for water backup and sump pump cover?

39) What is the purpose of an automatic increase in insurance?

Chapter Review

Table 3.4. Chapter 3 Review: Personal Dwelling Policies	
Standard Dwelling Policy Components	
Parts of the policy	• insuring agreement • definitions • deductibles • coverages and other coverages • covered perils • exclusions • coverage conditions
Dwelling Coverage Forms	
Basic	• DP-1 • includes only named basic perils • no minimum required
Broad	• DP-2 • covers perils named in the declarations • covers basic and broad perils, plus extended coverage perils • includes protection for malicious mischief and vandalism
Special	• DP-3 • protects on an open-peril basis • covers basic and broad perils • includes protection for malicious mischief and vandalism
Types of Property Covered	
Coverage A - Dwelling	• defines which coverage applies to the dwelling itself • for residential properties
Coverage B - Other Structures	• includes outdoor structures at the same location • includes detached structures (e.g., barns, fences)
Coverage C - Personal Property	• applies to the possessions of the owner or her visitors that are located inside the dwelling

Table 3.4. Chapter 3 Review: Personal Dwelling Policies	
Coverage D - Fair Rental Value	• reimburses the insured for rent paid while the dwelling is being repaired • applies if the dwelling has been destroyed or damaged by a covered peril
Coverage E - Additional Living Expenses	• covers increases in living expenses while the dwelling is being repaired • includes expenses needed for everyday life (e.g., tolls, laundry, hotel)

Answer Key

1. A detached structure is a permanently installed building or feature that does not form part of the main dwelling. Examples include separate garages, sheds, pools, and fences.

2. A dwelling policy is typically obtained by people who need coverage for a seasonal home, a rental home, properties that are in the process of being built, or permanently installed mobile homes.

3. The DP-1: Basic Form is a named peril policy and includes perils such as frozen pipes, lightning, explosion, vandalism, wind, and smoke.

4. The named perils on the DP-1: Basic Form are all similar in that they are sudden and accidental versus perils that gradually damage a property over time.

5. One example of a covered claim for floor damage from a water discharge would involve a sudden and accidental leak from a hot water heater.

6. The named insured must ensure the dwelling was kept at a reasonable temperature when the cold snap came through, and they must have been in residence for at least sixty consecutive days before the event occurred.

7. The peril of collapse can include situations such as the use of defective materials having been used, the weight of rain or snow causing the roof to collapse, decay damage that was hidden, or the weight of animals or people.

8. An open peril policy (DP-3: Special Form) covers any damage—no matter the cause—as long as it is not one of the named exclusions.

9. Common exclusions on the DP-3: Special Form include ordinance or law, flooding, movement of the earth, or war.

10. Direct damage is when a peril is responsible for the actual cause of the loss or damage, such as when wind blows away a few shingles from a roof. Indirect damage is when a peril causes a domino effect whereby the initial property is not physically damaged (or sustains only minor damage), but the peril allows something else to be damaged, such as when wind lifts a few shingles from a house, causing rain to seep in and destroy a ceiling in the home's interior.

11. Coverages A through D are part of all dwelling policies, but part D is considered an indirect coverage.

12. The main structure being utilized as a dwelling—and everything attached to it—would be insured under Coverage A.

13. Any construction materials located on or next to the dwelling and being used during the construction or repair of a structure on the described policy would be covered.

14. Examples of properties covered by Coverage B - Other Structures include a pool, fence, barn, shed, detached garage, and tree house.

15. Because the renter uses the space for his auto repair business, there is no coverage. Ideally, the renter should have business insurance that will cover any losses for his tools, clients' vehicles, etc.

16. The DP-3: Special Form covers personal property that is not considered a vehicle or vehicle part, so only the CDs would be covered as long as the policy includes theft protection.

17. While fire is a covered peril, the DP-3: Special Form excludes coverage for money or currency. The model airplane and two dining room chairs would be covered; the cash would not be covered.

18. In order for the insured to be able to claim loss of rent, the cause of the loss must be covered. If the policy excludes flooding, the claim will not be paid.

19. The coverage for Coverage D - Fair Rental Value ends once the dwelling is considered habitable, even if the policy has expired.

20. Coverage E typically only applies if the home is rendered uninhabitable from a covered cause of loss, such as wind, but no coverage is usually afforded if the home is rendered uninhabitable because of flooding.

21. Additional living expenses are reimbursable.

22. The insured can claim any expenses to remove the tree or limbs off covered property that has been damaged by a peril.

23. If shed debris removal is due to a covered peril, the payment would be made from the Coverage B - Other Structures coverage.

24. Under the DP-1: Basic Form, the insured has coverage for this peril for five days from the date the artwork is moved; under the DP-2 and DP-3 policies, the coverage lasts for thirty days.

25. The policy provides coverage up to 10 percent of the Coverage C - Personal Property limit.

26. The insurer would investigate whether or not there was neglect on the part of the insured, and if he is found guilty of neglect, the loss would be excluded.

27. If the loss was deliberately caused by the insured's son, the loss would be excluded.

28. Both maintenance and wear-and-tear issues are excluded by the DP-3: Special Form.

29. Rioting is covered under the extended coverage perils in DP-2 and DP-3 policies, so broken windows caused by rioters would be covered.

30. In order to meet the "Conditions" section of the policy, the insured must file suit within two years of the date of loss.

31. The insurer has ten days to notify the mortgage company before the date of cancellation or nonrenewal takes effect.

32. The policy covers the legal representative of the insured for property covered under the policy at the time of the insured's death.

33. The insured must comply with all of the "Duties After Loss," or coverage of the claim could be denied

34. An insured can only assign the ownership of a policy to someone else if the insured advises the insurer and the insurer gives the insured written consent.

35. Endorsements can be added to policies at an additional cost.

36. While the policy does not cover movement of the earth, there is an endorsement for sinkholes available in some states where it may be required.

37. The endorsement for owners of condominiums covers out-of-pocket expenses for the insured's portion of the deductible paid by the condominium association's master policy on a loss.

38. The endorsement for water backup and sump pump covers damage to flooring or walls affected by non-domestic sewage water that backs up into the home from outside the property

39. An automatic increase in insurance covers the insured's cost(s) should prices for labor or materials suddenly increase due to unforeseen circumstances (e.g., inflation).

4. Homeowners Policies

The Basics of Homeowners Policies

Purpose of Homeowners Insurance

Homeowners policies are comprehensive policies that are uniquely designed to cover different types of residential risks. The policies cover the structure of the home, the contents inside, and other structures on the property. These policies also include liability coverage to protect homeowners if someone gets hurt at the home or if a resident of the home accidentally damages another person's (e.g., a visitor's) property at the home.

It is important for homeowners to purchase the right type of home insurance for the dwellings they live in. For that reason, homeowner policy forms are designated by "HO-" followed by a number that relates to the type of home the policy covers.

In contrast, **dwelling insurance policies** only cover the structure of a building and the owner's liability, but not the contents or any structures or property outside the home.

People live in various types of residences covered by home insurance, including

- single-family homes,
- townhomes,
- condos or co-ops, and
- mobile homes.

The main components of a homeowner insurance policy are the property coverage (the structure and the insured's personal property) and liability portions of the policy.

Quick Review Questions

1) What is the PRIMARY purpose of homeowners policies?

2) What are the two main parts of a homeowner policy?

3) How are dwelling policies different from homeowners policies?

Homeowner Policy Definitions

To clarify policy coverages, a homeowner insurance policy has a section that specifically defines important terms used within the policy. Common homeowner policy definitions are described below.

An **insured** is anyone who is insurable under the homeowner policy. A **named insured** is the person(s) named on the policy and that person's spouse if the spouse is a resident of the same household. Other **unnamed insureds** are also covered under a homeowner policy. They include

- anyone else living at the residence who is related to the named insured by blood, marriage, or adoption;
- children under age 21 who are under the care of the insured; and
- full-time students under age 24 who are relatives of the named insured and who lived at the residence before moving away to attend school or are age 21 and in the insured's care.

Did You Know?

Tenant insurance policies (HO-4) are considered homeowners policies even though the residents do not own the building. This policy covers the personal property of the residents and gives them liability protection in case someone gets injured while visiting them or they are personally liable for damage to the building.

The **insured location** is the address on a homeowner policy, along with any other locations listed on the policy. Locations under a homeowner policy include

- the address shown on the policy that is being used as a residence by the named insured;
- other structures and grounds used by the insured as a residence;
- a residence the named insured acquires during the policy period that is being used as a residence;
- a non-owned residence being used as a temporary residence;
- vacant land that is not farmland that is owned by or rented to an insured;
- land that an insured owns or rents which is being built as a one-, two-,three-, or four-family dwelling that is being constructed as the insured's residence;
- individual cemetery plots or burial plots purchased by an insured; and
- residences and their premises that an insured occasionally rents.

Coverage under **bodily injury** includes the loss of essential services such as making meals, mowing the lawn, and doing the laundry. Bodily injury also covers the cost of care, including medical bills, ambulance fees, rehabilitation services, and death-related services.

The policy also covers **business** conducted on the property. It can be any full or part-time trade or profession or any activity performed for compensation on the insured property.

Policies usually define one **occurrence** as one event involving bodily injury or property damage, including those that are continuous or that may expose people or property to the same harmful conditions.

Property damage is any damage to real or personal property that happens because of negligence, an act of nature, or willful destruction.

> **Did You Know?**
>
> Claims adjusters often refer back to these definitions when adjusting a claim to help clarify why an incident may or may not be covered under the policy.

The **residence premises** is the part of a structure where an insured lives as well as other structures on the premises and the grounds on the premises.

A **residence employee** is an insured's employee or an employee covered by a contract with a labor leasing firm whose role is to provide household duties, domestic services, or maintenance.

Quick Review Questions

4) Does an insured location refer only to an insured's primary residence?

5) Would an individual who provides regular house-cleaning services to a named insured be covered under a homeowner policy?

6) If a dog bites a child who is visiting the insured's home, is that considered an occurrence?

Coverage Forms

Coverage Forms Overview

The Insurance Services Office, Inc. (ISO) created different HO forms for different types of properties. Each form includes certain types of **perils** that can cause loss for the policyholder. Each policy form lists the exact perils that will be covered under that policy.

Some forms include **named perils** or **broad perils**; in such cases, the policy form will actually list the specific perils the policy covers. Other forms include **open perils**, which means that the policy covers all risks except those that are specifically excluded.

Homeowners policies are different than dwelling policies in that dwelling policies are designed in three tiers with the lowest tier having the least coverage and the highest tier having the most coverage. Unlike dwelling policies, homeowners policies are designed according to the types of residences they will insure.

Table 4.1. shows the various HO forms and the types of residences that can be insured with each form. The table also shows whether the form includes open perils, named perils, or open perils for one part of the coverage and named perils for another part of the coverage.

Table 4.1. HO Insurance Forms

Form Name and Number	Peril Type	Residential Dwelling Use
Broad Form HO 00 02 or HO-2	named peril	1 – 4 units; owner-occupied
Special Form	open peril and named peril	1 – 4 units; owner-occupied

Form Name and Number	Peril Type	Residential Dwelling Use
HO 00 03 or HO-3		
Renters or Tenants Form HO 00 04 or HO-4	named peril	occupied by tenant
Comprehensive Form HO 00 05 or HO-5	open peril	1 – 4 units; owner-occupied
Condominium Form HO 00 06 or HO-6	named peril	condominium unit; owner-occupied
Modified Form HO 00 08 or HO-8	named peril	1 – 4 units; owner-occupied; historic or older home

Table 4.1. HO Insurance Forms

The named perils include:

- fire or lightning
- windstorm or hail
- explosion
- riot or civil commotion
- aircraft
- vehicles
- smoke
- vandalism or malicious mischief
- theft
- falling objects
- the weight of ice, snow, or sleet
- accidental discharge or overflow of water or steam
- sudden and accidental tearing apart, cracking, burning, or bulging
- freezing
- sudden and accidental damage from artificially generated electrical current
- volcanic eruption

There are certain **general exclusions** that are common to all HO forms. They include:

- ordinance or law
- movement of the earth
- water damage
- power failure
- neglect
- war
- nuclear hazard
- intentional loss
- governmental action

Quick Review Questions

7) Which HO forms could apply to a 1 – 4 unit family dwelling?

8) Which HO form covers a non-owned residence?

Replacement Coverage for HO-2 through HO-5

All homeowners policies except HO-4 are designed to insure residences that are occupied by the owners and their family members, which may include spouses, children, extended family members, and two roomers or one additional family.

Also, homeowners policies cover an owner's primary residence only; they are not appropriate for vacation homes, secondary homes, or vacant homes.

In the event of a total loss where a residence must be replaced, homeowners policies will pay to rebuild the structure as long as it was insured immediately before the loss for at least 80 percent of the full cost to rebuild the structure. The 80 percent provision does not apply to excavation expenses, footings, piers, foundations, or materials used to support the structure.

If the home was insured for less than 80 percent of the replacement cost, the insurer will only pay up to the dwelling coverage limit stated on the policy.

Also, insurers will only pay for the actual cost value up to the policy limit while the structure is being built. They will pay the difference in the full replacement cost when the construction has been completed. Insurers will only replace the building with materials of like kind and quality and for similar uses. The insurer will pay the full replacement cost to replace the building without considering depreciation as long as the amount is necessary to replace the building.

Did You Know?

Homeowners policies cover foster children and any children who are in the care of the insured, even if the children are not listed on the policy.

Did You Know?

Homeowners may use up to 10 percent of the replacement coverage to cover any costs needed to add upgrades to meet ordinances or laws.

Homeowners may opt to rebuild the structure on a new site, but the insurer will not pay for more than the cost to rebuild the structure on the original site.

In all cases, homeowners must pay the deductible before the insurer will pay anything.

Quick Review Questions

9) Which types of homes are NOT covered by HO policies?

10) Can homeowners rebuild a property on a different location?

11) Is there a provision that allows the homeowner to bring the structure up to new codes or make improvements?

Individual Homeowner Coverage Forms (HO-2, HO-3, and HO-5)

An **HO-2** form is typically used for dwellings that insurers feel are risky to insure. This is a named peril policy for the dwelling and its contents and includes the following coverages:

- dwelling
- other structures
- personal property
- loss of use
- additional coverages
- liability
- medical payments

The exclusions on an HO-2 policy are as follows:

- ordinance or law
- movement of the earth
- water damage
- power failure
- neglect
- war
- nuclear hazard
- intentional loss
- governmental action

The HO-2 only covers personal property for named perils.

An **HO-3** form is commonly used for standard housing. It includes the following coverages:

- dwelling
- other structures
- personal property
- loss of use
- additional coverages
- liability
- medical payments

The exclusions on an HO-3 policy are as follows:

- ordinance or law
- movement of the earth
- water damage
- power failure
- neglect
- war
- nuclear hazard
- intentional loss
- governmental action

Did You Know?

Endorsements can be added to all HO forms to provide additional coverage for things like jewelry, fine arts, and sporting equipment; all are covered for open perils.

HO-3 policies cover the structure for open perils and the personal property for named perils.

An **HO-5** policy is the most comprehensive homeowner form. Because it offers more coverage, it is the most expensive of the HO forms. It is generally used for mid-range homes, upscale homes, and luxury homes. An HO-5 policy includes the following coverages:

- dwelling
- other structures
- personal property
- loss of use
- additional coverages
- liability
- medical payments

The exclusions on an HO-5 policy are as follows:

- ordinance or law
- movement of the earth
- water damage

- power failure
- neglect
- war
- nuclear hazard
- intentional loss
- governmental action

An HO-5 policy covers open perils for the structure and the contents.

Quick Review Questions

12) Why would someone choose an HO-2 policy?

13) Which HO form offers the most comprehensive coverage?

14) Which types of dwellings CANNOT be insured using an HO form?

15) Which types of homes are covered with HO-5 policies?

HO-4 Coverage for Tenants

HO-4 policies are only used for tenants who are renting dwellings of any kind. These types of policies include the following coverages:

- personal property
- loss of use
- additional coverages
- liability
- medical payments

The exclusions on an HO-4 policy are as follows:

- ordinance or law
- movement of the earth
- water damage
- power failure
- neglect
- war
- nuclear hazard
- intentional loss

- governmental action

This policy covers not only the tenant's personal belongings but also any personal liabilities the tenant may have for damage to the owner's property or liability for any guests who are injured while on the premises.

Quick Review Questions

16) Would a broken pipe cause by the tenant leaving the garage door open be covered under an HO-4 policy?

17) If a burglar breaks into the building and damages the property's windows, would the tenant be protected against any liability from that incident?

HO-6 Coverage for Condominium Owners

The correct HO form for a condo is an **HO-6** policy; it is called the **unit owners form**. A condo is a multi-unit dwelling where the owners own the building, but not the land it sits on. The surrounding property and external features of the buildings are covered by the condo owners' association insurance. In the event that an entire building sustains a loss, part of the building will be covered by the HO-6 policy and the remaining part will be covered by the condo association owners' policy. The HO-6 policy covers the interior of the unit where the condo association's policy coverage ends. The coverages on an HO-6 policy include the following:

- dwelling
- personal property
- loss of use
- additional coverages
- liability
- medical payments

Did You Know?

An HO-6 policy states exactly where the coverage begins. It could be from the studs inward, the wallboard inward, or the paint or wallpaper inward. The condo association's insurance policy covers all of the parts of the structure that the HO-6 policy does not cover.

The exclusions listed on an HO-6 policy are as follows:

- ordinance or law
- movement of the earth
- water damage
- power failure
- neglect
- war
- nuclear hazard
- intentional loss
- governmental action

The HO-6 policy is a named peril policy.

Quick Review Questions

18) Would an HO-6 policy cover a loss where a unit owner's guest got injured while working out at the fitness center on the common grounds of a condo complex?

19) Would an HO-6 policy cover water damage to the ceiling of a property?

HO-8 forms for Historical or Special Buildings

An **HO-8** form is also called a modified coverage form. These forms cover residential dwellings that are older and have outdated construction or custom features that do not qualify for other HO forms. Such homes would cost more to replace than the home's market value. Examples of residential dwellings that are appropriate for an HO-8 policy include the following:

- homes that are registered landmarks
- homes with unique architectural features
- homes built with materials that are hard to replace
- homes that do not meet the standards for cosmetic and structural requirements for other HO forms

An HO-8 form is different from other HO forms because it requires owners to repair or rebuild within 180 days of the loss. If owners comply with this condition, the policy will pay up to the dwelling limit only, and owners may only rebuild using common construction materials and methods. The materials may be of like kind and quality but they must cost less than obsolete, antique, or custom construction methods and materials. The perils covered under an HO-8 policy include the following:

- fire or lightning
- windstorm or hail
- explosion
- riot or civil commotion
- aircraft
- vehicles
- smoke
- vandalism or malicious mischief
- theft
- volcanic eruption

Did You Know?

An HO-8 policy works well for these types of dwellings if the owner does not want to make significant renovations or upgrades to the home when rebuilding.

The exclusions on an HO-8 policy are as follows:

- ordinance or law

- movement of the earth
- water damage
- power failure
- neglect
- war
- nuclear hazard
- intentional loss
- governmental action

HO-8 policies are named peril policies.

Quick Review Questions

20) A home that was once the main residence on a former plantation was just purchased. Would this home be appropriate for an HO-8 policy?

21) An older home with a thatched roof was destroyed in a fire. Under the insured's HO-8 policy, would the owner be able to rebuild the home to include a thatched roof?

Property Coverages in Section I of HO Policies

Property coverages for homeowners are similar to the property coverages for dwelling policies as described in Chapter 3; they are listed in the first section of HO policies. Property coverages generally cover the dwelling, other structures, personal property, and loss of use. Each HO form includes different property coverages as noted in Table 4.2.

Since tenants do not own their dwellings, the dwelling and other structures are not covered under the "Property" section of HO-4. On an HO-6 form, the coverage for other structures is included with the dwelling coverage; otherwise, direct and indirect losses are covered under all HO forms.

Table 4.2. HO Policy Coverages

Coverage Name	Damage Type	HO-2	HO-3	HO-4	HO-5	HO-6	HO-8
A (Dwelling)	direct	X	X	none	X	X	X
B (Other structures)	direct	X	X	none	X	in Coverage A	X
C (Personal property)	direct	X	X	X	X	X	X
D	indirect	X	X	X	X	X	X

Table 4.2. HO Policy Coverages							
Coverage Name	**Damage Type**	**HO-2**	**HO-3**	**HO-4**	**HO-5**	**HO-6**	**HO-8**
(Loss of use)							

Coverage A - Dwelling

Coverage A on a homeowner policy is called the dwelling coverage, and it is important not to confuse this term with a dwelling fire (DP) policy. A dwelling fire policy is designed for tenant-occupied dwellings and vacant dwellings where the owner has minimal personal property at the dwelling.

By contrast, Coverage A on a homeowner policy refers to insuring a residence structure. HO forms provide more coverage for personal property than DP forms as the owners live in the residence and have all their furniture, tools, clothing, and other personal items in their homes.

Coverage A includes structures attached to the dwelling and materials on or adjacent to the residence premises that are used to construct, repair, or alter the dwelling or other structures on the premises where the residence is located. For example, Coverage A includes awnings and screened-in porches because they are attached to the dwelling. It also includes structures owned by the property owner that exist on the residence premises, such as a fence, shed, or detached garage.

Did You Know?

Insurance policies can cover almost anything, but they never cover the land itself.

For policy forms HO-2, HO-3, HO-5, and HO-8, Coverage A refers to the structure of the residence, structures that are attached to it, and materials on the residence premises that are being used to construct, renovate, or repair the building. Coverage A for the HO-4 and HO-6 policies works a bit differently:

- With an HO-4 policy, there is no Coverage A because the landlord insures the structure under a DP policy. Tenants need an HO-4 policy to cover their personal property and liability.
- Likewise, Coverage A for an HO-6 policy covers improvements and betterments; these include alterations, appliances, fixtures, and improvements inside the condo unit. The policy does not cover the outside of the building or any other structures on the property.

One example of Coverage A would be if a kitchen fire breaks out in a single-family home and causes damage to the interior and exterior of the residence. The Coverage A amount on the home is $350,000 and the deductible is $1,000. The cost to repair the exterior of the dwelling is $85,000. The kitchen sustained damage in the amount of $20,000. The cost to replace the awning is $2,000. The owners lost personal property in the kitchen in the amount of $2,000. In this scenario, the insurer would have paid out $106,000 in total:

- Coverage A would cover the $85,000 for the exterior, $20,000 for the kitchen, and $2,000 for the awning since it was attached to the home.
    - This all totals $107,000.
- After subtracting the $1,000 deductible, the total payment is $106,000.

The personal property in the kitchen would also be covered under Coverage C, but that will be discussed later in the chapter.

Quick Review Questions

22) A condo owner permanently installed two bookcases in her unit. Would the bookcases be covered under Coverage A in the event of a fire?

23) A homeowner stacked $3,000 of lumber, which was to be used to finish the basement, inside an attached garage; the lumber ended up being stolen during the night. Would it be covered under Coverage A?

Coverage B - Other Structures

For HO forms HO-2, HO-3, HO-5, and HO-8, Coverage B covers structures other than the residence as long as they are located on the premises. Buildings and other items are considered other structures if they are separated by a clear space from the main dwelling. Structures connected only by a fence or utility line are also covered.

Examples of other structures include the following:

- detached garage
- shed
- pole barn
- barn
- fence
- mailbox
- in-ground swimming pool
- gazebo
- guest house
- workshop
- barn

Certain other structures are not covered and include the following:

- the land the structure sits on
- a garage that is being rented to someone who is not a household resident
- structures where a business is conducted
- structures used to store business property (A structure that contains business property by a resident or tenant of the dwelling is covered if it does not include gases or liquid fuel, excluding fuel in a parked vehicle.)

Did You Know?

Other structures are not always types of buildings. For example, fences and mailboxes are considered other structures and are therefore covered.

Coverage B is limited to 10 percent of the Coverage A amount. For example, if Coverage A amount is $300,000, the Coverage B amount would be 10 percent of that, or $30,000. An endorsement may be added to the policy to increase the limit to 20 percent or more, and the premium would then be higher.

For HO-4 policies, other structures are not covered at all because if there are any other structures on the premises, the landlord is responsible for insuring them.

For HO-6 policies, other structures that are on the resident premises and are owned by the resident are covered under Coverage A—not Coverage B. HO-6 policies do not cover structures rented to anyone who is not a resident of the dwelling unless the structure is being used solely as a private garage. The HO-6 form does not cover land or structures where business is conducted. Business property stored in other structures is not covered. Business property owned by a resident or tenant of the residence is covered in other structures if it is being contained there and does not include gases or liquid fuel (unless the fuel is in a parked vehicle).

There is a notable difference in Coverage B between dwelling policies and homeowners policies. Dwelling policies do not cover grave markers or mausoleums; homeowners policies do.

As an example of Coverage B, a home is being covered under an HO-5 policy with a dwelling amount of $250,000. A strong wind collapses a detached garage, which will cost $20,000 to rebuild. The detached garage would be covered under Coverage B for 10 percent of the Coverage A amount, which is $25,000.

Did You Know?

A homeowner's policy will cover many types of outdoor structures, but it typically will not cover an antenna or satellite dish.

Quick Review Questions

24) A homeowner wakes up in the morning to find that vandals have torn down her fence and destroyed her mailbox. Would these be covered losses under Coverage B?

25) If the home in the preceding question is covered for $200,000, and the damage to the fence and mailbox total $23,000 to repair, would they be covered under Coverage B?

Coverage C - Personal Property

Personal property is often referred to as anything that can be picked up and carried out of the residence. It includes furniture, clothing, dishes, and more.

Forms HO-2,HO-3, H0-4, HO-5, HO-6, and HO-8 also cover the following property:

- property on the residence premises the owner occupies that belongs to someone else
- a guest's or residence employee's personal property that is in a residence occupied by the insured
- HO-8: motor vehicles that are not required to be registered and are used to service the property (e.g., riding lawnmowers, golf carts)

The automatic coverage limit for Coverage C is 50 percent of Coverage A. Policyholders with an HO-4 or HO-6 policy choose their own limits as long as they abide by state-mandated minimums. Homeowners policies do not cover the following:

- items that are insured by other policies
- animals, birds, and fish
- motor vehicles and their accessories, parts, and equipment
- aircraft and its parts (if they are used to carry people or cargo)
- hovercraft and its parts
- property of other tenants, boarders, and roomers—except for relatives of the insured
- property rented or held for rental to others off premises
- business data (e.g., accounting books, drawings, paper records, computers, and related equipment; exceptions: blank recording storage media/prerecorded computer programs available on the retail market
- credit cards and EFT transfer cards
- water or steam

Did You Know?

The personal property coverage on a homeowner policy provides coverage for the property anywhere in the world.

There is a limit of 10 percent, or $1,000—whichever is greater—of the Coverage C limit for personal property at other residences. This limit does not apply to property that is being moved while a residence is being repaired, rebuilt, or renovated and is not fit for residency. This limit also does not apply to property a resident is moving into a newly acquired principal residence for thirty days from the time the owner starts moving property there.

Homeowners policies have special limits of liability per loss for certain types of property as follows:

- $200: bank notes, money, bullion, silver and gold coins (not goldware/silverware), medals, scrip, stored value, cards, and smart cards
- $1,500: securities, deeds, accounts, evidences of debt, manuscripts, personal records, non-bank notes, tickets, stamps, and passports.
- $1,500: watercraft including trailers, furnishings, motors, and equipment
- $1,500: trailers or semi-trailers not used for watercraft
- $1,500: furs, jewelry, watches, and precious and semi-precious stones for loss by theft
- $2,500: firearms and related equipment for loss by theft
- $2,500: silverware, goldware, platinum-ware, silver-plated ware, gold-plated ware, platinum-plated ware, and pewterware; hollow-ware, tea sets, flatware, and trophies and trays made of or including silver, gold, or pewter
- $2,500: business property used primarily for business purposes on the residence premises
- $500: property used for business purposes away from the residence premises

- $1,500: electronic apparatus and accessories that are in or on a motor vehicle as long as they can be operated by the motor vehicle's system and other power sources
- $1,500: electronic apparatus and accessories used primarily for business use off the residence premises (not in a vehicle and must be able to power from a motor vehicle and other power sources)

The personal property coverage for homeowners policies is different than for dwelling policies. Dwelling policies cover personal property that is owned by the owner or is used by the owners and family members while it is at the dwelling, such as lawnmowers or landscaping tools.

Unlike homeowners policies, dwelling policies do not cover money, bank notes, bullion, coins, gold, passports, personal records, gold, silver, platinum, stamps, scrip, stored value cards, smart cards, and similar items. Dwelling policies also do not cover the list of items not covered under homeowners policies nor do they cover grave markers, including mausoleums.

One example that explains how Coverage C will respond to a claim is if a burglar breaks into a resident's home that has a dwelling amount of $350,000 and steals $5,000 worth of computer equipment. The door breaks as well and requires $700 to be replaced. The resident would receive $700 under Coverage A and $5,000 under Coverage C less their deductible. (The Coverage C limit is 50 percent of Coverage A, which is $175,000.)

Quick Review Questions

26) A fire breaks out at a residence, and the owners lose a pedigree show dog worth $2,000. How much will the policy cover?

27) A resident hides $5,000 in cash under his mattress, and the money gets stolen. Will the resident recover the full $5,000 from the insurer?

28) A tree falls in a windstorm and breaks through the roof, causing $10,000 in damage to the living room furniture. The dwelling amount is $75,000. Will the furniture be covered?

29) A couple goes on vacation, and a hotel employee steals a leather jacket from their baggage. Is this loss covered?

Coverage D - Loss of Use

This portion of a homeowner policy is designed to provide coverage if a homeowner cannot live in the residence because of a covered loss. There are four parts to the "Loss of Use" section:

1. **Additional living expense** coverage pays for necessary increases in living expenses the resident incurs so that the household can maintain its normal standard of living. The policy pays for the shortest time required to repair or replace the dwelling and covers costs for eating out, laundry, extra expenses for traveling farther to work, etc.
2. **Fair rental value** coverage ensures payment for the loss of a tenant's rent less any expenses that do not continue. This means that if a resident rents out a room in her home and the tenant

cannot live there while the home is being repaired, the owner will be entitled to the rent that the tenant was paying.

3. A **civil authority prohibits use** clause covers expenses incurred when the resident cannot use the residence because a neighboring property is damaged by a covered peril.
4. The **loss or expenses not covered** clause explains that homeowners policies will not cover losses if a lease or agreement is cancelled.

Unlike a homeowner policy, additional living expenses are not covered under a dwelling policy since the homeowner lives in the primary residence. A dwelling policy does cover fair rental value as well as incidents that involve a civil authority prohibiting the use of the premises. Like a homeowner policy, the coverages continue even if the policy expires, and losses or expenses will not be covered if a lease or agreement is cancelled.

Did You Know?

A homeowner policy covers an in-law suite that an insured rents to others.

An example of Coverage D would be if a homeowner has an HO-5 policy with a Coverage A limit of $200,000. If there is a fire in the home and the residents have to move into a hotel for two weeks, the policy will cover a maximum of up to 30 percent of Coverage A. This comes to $60,000 to pay for lodging, food, transportation, and other additional expenses.

Table 4.3. explains the percentages of Coverage A that will be paid under the various HO forms.

Table 4.3. HO Policy Coverage D (Loss of Use)

Coverage Name	HO-2	HO-3	HO-4	HO-5	HO-6	HO-8
A (Dwelling)	$15,000 minimum	$20,000 minimum	not covered	$30,000 minimum	$1,000	$15,000 minimum
B (Other structures)	10% of A	10% of A	not covered	10% of A	part of A	10% of A
C (Personal property)	50% of A	50% of A	varies by state	50% of A	varies by state	50% of A
D (Loss of use)	30% of A	30% of A	30% of C	30% of A	50% of C	10% of A

Quick Review Questions

30) A neighbor's house, which is within several feet of the resident's home, is damaged by a tornado, but the resident's home does not sustain damage. The emergency authorities order the residents to vacate the premises for two days while the demolition crews tear down the remains of the neighbor's house. Will the residents be entitled to loss of use coverage?

31) A resident with an HO-6 policy sustains lightning damage which affects the electrical system in the condo. The resident decides to go on vacation for a month while the repairs are being done, but the workers finish in one week. Will the vacation be covered?

Liability Coverages in Section II of Homeowners Policies

Coverage E - Personal Liability

Personal liability coverage pays for claims against a resident for bodily injury or property damage. The policy will pay up to the policy limit for damages for which the resident is legally liable.

The coverage includes defense costs by the insurer's attorney. Liability coverage applies even when a lawsuit is fraudulent, groundless, or false. The insurer's responsibility terminates when the limit of liability has been reached or a settlement or judgment has been ordered.

The insured chooses the liability limits. If an insured wants additional liability coverage, he can purchase an umbrella liability policy which will cover in excess of the homeowner policy liability.

There are certain exclusions on personal liability on a homeowner policy. These include the following:

- motor vehicle liability
- watercraft liability
- aircraft liability
- hovercraft liability

Personal liability coverage also does not apply to the following situations:

- expected or intended injury
- claims arising out of or in connection with a business
- claims arising out of or in connection with professional services
- occurrences that are not at an insured location
- war
- communicable diseases
- sexual molestation, corporal punishment, or physical or mental abuse
- the use of controlled substances

Did You Know?

Insureds who have extra risks (e.g., owning more than one property, a trampoline, or swimming pool) are best protected by adding an umbrella policy.

For example, a guest spends time at a resident's home and the resident's dog bites the guest. The resident has $300,000 of liability coverage. The ambulance bill is $800, the emergency room visit costs $2,000, and the ensuing medical bills are $20,000; the total is $22,800. The $300,000 liability limit would cover the entire claim.

Quick Review Questions

32) A resident has a pilot's license and $300,000 of personal liability on his homeowner policy. The resident takes a friend and the friend's spouse up in a small private plane he owns. The friend dies and the spouse is badly injured. Will the medical costs be covered?

33) At a homeowner's party, the deck collapses, injuring multiple guests. Will this type of claim cover the guest's injuries?

Coverage F - Medical Payments to Others

Coverage F refers to medical payments to others. The limit for medical payments is much smaller than for personal liability. The medical payments coverage pays for reasonable fees for the following:

- medical and surgical services
- X-rays
- dental services
- ambulance fees
- hospital bills
- professional nursing services
- prosthetic devices
- funeral services

The coverage only covers guests to the residence. It does not cover regular residents of the household unless they are resident employees.

In order for the event to be covered, occurrences must happen at an insured location with the insured's permission.

Coverage applies if an occurrence happens off the insured location yet

- arises due to a condition on the insured location or an area that adjoins it,
- is caused by activities of an insured,
- is caused by a residence employee while on the job, and/or
- is caused by an animal the insured is caring for.

Did You Know?

Coverages for medical bills are paid regardless of fault, and they can prevent costly lawsuits.

Medical payments are limited to medical bills that are incurred and submitted within three years of the date of the bodily injury occurrence. As with personal liability, the following are excluded from medical payments coverage:

- motor vehicle liability
- watercraft liability

- aircraft liability
- hovercraft liability

Medical payments coverage also does not apply to the following situations:

- expected or intended injury
- claims arising out of or in connection with a business
- claims arising out of or in connection with professional services
- occurrences that are not an insured location
- war
- communicable diseases
- sexual molestation, corporal punishment, or physical or mental abuse
- the use of controlled substances

An example of medical payments coverage would be if a child visits an insured's home, slams her finger in the door, and requires stitches in the emergency room. The homeowner has $15,000 in medical payments coverage on his homeowner policy. The cost of the medical bills is $1,000. Since this is a small amount and there is sufficient coverage under medical payments, it would be covered under medical payments rather than personal liability. The policy would pay the bill to avoid a lawsuit.

Quick Review Questions

34) A child is playing at a resident's home, trips over a rug, and knocks out a tooth. The medical payments coverage on the homeowner policy is $20,000. The child's dental work amounts $5,000. Will the medical payments coverage apply?

35) The owner and a friend are making repairs to the owner's hovercraft when it falls and crushes the friend's toe. Is this a covered expense?

Additional Coverages

All homeowner forms list additional coverages, also called coverage extensions, that insurers cover at no cost to the insureds. Additional coverages may have certain criteria, and each additional coverage may have individual policy limits. The specifics for each additional coverage will be outlined in the policy wording under "Additional Coverages." The following twelve additional coverages are found in HO-2, HO-3, HO-4, HO-5, HO-6, and HO-8 policies:

Debris Removal

The insurer will pay for the reasonable expenses to remove debris from the property due to a covered peril. If the debris removal is more than the limit of liability, the company will pay an additional 5 percent for debris removal. The insurer will also pay up to $500 per tree, or $1,000 for removing trees due to wind, hail, or the weight of ice, snow, or sleet. It also covers a neighbor's tree that falls due to a covered loss if it damages a structure or blocks a driveway or handicap ramp.

Reasonable Repairs

The insurer will pay reasonable costs for an insured to take necessary measures to protect his property from further damage due to a covered loss. This additional coverage does not increase the limit of liability that corresponds to the property being repaired.

Trees, Shrubs, and Other Plants

Homeowners policies will pay for trees, shrubs, lawns, and other plants that get damaged by one of the following causes of loss: fire or lightning, riot or civil commotion, explosion, aircraft, vehicles not owned or operated by a resident, vandalism, or theft. Policies will pay up to $500 for any one tree, shrub, or plant, and up to 5 percent of the limit of liability that applies to trees, shrubs, and plants.

Fire Department Service Charge

Policies pay up to $500 for fire department service charges when they respond to fight a fire on the property covered by the policy. Coverage is excluded for a property that lies within city limits, a municipality, or protection district that furnishes fire protection services. Coverage applies without regard to a deductible.

Property Removed

This coverage pays for covered property from a direct loss of any kind while someone moves it away from the premises to get it out of danger. The coverage lasts for thirty days or less while it is being removed from the residence premises. The coverage does not change the limit of liability for the property being relocated.

Credit Card, Electronic Fund Transfer Card/Access Device, Forgery, and Counterfeit Money

Homeowners policies pay up to $500 for the following with no deductible:

- an insured's legal obligation to pay for unauthorized credit card usage or theft of credit cards in an insured's name
- loss from the unauthorized use of an electronic funds transfer card or access device used for deposits and withdrawals issued in an insured's name
- loss caused by forgery or altered checks
- loss due to accepting counterfeit currency in good faith

Loss Assessment

Homeowners policies pay up to $1,000 for the insured's share of a loss assessment fee by a corporation or property owners' association. There are exclusions for this coverage, such as earthquakes and assessments by governmental bodies.

Collapse

This additional coverage applies to Coverages A and B only (primary structure and other structures) for structures that cave in or are in a state of collapse.

Glass or Safety Glazing Material

This coverage applies to broken glass or glazing material that is part of storm doors, windows, or the building. Coverage does not apply to vacant dwellings or accidental breakage.

Landlord's Furnishings

The coverage pays $2,500 for a landlord's furnishings (carpet and other furnishings) in each apartment that is regularly rented or held for rental to others by an insured for certain specified losses.

Ordinance or Law

Homeowners policies allow insureds to use up to 10 percent of the limit of liability for Coverage A for increased costs for the enforcement of ordinances or laws related to construction, demolition, remodeling, or renovations.

Grave Markers

The coverage pays up to $5,000 for grave markers/mausoleums on or away from the residence premises for covered perils.

Additional coverages are also available under Section II for liability, and they include the following:

claim expenses: pay for defense costs and related taxes, loss of earnings, premiums on bonds, and accrued interest on judgments under certain circumstances

first aid expenses: pay for first aid expenses to others for bodily injury covered under the policy

damage to property of others: pays up to $1,000 for damage an insured causes to someone else's property under certain conditions

loss assessment: pays up to $1,000 for loss assessments when an insured causes bodily injury or property damage under certain conditions

Along with the additional coverages, certain insurers may allow insureds to add coverage through endorsements (for an extra premium) for surface-water floods, earthquakes, mobile homes, personal watercrafts (e.g., small boats, Jet Skis), or other inland marine items (e.g., jewelry, watches, furs, sporting equipment, musical instruments, fine arts).

Insureds who desire additional liability may purchase a personal umbrella insurance policy, which is an excess liability policy that offers additional limits over and above the underlying policies. In the event of a claim, the underlying policy's liability coverage (home or auto) pays first, and the umbrella policy pays the remainder of the claim up to the umbrella liability limit.

Helpful Hint

Insureds can also purchase standalone policies for mobile homes, personal watercraft, and inland marine items. Insureds who are interested in flood insurance policies must purchase them from the National Flood Insurance Program (NFIP), which is a federal program.

Quick Review Questions

36) A storm blows through and topples three trees on an insured's property. How much will a homeowner policy pay for debris removal?

37) A homeowner in a rural area has a small kitchen fire and calls 911 to get help in putting it out. How much will the insurance pay toward that emergency call?

38) An insured borrows a set of China when hosting a party and then accidentally drops the box, causing $1,200 in damage. Will this loss be covered under additional coverages?

39) An insured notices that his foundation is bowing and is concerned that the structure could collapse. Will the insured be able to collect for a claim under additional coverages under collapse?

40) An insured has a homeowner policy with $300,000 in liability coverage. They also have a $1 million umbrella liability. One of the insured's children nearly drowns, and the medical bills are $500,000. Would the homeowner policy cover the entire loss?

Conditions

Conditions are provisions in an insurance policy that outline things that must happen before an insurer will pursue a claim. If the conditions are not met, the insurer is not obligated to pay. There are three types of conditions in all HO policy forms:

1. property conditions
2. liability conditions
3. conditions that apply to both

Property-Only Conditions

Policies list a number of conditions that apply to Coverage A – Property. A few of the common conditions that apply to a homeowner policy are explained in this section.

Appraisal

Insureds may request an appraisal if they cannot agree on the amount of the loss. Upon receiving a request for appraisal, both parties have twenty days to select an impartial appraiser. The appraisers jointly choose an umpire. If they cannot agree, a judge or court can select an umpire within fifteen days. Each appraiser writes up an appraisal. If the appraisals disagree, the umpire will decide the case. Each party pays its own appraiser and splits the cost of the umpire.

Duties of the Insured After a Loss

Insureds must attend to certain duties for an insurer to cover a loss. These include promptly notifying the insurance company, notifying the police if there is a theft, protecting property from further damage, preparing a detailed inventory list and sworn statement, providing receipts, and abiding by the specified number of days for submitting information.

Loss Settlement and Payout

Losses may be settled according to actual cash value, which accounts for depreciation or the actual replacement cost at the current market value. Property claims for personal property, structures that aren't buildings, and grave markers will be settled on an actual cash-value basis. Awnings, carpeting, outdoor antennas and equipment, and household appliances will also be settled on an actual cash-value basis. Buildings are covered on a replacement-cost basis as long as the amount of insurance is at least 80 percent of the full replacement cost of the building before the loss.

Other Insurance

Where other insurance policies or service agreements apply to a loss, insurers will only pay up to the limit of liability. Service agreements apply to a service plan, property restoration plan, or home warranty.

Mortgage Holders Clause

Where a mortgage holder exists, payments for claims will be made to the mortgage company and the insured. Mortgagees will be paid in the order in which they are listed on the policy. A claim for subrogation will not prevent the mortgagee from recovering the full amount due.

Loss Payable Clause

Where a different person is listed as a loss payee on a declarations page, the loss payee will be considered an insured. The insurer will notify the loss payee as well as the insured if there is an intention to cancel or not renew the policy.

Bankruptcy of an Insured

This provision states that an insurer must still satisfy its obligations under the policy, even if the insured files for bankruptcy or is insolvent.

Policy Period

The insurer is only obligated to pay for claims for bodily injury or property damage during the policy period. A claim that occurs before or after the effective dates of the policy will not be covered.

Quick Review Questions

41) In the event of a total loss of a residence due to a fire, will the home be rebuilt on an actual cash-value basis or on a replacement-cost basis?

42) A home has a first mortgage of $200,00 and a home equity line of credit of $100,000. If a covered loss is $50,000, which lender would be paid?

43) An insured and a claims adjuster disagree on the value of a property claim for a stolen television. Each party hires an appraiser and still cannot agree on an amount. What is the next step?

44) A home has a home warranty on it, and the home is destroyed by a tornado. Would the insurance company or the home warranty company pay for the loss?

Property and Liability Conditions

The following conditions apply to both the "Property" and "Liability" sections of a homeowner policy:

Liberalization Clause

If an insurance company changes a policy by broadening the coverage and does not charge the insured an additional premium, the change automatically applies to the policy at the time that the state in which the property is located approves the change. The change only applies when the implementation date is within sixty days before the policy issuance or during the policy period.

Waiver or Change of Policy Provisions

In order for a waiver or change in a policy to be valid, the change must be made in writing by the insurer.

Assignment

This condition states that the insurance policy will not be valid if it is transferred to another party unless the insurer gives written consent.

Subrogation

An insurer has the right to recover costs from a party it believes is responsible for a claim in a process called subrogation. Insureds must cooperate with the insurer during the subrogation process and submit all requested documents, photos, or other information.

Death

If an insured, the insured's spouse, or any resident of the household dies, the insurer will insure the deceased person's representative in matters that pertain to the deceased member's covered property and premises. This provision only applies if the spouse and other household members are living on the residence premises at the time of the death. Anyone who has proper temporary custody of the property until a legal representative is appointed is also insured by the insurer.

Cancellation

An insured may cancel a policy at any time by refusing to pay the premium, returning the policy, or notifying the insurer in writing. The insured can cancel for any reason if the policy has been in effect for at least sixty days and is not a renewal policy.

If the policy has been in effect for at least sixty days and is a renewal policy, the insured may cancel for the following reasons if at least thirty days' notice is given before the cancellation goes into effect:

- a material misrepresentation of fact which would have caused the insurer to decline the policy if it was aware of the misrepresentation
- a risk that has significantly changed since the policy was issued

Insurers may also legally cancel a policy that has been in force for a year by informing the insured at least thirty days before the cancellation/nonrenewal takes place. State laws determine whether an insured is entitled to a prorated refund.

Quick Review Questions

45) A neighbor drives his car into the side of a homeowner's house, and the homeowner files a claim, pays her deductible, and has her house repaired. If the insurer pursues the neighbor to pay for the damages to the home, under which condition does the process fall?

46) A homeowner received her new home insurance policy ninety days ago, but after getting quotes, the homeowner discovers that she can save significantly with another insurer. Will this policyholder be able to cancel her current policy?

Chapter Review

Table 4.4. Chapter 4 Review: Homeowners Policies	
Types of properties covered	• 1-to-4 family-owner-occupied residences • not more than two families or two roomers or boarders per unit • tenant in non-owned dwellings (HO-4) • residential condominiums (HO-6) • seasonal dwellings and secondary residences • other types of ownership (e.g., dwellings under construction)
Coverage forms	• *HO-2: Broad Form* - named peril • *HO-3: Special Form* - dwelling and other structures on an open peril basis; personal property covered only for broad perils • *HO-4: Tenant Broad Form* (contents) - insures personal property for broad perils • *HO-5: Comprehensive Form* - covers both the dwelling and other structures on an open peril basis • *HO-6: Condominium Form:* broadens coverage to include parts of the building • *HO-8: Modified Form:* used when replacement cost coverage is not practical
Property coverages	• *Coverage A (Dwelling):* dwelling and premises; must be used primarily for residential or dwelling purposes • *Coverage B (Other Structures):* separate structures at same location, such as detached garages or sheds • *Coverage C (Personal Property):* can be purchased to insure personal property common to a residence • *Coverage D (Loss of Use, Fair Rental):* applies if property covered under A, B, or C becomes damaged or is destroyed • *Coverage E (Additional Living Expenses):* only available if broad or special dwelling coverage is written

Answer Key

1. The primary purpose of homeowners (HO) policies is to insure residential risks.

2. A homeowner policy covers both the property and the owner's personal liability.

3. Dwelling policies only cover the dwelling structure and liability; they do not cover the owner's possessions or other structures on the property.

4. An insured location can be something other than the primary residence, including a secondary home, vacation home, an apartment being rented while the primary residence is being repaired, or a cemetery plot.

5. Yes, because the house cleaner is considered an employee who provides household duties.

6. Yes, because an occurrence is any accident that involves bodily injury or property damage that takes place in the insured's home.

7. The following homeowner (HO) forms could all apply to a family dwelling: HO-2, HO-3, and HO-5.

8. The homeowner (HO) form HO-4 is used for renters or tenants.

9. Homeowner (HO) policies do not cover vacation homes, second homes, or vacant properties.

10. They could, but the insurance would only pay the amount agreed upon to replace the original structure.

11. According to most policies, the homeowner can use up to 10 percent of the total cost to make improvements on the home.

12. An HO-2 policy provides coverage for risky-to-insure homes that are more likely to have claims

13. The HO-5 form covers all of the same coverages as the other HO forms, but it is the only one that offers open peril coverage for the dwelling and the owner's personal property.

14. Any dwelling that is not being used as a residence cannot be covered under HO forms.

15. HO-5 policies provide coverage for expensive homes that would be more costly than usual to replace.

16. The HO-4 policy would protect the tenant from any liability caused by his failure to properly secure the property.

17. The coverage for damage incurred during a burglary would be under the landlord's coverage since the damage was not cause by the tenant.

18. Because the incident occurred in a common area of the property, the condo association's policy would be responsible for the loss.

19. In this case, because the event affects the interior of the property, repairs to the unit's paint and drywall would be covered, but the damages to the roof would be covered under the condominium association's policy.

20. A plantation home would have been built in the 1800s and likely have unique architectural features on the interior and exterior; therefore, the replacement cost would far exceed the market value, making the HO-8 policy an appropriate choice.

21. The owner would have to replace the roof with common roofing materials, such as shake shingles, asphalt shingles, slate or ceramic tiles, or something similar that reflects modern construction guidelines.

22. The bookcases would be covered because they were permanently installed to the unit.

23. Although the lumber was to be used for construction in the residence, it would not be covered under Coverage A because any possessions inside the residence would be covered under Coverage C. If the lumber had been stored outside the residence, it would be covered under Coverage A.

24. Vandalism and malicious mischief are covered perils under an HO-3 policy, and fences and mailboxes are covered structures under Coverage B.

25. The total coverage for outdoor structures would be no more than $20,000, so $3,000 would have to be paid out-of-pocket by the owner.

26. Animals are not covered under homeowners policies.

27. No; Coverage C only provides $200 for money.

28. The value of furniture is covered under Coverage C for up to half of the dwelling coverage amount. The limit would be half of $75,000 which is $37,500—a sufficient amount to cover the $10,000 loss.

29. As long as the item's value is less than half of the policy's coverage for the entire dwelling, Coverage C will cover all personal possessions—regardless of where they were at the time of loss.

30. Loss of use is covered under the civil authority prohibits use provision.

31. The coverage for loss of use coverage applies until the repairs are complete, and then the resident will have to pay the expenses for the other three weeks.

32. Because the incident did not occur at an insured location, and incidents involving aircraft are excluded from personal liability coverage, the insurance would not cover the medical costs.

33. Because it was an unexpected occurrence at the covered property, the policy will pay for guests' injuries up to the policy limit.

34. Because this was an unexpected occurrence, and there is sufficient coverage to pay the $5,000 claim, the insurer would do so to avoid a lawsuit.

35. Hovercrafts are excluded from homeowner policy coverage.

36. While the policy will pay $500 per tree, it only pays a maximum of $1,000.

37. Since the home is not in a city, municipality, or fire protection district, the most the policy will pay is $500.

38. This loss would be paid under additional coverages for liability, and policies typically pay up to $1,000 for this type of loss.

39. This coverage is not triggered until a structure actually begins to collapse, so it would not be covered.

40. The homeowner policy is the underlying policy and would pay up to the maximum limit of $300,000, but the umbrella policy pays anything in excess of that, so it would pay the remaining $200,000.

41. The insurer will pay for the loss based on the replacement cost, provided the insured had a homeowner policy that insured the home to at least 80 percent of the replacement cost

42. The payment would be made to the first mortgagee, and the insured as the first mortgagee is listed first on the policy.

43. Both sides would agree to an umpire who will have the final word on the settlement amount.

44. The warranty company would be considered insurance, but it would be the secondary payer and would only pay if the homeowner policy limit is not sufficient to cover the loss.

45. The insurer has the right of subrogation, which allows the insurer to recover costs from the party who is responsible for damaging the home.

46. A homeowner can cancel a new policy at any time for any reason, as long as the policyholder notifies the insurer in writing.

5. Flood, Mobile Home, Farm Owners, and Other Personal Property Insurance

National Flood Insurance Program (NFIP)

The National Flood Insurance Program (NFIP) was created by the National Flood Insurance Act in 1968. The federal government developed the program with two goals in mind: to protect property owners and reduce flood damage in the future. The federal government transferred the NFIP to the Federal Emergency Management Agency (FEMA) in 1979.

Commercial and residential property owners can buy flood coverage through the NFIP because standard home and commercial policies do not cover flooding as a cause of loss.

The NFIP defines flooding as "a general and temporary condition of a partial or complete inundation of two or more acres of normally dry land area of two or more properties (at least one of which is the policyholder's property."

Flood waters must originate from one of the following sources:

- overflow of inland or tidal waters
- water from any source that is unusual and quickly accumulates or runs off from surface water
- mudslides caused by flooding over normally dry lands
- land that subsides or collapses along a body of water due to erosion caused by atypical waves or currents

NFIP policies are divided into the following three parts:

- insurance: The NFIP offers flood insurance to homeowners and commercial property owners whose property is in an NFIP-participating community.
- floodplain management: As members of the NFIP, communities must regulate land development according to the minimum standards laid out by the NFIP. NFIP offers lower rates on flood insurance for communities that go beyond the minimum standards.
- floodplain mapping: FEMA maps the **floodplain**, called the Special Flood Hazard Area (SFHA), and sets forth regulations to reduce flood damage in floodplains. FEMA also offers Flood Insurance Rate Maps that outline areas that that have high risks of flooding.

Did You Know?

Tenants may purchase flood insurance for the contents of the building if they rent a property in a designated flood area.

Quick Review Question

1) Why did the federal government enact the National Flood Insurance Act?

Participation and Coverage Limits in NFIP

Any property owner can purchase flood insurance; however, properties in designated flood zones will have higher rates than properties outside of designated flood zones.

The **Flood Disaster Protection Act (1973)** requires flood insurance for residential and commercial properties that are located in high-risk flood areas and have government-backed mortgages. Such properties will not be considered for future federal disaster aid if they do not abide by these rules, so it is in the best interest of owners to obtain this type of coverage when it is offered.

Residential property owners in designated floodplains may get protection against flooding for up to $250,000 for the structure and $100,000 for the contents. Commercial property owners may choose up to $500,000 of coverage on buildings and $500,000 on the contents of business properties in a floodplain.

Mortgage lenders also typically require property owners to purchase flood insurance and property insurance if the property is in a flood zone. Sometimes, mortgage lenders may require property owners to have flood insurance even if the property is located outside of a flood zone.

Private insurers may also offer flood insurance in addition to NFIP, but such policies are not backed by the federal government. The benefits of purchasing private flood insurance include

- higher policy limits,
- additional coverage beyond the structure and contents, and
- better customer service.

The NFIP also instituted the **Write-Your-Own (WYO)** program, which is a partnership between FEMA and private insurance companies. This program allows private insurance companies to write and provide services for a standard flood insurance policy under their own brands; however, private insurers must follow the coverage and rates as established by FEMA and the NFIP.

Quick Review Questions

2) A homeowner notices standing water on her one-acre property, but there is no water on the adjacent properties. According to the NFIP, would this be considered flooding?

3) A tenant purchased a flood insurance policy with $100,000 in contents coverage and a $500 deductible. When the property flooded, the tenant filed a claim for $105,000, but not all of it was covered. How much was paid out?

4) A homeowner who was insured by the NFIP filed a claim for flooding. The home was unsafe to live in because of mold damage, so the family moved into a rental home while the home was being repaired. Does flood insurance cover the family's temporary rental expenses?

5) A homeowner's garage was flooded, but the water never reached the living quarters above the garage. Does the flood policy cover the garage?

6.) A homeowner living in a designated flood zone files a claim for flooding under his NFIP policy. There is $200,000 in damage to the home and $125,000 in contents damage. The deductible is $1,000. How much will NFIP be required to pay the homeowner?

Eligibility to Participate in the NFIP

Communities that want to participate in the NFIP must adopt and enforce the established floodplain management regulations set by the NFIP standards. The NFIP not only requires communities to meet the minimum requirements, they also encourage communities to exceed them.

An NFIP flood policy has two parts: building property coverage and personal property.

The building property coverage includes the foundation walls, anchorage, and attached staircases. It also includes the following items:

- cisterns and water
- drywall and insulation for walls and ceilings in the basement
- circuit breaker boxes, electrical outlets, and switches
- solar energy equipment
- fuel tanks and fuel
- well water tanks and pumps
- appliances to service the building (e.g., HVAC, sump pumps)

NFIP policies exclude the following:

- carpeting and floor tiles
- drywall or ceilings not made of drywall
- paneling, window treatments, bookcases, and similar items
- personal property stored in the basement
- personal property valued at over $2,500
- additional living expenses

There are several reasons why FEMA may deny coverage for a flood claim:

- FEMA could not verify the homeowner's identity.
- The homeowner could not prove she occupied the home before the loss.
- The homeowner had coverage under another policy that was triggered first.

Did You Know?

A basic flood insurance policy through the NFIP covers repairs to a basement but not the contents being stored in the basement. Policy

- FEMA will not cover claims for landscaping or food spoilage.
- The homeowner requested rental assistance but failed to actually move his family during the repairs.

NFIP policies have a standard thirty-day waiting period; however, there are exceptions. For example, the **Biggert-Waters Flood Insurance Reform Act (2012)** waives the thirty-day waiting period for property owners and renters who are subject to flooding due to wildfires.

Quick Review Questions

7) The structure of a home was okay after a flood, but the wooden porch and wooden fence were badly damaged. Would the homeowner be able to file a claim for the damage to the deck and fence?

8) Would NFIP pay to replace a furnace damaged during a flood under the building coverage or personal property coverage?

9) A homeowner with an NFIP policy lost all of her children's winter clothing because of a flood in the basement. Would the clothing be covered under the flood insurance policy?

10)The basement in a home is covered by a flood policy and a homeowner policy with water backup coverage. The home experiences a flood, but the damage to the home is due to water backing up through the drains. Which policy would cover the loss?

Limits of Coverage for NFIP

The NFIP limits the amount of coverage for the building and its contents for single- and multi-family dwellings. Table 5.1. lists the maximum amounts the federal government will pay homeowners if their homes flood and the structures or contents get damaged by the water.

Table 5.1. Limits of Coverage for the NFIP

	Building	Contents
Single-family	$250,000	$100,000
Other residential	$250,000	$100,000

Did You Know?

Condo owners can get flood insurance for the same amount of protection as owners of single-family homes.

The process for a community to become eligible for the NFIP can be time-consuming. To allow residents to have some coverage during the application process, the federal government set up an NFIP emergency program.

The emergency program provides a limited amount of flood insurance coverage while a community is in the process of being officially recognized as a participating community in the NFIP. Residents can get flood insurance coverage at less than actuarial rates during this phase of the process.

Quick Review Questions

11) A single-family home is located in a community that is in the application phase of participating in the NFIP. Would it be possible for the homeowner to get coverage during the application phase?

12) How much coverage could a homeowner get if he wants to purchase flood insurance for his condo and its contents?

NFIP Deductibles

Homeowner and dwelling fire policies carry various exclusions that apply to water damage. They do not cover properties that are prone to flooding. These include newly constructed buildings in, on, or over water; underground equipment and structures; and containers.

In most cases, there is a thirty-day waiting period after paying the premium before flood coverage begins, although there are exceptions for homeowners who

- must get flood insurance coverage to satisfy lending requirements or,
- purchase flood insurance within sixty days of a wildfire on federal land that caused flooding.

There is a waiting period of one day for homes located in high-risk flood areas if the policy is purchased within thirteen months of a flood map update.

There are separate deductibles for the building and contents coverages, and the maximum deductible amounts are $10,000. The building deductible applies to the foundation, walls, flooring, and ceilings. The contents deductible applies to everything that can be picked up and carried out of the house (e.g., furniture, clothing, dishes, décor).

Homeowners must pay the deductible before the NFIP will pay their portion of the damages. If the building and contents are damaged, the homeowner may have to pay part or all of both deductibles.

Did You Know?

The higher the deductibles are, the lower the premium will be; in fact, homeowners can get up to a 40 percent discount if they choose $10,000 deductibles.

Homeowners can choose various increments of deductibles for the building and contents, and the deductibles do not have to be the same for both.

Quick Review Questions

13) Homeowners in an NFIP flood area purchased the maximum limits of NFIP for the dwelling and its contents. The policy has a $10,000 deductible for the building and $1,000 for the contents. If the damage to the building is $350,000, and the homeowner loses $50,000 in contents, how much will the NFIP pay for these losses?

14) A homeowner wants to refinance her home loan, and the lender requires her to increase the flood coverage to the maximum limit of $250,000. Would the thirty-day waiting period apply in this case?

Mobile Homes

Mobile homes and associated other structures may be insured under a traditional homeowners policy by endorsement. This means that all of the provisions of the homeowner policy apply; the mobile home endorsement outlines additions, conditions, and exclusions that apply to mobile homes.

Mobile homes are typically valued significantly less than homes on permanent foundations. For that reason, the limits of liability for these types of dwellings and other structures are designed to work a bit differently than for other homes. As with a standard home, the limit for the other structures coverage (Coverage B) is 10 percent of the limit for the dwelling (Coverage A). The exception is if 10 percent of the Coverage A limit is under $2,000. In that case, the insurance company will pay the full $2,000 for Coverage B, and it will not reduce the amount available for Coverage A.

One of the benefits of a mobile home is that it can be transferred to another location if it is in danger of being damaged. At any time, the homeowner may remove the home from the property to prevent it from being damaged by a covered peril. In this case, the insurer will pay any reasonable expenses in the amount of $500 or less for the homeowner to remove the home and return it to its original location. The deductible would not apply in this case.

Coverages A through F apply to mobile home policies. The list of the coverages and their descriptions are as follows:

- Coverage A - Dwelling: This covers the structure of the mobile home on the residence premises regardless of whether the structure is leased or owned—as long as it is being used as the principal residence of the homeowner.
- Coverage B - Other Structures: This covers any structures other than the mobile home (e.g., a shed, fence, mailbox) or any other structure on the residence premises.
- Coverage C - Personal Property: This section covers the insured's personal property anywhere in the world.
- Coverage D - Loss of Use: This covers additional living expenses and fair rental value if the insured cannot live in the home due to a covered peril.
- Coverage E - Additional Coverages: This covers debris removal, reasonable repairs, trees/shrubs/plants, fire department charges, emergency removal of the property, loss assessments, collapse, credit card fraud, glass damage, landlord's furnishings, ordinance or law, and grave markets.
- Coverage F - Personal Liability: This section covers any bodily injury and property damage for which the homeowner may be liable.

Did You Know?

To be eligible for a mobile home policy, the mobile home must be designed and set up for someone to live in it year-round. This means it must have adequate systems for heating, cooling, electrical, and plumbing.

The conditions, additions, and exclusions for the homeowner policy may also apply to the mobile home endorsement.

Quick Review Questions

15) A homeowner had purchased $150,000 coverage for his mobile home with a $1,000 deductible. Although the home itself did not sustain damage, a shed on the property valued at $9,000 was destroyed by wind. How much will the policy pay out?

16) A homeowner decides to move her mobile home to protect it from catching fire during a wildfire. She was able to temporarily move it to a vacant lot near town to get it away from the fire. The homeowner spent $3,000 to have the mobile home relocated and another $3,000 to have it returned. Will the costs to move the home to a safer area or to return it to the property be covered?

17) An individual purchases a used mobile home and puts it on a lot but has not yet connected the home to electricity or water. For what amount can the homeowner insure this mobile home?

18) A mobile home is damaged in a tornado, and it costs $5,000 to repair the damage to the structure. Will this be a covered loss? If so, how much will the homeowner receive?

Farm Owners Insurance

Farmers live and work on their properties. For these reasons, insurance companies designed **farm owners' insurance** that covers their homes along with the liability and property of their farming operations. The design of farm owners' insurance is much like that of a commercial property package.

> **Helpful Hint**
>
> A farmer can opt to insure the home on one policy and the farm property and operations on a separate business policy.

Farm owners policies cover family homes and everything in them as well as personal liability for farmers and their families. Farm owners insurance also covers farming equipment, livestock, and farming products. Such policies, however, generally exclude coverage for unharvested crops. Farmers can get coverage for harvested crops up to the limit stated in the policy.

Insurance companies are highly concerned with risks, and there are a lot of risks in farming. Underwriters will want to know about the following variables:

- the types of farming operations (e.g., dairy, poultry, ranch, vegetables, grains, or a combination of operations)
- acreage and what the farmer uses the land for
- the type and number of animals on the property
- the number of residences on the property
- an inventory of all farming vehicles and equipment
- the number of barns and other structures

> **Did You Know?**
>
> Like DP and HO policies, farm owners insurance policies come in basic, broad, or special coverage forms.

Farm owners insurance policies comprise several different insurance forms, including one or more farm coverage forms, the Home Form, the common policy declarations, and the common policy conditions forms.

Every farming operation is different, which is why farm owners insurance policies are highly customizable. Farmers can add endorsements to modify their farm owners policies to include farm computers, pollutant cleanup, sump overflow and backup, blanket barns and outbuildings, borrowed farm equipment, and many other items. Farm owners receive coverage for the causes of losses that are listed on the declarations page.

Quick Review Questions

19) Would a person who does not earn full income from farming be eligible to purchase farm owners insurance?

20) A farmer decides to rent out the dwelling that is located on his farm's premises. Can he get farm owners insurance?

21) A farmer retires, and his children decide to lease out all the farmland, sell the animals, and stop farming altogether. When it is time for the farm owners policy renewal, will the farm still be eligible?

22) A tornado blows through a farm, destroying the ten acres of corn in the field as well as the corn that is stored in a silo. Will the farmer be entitled to receive payment for the corn lost in the field, the corn stored in the silo, or both?

Builder's Risk

A **builder's risk** insurance policy protects jobsites against damage and loss during a building's construction. Builder's risk policies can cover new construction or the remodeling of preexisting buildings. Commercial contractors typically purchase builder's risk policies, but they are also appropriate for homeowners, property owners, and house flippers.

Builder's risk policies cover various causes of losses depending on the policy. The most comprehensive builder's risk policies generally cover the following types of losses:

- theft
- vandalism
- property damage
- collapse
- arson
- fire or lightning
- debris removal
- materials in transit
- backup of sewers, drains, and pumps
- windstorm or hail

> **Helpful Hint**
>
> Builder's risk also covers supplies; equipment (on the jobsite, in transit, in storage); and materials.

Builder's risk policies generally use one of two ways to determine the amount of insurance. They can use the **completed value form** to report on the construction of just one project. In contrast, the **reporting form** is used for projects in which multiple buildings are under construction. In such cases, the insured must update the insurance company monthly on the progress of the projects.

The dates on which coverage becomes effective and the dates on which coverage ends can be tricky with builder's risk policies. The trigger that starts coverage is generally when the materials are moved to the jobsite, but the policy may describe some other trigger. Coverage can end at various points in construction, but may include any of the following:

- when the project has been completed
- when the project is ready for its intended use
- when the owner and contractor agree it will end
- when the project receives a certificate of occupancy
- when the building becomes occupied

The policy will explicitly describe the termination date trigger.

Builder's risk policies typically include certain additional coverages which will be listed on the policy. Common additional coverages include the following:

- debris removal: covers cleanup costs after the property has been damaged
- preservation of property: requires insureds to do whatever they can to preserve property at risk of being damaged; required by insurance policies; pays for damage to the property while it is being removed and returned to the property if it was removed to protect it from a covered loss
- fire department service charge: covers charges by a fire department for services rendered
- pollutant cleanup and removal: covers losses for which the insured is liable if land or water pollutants cause damage to another party or their property

Insureds have the option of adding coverage extensions to cover extended time periods for various circumstances.

For example, if an insured wishes to have coverage for temporary structures like scaffolding, property while it is being stored temporarily, or property such as elevators or HVAC systems, these can be added as extensions for an extra fee.

Quick Review Questions

23) A homeowner decides to construct a second-story addition to her home. The addition would include a bedroom, bathroom, and bonus room. Would this type of project be covered under a homeowners insurance policy or would a builder's risk policy be required?

24) A developer purchases several hundred acres of land on which he plans to put a school and a subdivision of 200 homes. Which builder's risk form would be appropriate for this type of project: the completed value form or the reporting form?

25) A windstorm blows through, damaging a partially constructed building and scattering debris throughout the construction site. Will the cost of removing the debris be covered under the builder's risk policy?

Additional Homeowners Coverage

Earthquake

In the insurance industry, earthquakes are considered catastrophes because they can damage homes, other structures on the property, and contents inside the home.

For the purpose of insurance, an earthquake occurs when the earth shakes or trembles because of a volcano, tectonic processes, or some other cause.

Damage by an earthquake is rarely covered under standard homeowners policies, but homeowners can add earthquake coverage for an additional premium by adding conditions to a policy or by purchasing a standalone policy that covers earthquakes.

Earthquake coverage also covers the cost of emergency repairs that are necessary to protect the home from further damage, such as removing broken glass and boarding up windows.

The deductible for earthquake coverage is typically a percentage of the dwelling and personal property coverages. While the deductibles for earthquake coverages can be high, earthquake policies provide much of the necessary funds to rebuild a home after a devastating loss.

Did You Know?

Anyone can purchase an earthquake policy regardless of whether earthquakes have happened in their area in the past.

Quick Review Questions

26) A homeowner wants to get insurance protection just in case earthquake activity occurs. Will the homeowner be eligible to purchase a standalone earthquake policy, earthquake coverage by endorsement, or neither?

27) A homeowner and his family safely escape from the home during an earthquake. Will the insured's earthquake policy cover any damage caused by the quake?

Watercraft

Insureds who own or use a boat may be interested in adding an endorsement to their homeowners policies to cover liability for damages caused while operating a boat or damages to a boat that is docked. The watercraft endorsement also covers liability and medical payments for injuries caused by the insured while operating a boat.

> **Did You Know?**
>
> Tornadoes cause extremely high winds, but there is no such thing as tornado insurance. Damage by tornadoes is covered under wind or windstorm coverage.

Watercraft endorsements do not cover personal watercrafts (e.g., Jet Skis). The endorsement also excludes boats with inboard engines that have more than fifty horsepower. Outboard motorboats must be twenty-five horsepower or lower to be covered under this endorsement.

Quick Review Questions

28) A homeowner was partying on his neighbor's pontoon when the homeowner steered the boat into another boat, causing damage to both crafts. Would the watercraft endorsement on the homeowner's home insurance policy cover the damage to both boats?

29) While the homeowner is fishing on her boat, she casts a fishing line that accidentally catches the finger of a child in a neighboring boat. Will the child's $500 doctor's bill be covered under the homeowner watercraft endorsement?

Windstorm

Wind is defined as a current of air blowing in a certain direction. A windstorm is defined as wind that is caused by straight-line winds or thunderstorms, such as cyclones, tornadoes, and hurricanes. Wind damage is often excluded from homeowner policies in states where wind damage has caused major destruction. When this is the case, the policy wording will state wind as an exclusion when the insurer will not cover it, although homeowners may be able to purchase wind coverage separately.

Most—but not all—standard homeowners policies cover the perils of windstorms, especially in coastal areas. In states where homeowners insurance companies do not include wind as a cause of loss, private companies sell wind insurance policies separately. Such policies are also sometimes called hurricane insurance policies. In some states, the state sponsors separate wind insurance coverage. While homeowners insurance is in force at all times during the policy term, wind or hurricane coverage may only be in effect during certain conditions.

In Florida, for example, coverage for wind policies may only be triggered when the National Weather Service issues a certain type of storm warning, such as a hurricane. In Texas, wind coverage includes not only losses for high winds, but also fire and theft.

Wind insurance covers the structure of a home that is damaged as a direct cause of wind and windstorms. It will also cover water damage caused by winds. For example, if a hurricane blows the roof off of a home and water enters the home, a wind policy will cover the water damage. Wind policies only cover water damage that is caused by wind.

The deductible for a wind policy or endorsement may be a flat fee; however, it is commonly a percentage of the dwelling coverage amount. Homeowners policies may have flat fees for the deductible, and percentages of the dwelling coverage as a deductible for wind claims only. The percentage for a deductible for a wind-based claim is typically between 1 and 5 percent.

Quick Review Questions

30) A homeowner has wind coverage in a policy with a $1,000 deductible and a wind deductible of 1 percent of Coverage A - Dwelling coverage ($200,000). How much would the insurance company pay if a tornado caused this loss?

31) A homeowner in Florida purchases an endorsement on his homeowners policy to cover wind. The National Weather Service issues a warning that a hurricane is coming; during the hurricane, a portion of the roof collapses, and rain destroys the kitchen. Will the water damage be covered under the homeowners policy?

Chapter Review

Table 5.2. Chapter 5 Review: Flood, Mobile Home, Farmowners, and Other Personal Property Insurance	
National Flood Insurance Program (NFIP)	
Parts of the program	• an insuring agreement to protect against flooding and damage from backed up water • floodplain management and mapping

Types of policies	• identical insurance coverage with choice of two policies:
	    • those purchased from NFIP
	    • those purchased from Write-Your-Own (WYO) program

Coverage eligibility criteria	• Location must meet floodplain management guidelines. • Structures must have a roof, two solid walls, and be above ground. • There is a 30-day waiting period. • Covers damage resulting from floods.
Definitions	• the rapid accumulation of runoff from any source • the overflow of inland or coastal waters • includes mudflow and collapse • collapse that exceeds typical cycles of water flow
Mobile Home Coverage	
Structure	• similar to homeowners policies • covers the structure up to 40%
Transportation	• pays $500 to move the mobile home to a safer location • transportation endorsement often purchased to ensure that any damage that occurs through transportation is covered • covers collision, upset, standing, or sinking
Coverage area	• continental US and Canada • up to 30 days after peril event
Farm owners Insurance	
Coverage	• hybrid of business and personal policies • covers both property and liability • can be written in a package or monoline • must include a farm Declarations Form

Table 5.2. Chapter 5 Review: Flood, Mobile Home, Farmowners, and Other Personal Property Insurance	
	• can cover basic, broad, or special perils
Coverage forms	• farm property • farm liability • agricultural machinery and equipment • livestock
Builder's Risk	
Coverage	• also known as "course of construction" insurance • protects against basic perils • materials, supplies, and equipment
Insureds	• contractors • property owners • subcontractors • lenders • architects
Watercraft	
Basics and coverage	• can be added as an endorsement to a homeowner policy • covers liability for damages caused while operating a boat or damages to a boat that is docked • covers liability and medical payments for injuries caused when an insured is operating the boat • does not cover personal watercrafts (e.g., Jet Skis) • excludes boats with inboard engines that have more than fifty horsepower • very low limit for coverage—usually around $1,000

Answer Key

1. The federal government enacted the National Flood Insurance Act to protect property owners by informing them of their risk of flood damage and reducing flood damage by mapping out areas that are prone to flooding.

2. No. The National Flood Insurance Program (NFIP) definition states that the affected property must be at least two acres or affect more than one property.

3. The policyholder would get the maximum limit of $100,000 after paying his $500 deductible.

4. No. Unlike standard homeowners policies, flood insurance policies do not cover additional living expenses.

5. Since the built-in garage is part of the structure, it would be covered under the dwelling coverage.

6. The will receive the maximum limits of $200,000 for damage to the structure, along with $100,000 for contents coverage minus the $1,000 deductible, for a total of $299,000.

7. The National Flood Insurance Program (NFIP) flood insurance policies only cover the structure and contents of the home; they do not cover items outside the home (e.g., decks, swimming pools, fences).

8. Items that are used to service the building, such as furnaces, water heaters, and so forth are included under the National Flood Insurance Program's (NFIP's) building coverage.

9. Personal property being stored in a basement would only be covered if the homeowner had purchased contents coverage.

10. National Flood Insurance Program (NFIP) policies only cover damage caused by surface water; they do not cover losses where another insurance carrier covers the loss.

11. Yes; however, the homeowner would only be able to get a limited amount of flood insurance until the community is fully admitted into the National Flood Insurance Program (NFIP), at which time, the homeowner would be able to purchase the full amount of coverage.

12. If the homeowner's community already participates in the National Flood Insurance Program (NFIP), the homeowner may purchase the maximum limits for the building ($250,000) and its contents ($100,000).

13. The claim amount for the building would be $240,000 ($250,000 – $10,000); for the contents it would be $49,000 ($50,000 – $1,000). The total payment would therefore be $289,000.

14. The waiting period is waived if a mortgage lender requires a homeowner to increase the flood insurance coverage.

15. The homeowner will receive a claim payment for $8,000, which would equal $9,000 minus the $1,000 deductible.

16. The homeowner policy covers the peril of fire and relocation of the home, so the insured would be entitled to the full $6,000 without having to meet a deductible.

17. A mobile home is only eligible for coverage if it is fit for habitation. Once the electrical and plumbing issues are fixed, the owner of the mobile home can purchase coverage for it.

18. Because wind damage is a covered loss, the homeowner will receive $4,000, which is the full $5,000 minus the $1,000 deductible.

19. Farmowners insurance policies cover all types of farming operations, including hobby farms.

20. To be eligible for farmowners policies, the farmer must have a primary residence on the farm and be living in it full time.

21. To have farmowners insurance policies, farmers must be actively engaged in operating their farms.

22. The stored corn would only be insured for the limit shown on the policy for stored crops. The farmer will therefore not be able to recoup the loss of the corn in the field unless he had previously added that type of coverage to the farmowner policy.

23. The homeowner would need a builder's risk policy because a homeowners policy would not be sufficient for such a large construction project.

24. The reporting form updates the insurance company every month about how much progress has been made on each building in that time, so this would be the most appropriate form in this scenario.

25. Debris removal is commonly listed as an additional coverage on builder's risk policies.

26. Since earthquake activity does not need to be active for a homeowner to obtain coverage, the homeowner could purchase either a standalone earthquake policy or earthquake coverage by endorsement.

27. The policy would cover damage to the house, fence, and mailbox, but the owner's auto coverage should cover damage to the insured's vehicles.

28. Pontoon boats have a minimum horsepower of 115, which is way over the outboard limit of 25 horsepower, so the accident would not be covered.

29. The watercraft endorsement covers liability, and the medical bill is under the $1,000 limit, so the child's medical bill would be covered.

30. The insurance company would pay $200,000 less the 1 percent deductible of $2,000, which equals $198,000.

31. Because the National Weather Service issued a hurricane warning and the windstorm caused the roof to collapse, resulting in water damage, all damage to the structure of the house and everything in the house will be covered up to the policy limits.

6. Personal Auto Policies (PAP)

Introduction to PAP

A **personal auto policy (PAP)** provides coverage for someone's vehicle as well as liability coverage in cases where the driver is responsible for injuries to someone else or damage to someone else's property. A typical policy has six sections which will be discussed in greater detail in this chapter. All PAPs must meet the minimum liability and property damage coverage requirements of the policyholder's home state. The six sections in a typical PAP are as follows:

- liability
- medical payments
- uninsured motorist coverage
- property damage to the insured's vehicle
- duties after a loss
- general provisions

Some examples of coverage provided by a PAP include damage to an insured's vehicle due to an accident, theft, or natural disaster; medical payments for injuries sustained by an insured and caused by a covered loss; and payments to others for damage caused by the insured due to the insured's negligence.

Quick Review Questions

1) What does a PAP typically cover?

2) Which type of coverage does a PAP provide for the insured's vehicle?

3) Which level of coverage do most states require vehicle owners to have?

Definitions

A PAP begins by stating that it is an agreement between the policyholder and the carrier to provide coverage in exchange for the payment of a premium. Immediately following this, the PAP has a section devoted to definitions for language provided in the policy. Some of the following terms are defined as follows:

- **bodily injury:** harm, injury, sickness, disease, or death that results from the loss
- **property damage:** physical damage, destruction, or loss of use to tangible property
- **family member:** any person who is related to the policyholder by blood, marriage, or adoption who resides in the same household (may include a ward or foster child)

- **your covered auto:** the vehicle shown in the declarations page, a newly acquired vehicle, a trailer owned by the policyholder, or a vehicle that is not owned by the policyholder provided it meets certain criteria
- **trailer:** a vehicle designed to be pulled by another vehicle
- **newly acquired auto (NAC):** can include a vehicle the policyholder just purchased in addition to the policyholder's other vehicles or to replace one of the vehicles that is already insured
- **collision:** coverage that begins on the date the policyholder becomes the owner of the newly acquired vehicle as long as the carrier is advised of the new vehicle within fourteen days if the currently insured vehicle has collision coverage, or within four days if the current vehicle does not have collision coverage, but the policyholder wants to add the coverage to the existing policy
- **other-than-collision:** has the same definition as the term *collision*; however, it applies to losses that occur due to other causes that are not associated with a collision.

Helpful Hint

Vehicles covered under a PAP typically include private passenger cars, vans, pickup trucks, trailers, newly acquired vehicles, and in certain circumstances, non-owned vehicles.

Quick Review Questions

4) Why do insurance policies have sections for definitions?

5) What qualifies as an NAC?

6) What is the difference between collision coverage and other-than-collision coverage?

7) Which types of vehicles are covered under a PAP?

Parts of the Document

Liability Coverages (Part A)

The insuring agreement lays out that the coverage pays for any bodily injury or property damage cause by the insured. It can also include any **prejudgment interest** that may accrue between the time the judgment is entered at trial and when the claim is paid, along with the costs associated with settling or defending a lawsuit in court.

The "insured" in the Liability section of the policy can be the policyholder or any family member related to the ownership, maintenance, or use of any automobile or trailer. It includes any person using the insured's covered auto policy with the policyholder's expressed or implied permission or with legal responsibilities for acts or omissions of a person for whom coverage is afforded under that section (such as a minor who has a driver's license).

Helpful Hint

The carrier's duty to settle or defend the insured ends when the limit of liability has been exhausted.

Supplementary payments include bail bonds that are required because of a car accident that results in bodily injury or property damage. Payments can also include premiums on appeal bonds, loss of earnings when an insured must attend a hearing or trial, any expenses incurred by the insured when rendering first aid to others at the time of the accident, and any other reasonable expenses incurred by the insured at the request of the insurance carrier.

> **Did You Know?**
>
> Drivers who use their personal vehicles in affiliation with rideshare companies are not covered by PAP. When drivers accept trips through their rideshare apps, these trips are not covered under PAP or company coverage; once the driver sets out to meet the client, the company insurance kicks in.

Exclusions can vary depending on the carrier and the state; however, the following are common exclusions. Note that there is no liability coverage for any of the following cases:

- an insured who intentionally causes injury or property damage
- property owned or being transported by the insured
- damage to property rented, used by, or in the care of the insured
- injury to an employee of an insured during the course of employment
- the insured's liability arising out of the ownership or use of a vehicle while being used as a public or livery conveyance
- any insured using any vehicle while employed in the pickup or delivery of newspapers or magazines, food, or any products for compensation
- situations in which the insured is employed or otherwise engaged in selling, repairing, servicing, storing, or parking vehicles designed for use mainly on public highways
- any insured who is maintaining or using any vehicle while employed or engaged in any business not described in the "Exclusions" section
- any insured who is using a vehicle without the express or implied permission of the vehicle owner
- for the payment of any punitive or exemplary damages awarded against an insured

The "Exclusions" section also states that no liability coverage is provided for the ownership, maintenance, or use of the following:

- any vehicle with less than four wheels or designed mainly for use off public roads
- any vehicle, other than the covered auto, that is owned by the insured or furnished for the insured's regular use
- any vehicle, other than a covered auto, that is owned by any family member or furnished for regular use of any family member
- any vehicle located inside a facility designed for racing, competing, or practicing for any speed contest

The limits of liability on a car insurance policy are typically shown as three separate numbers, side by side. For example, the declarations page or the insured's insurance wallet card might show "$25,000/$50,000/$25,000," which translates as follows:

- The first number represents the policy limit for bodily injury per person, per accident for care, loss of services, or death.
- The second number represents the policy limit for bodily injury for all injured claimants per vehicle, per accident for care, loss of services, or death.
- The third number represents the policy limit for damage to the claimant's vehicle per accident.

> **Helpful Hint**
>
> In the US, most states require a minimum limit of liability coverage on an auto policy for all vehicles.

The limits of liability are the most the policy will pay regardless of the number of insureds, claims made, vehicles or premiums shown on the declaration page, or vehicles involved in the accident. The State of Texas requires that insurers provide the following minimum coverage:

- bodily injury (per person): $30,000
- bodily injury (per accident): $60,000
- property damage (per accident): $25,000
- uninsured motorist: not required

If an auto accident to which the insured's policy applies occurs out of state and that particular state's minimum liability policy limit requirements are higher than those of the state in which the insured resides, the insured's policy will provide the higher necessary limit required by that state. This portion of the policy also provides the required minimum amounts and types of coverages for nonresidents to maintain insurance whenever the nonresident uses a vehicle in the state requiring the coverage.

If there is other applicable liability insurance available for a loss, each carrier will pay its fair share of the loss. That share is the proportion of the limit of liability the insured's policy bears to the total of all applicable limits; however, any insurance provided to an insured for a vehicle not owned by the insured, such as a temporary substitute vehicle, will be in excess over any other collectible insurance.

Quick Review Questions

8) What is a bodily injury liability claim?

9) What is a property damage liability claim?

10) What does the middle number of the three liability limits represent?

11) Can the insured claim damage to his built-in stereo system from the rear-end loss?

Medical Coverages (Part B)

Part B provides coverage for expenses incurred for medical treatment and funeral services because of bodily injury caused by an accident and sustained by an insured. The expenses must be incurred within three years from the date of the loss.

Under this section of the policy, an insured can be the policyholder or any member of that person's family while occupying the vehicle, or as a pedestrian when struck by a motor vehicle that is designed for use mainly on public roads. An insured can also be any other person occupying the insured's covered vehicle.

For example, if the insured's child is struck by a car while walking across the street, the insured's auto policy will cover the child's medical care expenses for up to three years from the date of loss or until the policy limit is exhausted, whichever comes first.

> **Helpful Hint**
>
> It is important to read the entire list of exclusions; there may be sections where the they do not apply to the insured.

The policy excludes medical payments for bodily injuries sustained while

- occupying a vehicle with less than four wheels;
- riding in a vehicle being used as a public or livery conveyance;
- riding in a vehicle being used as a residence;
- using a vehicle in the course of employment if worker's comp benefits are available;
- occupying or being struck by any vehicle other than the vehicle covered by the insured's policy;
- occupying a vehicle without the reasonable belief that the person is allowed to be in the vehicle;
- occupying a vehicle when it is being used in the vehicle owner's business;
- riding in a vehicle damaged by or as a consequence of nuclear weapons, war, civil war, insurrection, or rebellion; and
- occupying a vehicle located inside a facility designed for racing, competing, or practicing for any prearranged or organized race or speed contest.

No one can receive duplicate payments for the same elements of loss under a PAP. The language in the other insurance is much the same as it is in Part A.

Quick Review Questions

12) What does the concept of "other insurance" mean?

13) Who does the medical payments coverage protect?

14) Can the insured's employee, while on the clock, claim medical payments coverage for injuries caused while riding in the insured's vehicle as a passenger?

15) Can the insured claim medical bills for injuries he sustains during practice at the raceway caused by the excessive speed of his vehicle at the time of impact?

Protection Against Uninsured Motorists (Part C)

Uninsured motorist (UM) coverage offers an insured peace of mind in cases where there are injuries caused by an accident where the driver of the other vehicle is liable and has no insurance on their vehicle.

The policy defines an insured in this section as the policyholder, any of the policyholder's family members, or any other person occupying the policyholder's covered auto. An uninsured motor vehicle is defined as a land motor vehicle or trailer of any type that meets the following criteria:

- has no bodily injury liability bond or PAP policy at the time of the accident
- has the bodily injury bond or policy, but the limits are lower than those required by the state where the policyholder's covered auto is principally garaged
- is involved in a "hit-and-run" involving the covered auto, the insured, or any vehicle occupied by the insured when the liable vehicle or operator cannot be identified
- has a bodily injury bond or PAP at the time of the accident, but the bonding or insurance company denies coverage or is/becomes insolvent

Did You Know?

In most places, between 10 and 20 percent of drivers are insured.

The policy then states that an uninsured vehicle does not include any vehicle or equipment that meets the following criteria:

- owned by, furnished, or available for the regular use of the policyholder or any family member
- owned or operated by a self-insurer unless the self-insurer is or becomes insolvent
- owned by any governmental unit or agency
- operated on rails (trains) or crawler treads (continuous track—e.g., a military tank)
- designed for use mainly off public roads
- while located for use as a residence or premises

There is no uninsured motorists coverage if the at-fault vehicle is owned by the same policyholder or if one of the insured's family members is occupying or struck by an at-fault vehicle that is owned or insured by the same policyholder.

For example, if Chris uses his dad's old Honda to go to his after-school job and accidentally damages his mom's BMW on the way out of the garage, there is no coverage to repair the dent in the BMW.

This section of Part C is similar to the same section in Parts A and B. The limit includes two amounts side by side, with the first amount applying to the limit for any one person per accident and the second amount applying to the total limit for all bodily injury claims for insureds related to one accident. So, if the declarations page states the limit is $\frac{25}{50}$, this means that there is a $25,000 limit per person, per accident, and a limit of $50,000 for all insureds involved in the accident.

For example, Billy (the insured) is involved in an accident with an uninsured vehicle. Billy has two passengers in his covered vehicle and all three of them sustain injuries. The following scenarios could play out:

Scenario 1:

- $Billy's\ medical\ expenses\ total\ =\ 10{,}000.$
- Passenger 1 expenses total $30,000.
- Passenger 2 expenses total $4,000.

- $The\ total\ =\ \$44{,}000.$

If policy limits under this coverage are $\frac{25}{50}$, then each passenger has up to \$25,000 in coverage, so passenger 1 will be over limits by \$5,000. Even though the total of \$44,000 is below the \$50,000 total limit, the policy will only cover up to \$25,000 for passenger 1.

Scenario 2:

- $Billy's\ medical\ expenses\ total\ =\ \$21{,}000.$
- $Passenger\ 1\ expenses\ total\ =\ \$24{,}000.$
- $Passenger\ 2\ expenses\ total\ =\ \$20{,}000.$
- $The\ total\ =\ \$65{,}000.$

In this scenario, each occupant in the vehicle has medical expenses totaling less than the \$25,000 limit; however, the total for the accident of \$65,000 falls over the \$50,000 limit for all occupants, so this claim would be \$15,000 over limits. Other types of insurance, such as medical, may cover these additional costs.

Helpful Hint

There is no coverage for bodily injuries sustained by an insured if that insured or their legal representative settles the claim without the consent of the insurance carrier. In essence, the insured waives the coverage when settling the claim with the other driver's insurance.

Quick Review Questions

16) Name three examples of uninsured motor vehicles.

17) Can a four-wheeler be considered an uninsured vehicle?

18) Will coverage be provided for medical bills presented by an insured if the two involved vehicles are owned by family members living in the same household?

Coverage for Damage to Policyholder's Car (Part D)

In this section, "your auto" can signify the following:

- the policyholder's vehicle, including while family members or people with implied or expressed permission drive it
- any private passenger auto, pickup truck, van, or trailer not owned by, furnished, or available for regular use of the policyholder or any family member while in the custody of or being operated by the policyholder or family member
- any auto or trailer the policyholder does not own while used as a temporary substitute for the covered auto, which is out of normal use because of reasons such as breakdown, repair, servicing, loss or destruction

Now that there is an understanding of what is covered, the coverage itself can be defined. The insuring agreement states that the policy will provide coverage for direct and accidental losses to the covered auto or non-owned auto. A policy deductible will be deducted from any payments owed at the time of settlement. Direct and accidental loss can mean the following:

- **collision:** coverage for when the insured vehicle accidentally collides with another vehicle or object
- **other than collision:** sometimes referred to as comprehensive coverage, which protects against damage caused by other losses (e.g., windstorms, hail, flood, theft, fires, explosions).

For example, damage caused by a tree could be a covered loss under either type of damage. If the insured is distracted while driving and hits a tree head-on with his vehicle, that would be a collision. If the insured parks his car under the same tree, and lightning hits it and causes a large branch to break and crush the car, that would be covered under the "Other-than-Collision" section.

Transportation expenses cover the temporary rental of a vehicle that the policyholder can use while her own vehicle is either being repaired or is unavailable due to a covered loss. A policyholder can elect to add this coverage to the policy by selecting the desired limit based on what is offered by the carrier. Two common limits found are either $20 per day with a $600 limit or $25 per day with a $750 limit.

Stipulations or provisions in the policies require that there must be a loss to the covered auto that is either due to a collision or an other-than-collision event.

For example, if the insured is renting a car while his is being repaired for hail damage and he only has collision coverage, transportation expenses would not apply in this situation since the loss is not covered by his policy due to the policy not having "other than collision" coverage.

Transportation expenses can also include expenses the policyholder becomes legally responsible for in the event of a loss to a non-owned auto. The same limitations apply here as above, so if the loss is caused by fire and the insured only has collision coverage, then the policy would not provide coverage for the expenses for that non-owned auto.

The next section under transportation expenses is subject to the provisions described above and adds a limit to the coverage time frame:

- If the loss is due to a total theft, the coverage begins forty-eight hours after the theft and ends when the covered auto or non-owned auto is returned to use or payment has been made for the loss.
- In all other covered situations other than theft, the coverage begins twenty-four hours after the vehicle is withdrawn from use.

The payment will be limited to the period of time reasonably required to repair or replace the vehicle or once the limit has been exhausted.

The following are exclusions one would typically see in most auto policies. It is important to recognize there may be fewer or more exclusions depending on the state in which the vehicle is mainly garaged and the insurance carrier. The policy will not pay for the following:

- loss to the covered auto that happens while the auto is being used as a public or livery conveyance
- damage due and confined to wear, tear, freezing, mechanical or electrical breakdown, or road damage to tires—unless that damage results from the total theft of the auto

- loss due to or because of radioactive contamination, nuclear weapon discharge, war, insurrection, or rebellion
- any electronic equipment not permanently attached to the vehicle (e.g., radios, GPS, DVD players, and the media these items use)
- a total loss to the auto or non-owned auto due to destruction or confiscation by the government or civil authorities (does not apply to lien holders)
- losses to trailers, camper bodies, or motor homes (or any equipment used with them) that are not listed in the declarations
- loss to any non-owned-auto when used by the policyholder or the policyholder's family members without a reasonable belief that they have permission to use the auto
- loss to any custom furnishings or equipment such as special carpeting or insulation, furniture, height-extending roofs, custom murals, paintings, or other types of decals or graphics in or on a pickup or van (exceptions: caps, covers, bed liners on pickup trucks owned by the policyholder)
- loss to a non-owned auto being maintained or used by any person while employed or engaged in the business of selling, repairing, servicing, storing, or parking vehicles designed for use on public highways
- losses to covered autos or a non-owned autos located inside a facility designed for racing or speed competitions
- loss to or loss of the use of a non-owned auto that is rented by the policyholder or the policyholder's family member if the rental company is not allowed to recover from the loss based on the terms of the rental contract or a state law

The limit of liability for Part D is the lesser of the

- actual cash value of the stolen or damaged property; or
- the amount it will cost to repair or replace the property with other property of like, kind, and quality.

If the vehicle is stolen and never recovered or if it is recovered with enough damage to be deemed a total loss, the payment would be the actual cash value of the vehicle at the time of the loss based on the year, make, model, mileage, condition, and options (less any applicable deductibles).

Helpful Hint

Some policies may have additional exclusions for damage or loss arising out of neglect. Neglect means the failure to adequately maintain the covered auto or non-owned auto after a loss.

If the vehicle is involved in a loss and parts need to be replaced, the payment would be the cost of those parts that are of like, kind, and quality to what the vehicle had at the time of the loss, plus the labor (less any applicable deductibles).

The policy further states that the maximum amount that can be paid for a non-owned auto, which is a trailer, is $1,500. It also states that certain audio, visual, or data-producing electronic equipment that is permanently installed in the auto—but in locations in which the auto manufacturer did not design them to be installed—will have a $1,000 limit.

If the repair or the replacement results in betterment, or better than "like, kind, and quality," the insurer does not owe any additional amount for the improvement.

In Part D, the payment for the loss may be made in cash, repairs, or replacement of the damaged or stolen property to make the policyholder's vehicle whole again. If the stolen property is recovered, it may be returned at the insurer's expense and, if it is returned, the insurer will pay for any damage resulting from the theft. The insurer can also keep all or part of the recovered stolen property at an agreed-upon or appraised value. If the payment is made with money, it will include any applicable sales tax owed for the damaged or stolen property.

Helpful Hint

PAP will not directly or indirectly benefit a carrier or any other bailee that is hired to transport a vehicle.

If there are other sources of recovery available, then the policy only covers its share of the loss, which is the proportion that its limit of liability bears to the total of all the applicable limits. The policy, however, will be excess over any other collectible source of recovery in a situation where a non-owned auto is involved. This would include any coverage provided by the owner of that non-owned auto, any other applicable physical damage insurance on that vehicle, or any other source of recovery applicable to the loss.

As is the case with most property insurance, if the insurer and the policyholder cannot agree on the amount of a loss, either party has the right to demand an appraisal of the vehicle. Each party will select an appraiser, and both appraisers will agree on an umpire. Each appraiser will state the amount of the loss and if the appraisers fail to agree, they will submit their differences to the umpire.

Quick Review Questions

19) What does Part D include?

20) What is the difference between collision coverage and other-than-collision coverage?

21) What is the transportation coverage used for?

22) What happens if the insured and the insurer disagree about the value of the covered vehicle?

Policyholder Duties after an Accident (Part E)

Coverage may be denied if the policyholder fails to comply with the duties in this section, so it is important that policyholders communicate properly with their insurers about any damages that occur. The insured must promptly provide the carrier with the following information:

- how, when, and where the accident or loss happened
- the names and addresses of any injured persons
- the names and addresses of any witnesses
- any police reports describing what happened
- any legal documents connected to the case

Did You Know?

A person who is seeking uninsured motorist coverage must also notify the police promptly if a hit-and-run driver is involved and submit copies of legal papers if a suit is brought.

Any person seeking coverage must cooperate with the insurer while there is an investigation, settlement, or defense of any claim or suit. The person seeking coverage will also be required to submit to any necessary physical exams by physicians or to any examinations under oath, with expenses being paid by the insurer. Lastly, the person seeking coverage must authorize the insurer to obtain medical reports and other pertinent records related to the loss and submit a proof of loss when required. Of course, the insurer must be allowed to inspect the damaged property before it is repaired or disposed of.

Quick Review Questions

23) What are the main duties of the insured when there is a loss or accident?

24) What must any person seeking coverage from the covered auto's policy do when involved in a loss or accident?

General Conditions (Part F)

While the duties after a loss pertain to any insured under the policy, general conditions requirements apply to both the insured and the insurer. This section describes the conditions which must be met throughout all parts of this policy as well as through individual coverages. Much of this information repeats content from earlier parts of the chapter; these conditions are not repeated here. The remaining conditions include the following:

- **Bankruptcy** or insolvency of the policyholder will not relieve the insurer of any obligations under the policy.
- Insureds cannot bring **legal action** against the insurer unless there has been full compliance with all the terms of the policy; furthermore, no legal action can be brought against the insurer until it is clear how much the payment will be. It also states no one can sue the insurer to determine the liability of the insured.
- Insurers have the right to **subrogation**, meaning that the insured has the obligation to help the insurer recover any money paid out for a claim; if the individual receives any money from another company, it will be held in trust until the case is settled and the insurance company receives its money.

The policy **transfers** the insured's rights and duties only with the insurer's written consent; however, if the insured dies, coverage will be provided for the surviving partner or legal representative.

- If the insurer issues **more than one** auto policy to an insured, and both policies can apply to the same loss or accident, the maximum limit cannot exceed the highest applicable limit under any one policy.

As with many types of policies, PAP contains a lengthy section on conditions for termination or the nonrenewal of coverage. The following may take place within the first sixty days:

- Either party may cancel the policy by notifying the other party in writing.
- Insurers can cancel the policy with ten days' notice.

After the policy is in effect for sixty days, or if it is a renewal or continuation policy, the insurer may cancel for the following reasons:

- nonpayment of premium
- revocation of driver's license
- material misrepresentation

The **"non-termination"** condition requires that if the insurer offers to continue the policy and the insured does not accept, the policy will automatically terminate at the end of the policy period. When the insured obtains other insurance on the same vehicle, any previous coverage will end when the new policy takes effect.

Lastly, there are conditions about what will happen when the policy terminates:

- A **notice of termination** can be mailed or delivered in person.
- Any **premium refunds** will be computed based on the insurer's manuals.
- The **effective date of cancellation** on the notice is the end of the coverage.

Quick Review Questions

25) What does the right to recover payment mean?

26) What are some different reasons for the termination of an insurance policy?

27) Which policy would be considered primary if the insureds have more than one policy that provides coverage for a loss or accident?

28) What does transfer of interest mean?

Individual Named Insured Endorsement and DOC Endorsement

The **individual named insured endorsement** covers named insureds (i.e., sole proprietors) who use the cars listed on their commercial auto policies for personal use. Insureds with this endorsement are also covered when they lease, borrow, or even test drive a vehicle. In other words, the endorsement provides coverage for named insureds when they must drive vehicles other than those listed on their commercial auto policies. This endorsement is included in most commercial auto policies.

Similar to the individual named insured endorsement, the **drive other car (DOC) endorsement** covers individuals, such as employees and their spouses, who use those vehicles listed in the named insured's commercial auto policy or that the named insured borrows. For example, an employee and his spouse drive the employee's company car for both business and personal use and do not have another vehicle. Because they do not have a personal auto, the employee and his spouse do not have an auto policy of their own. The DOC endorsement purchased by the named insured provides non-owned coverage to the employee and his spouse for using the company vehicle. DOC endorsements can be purchased by corporations and partnerships as add-ons to commercial auto policies.

Quick Review Questions

29) What does the DOC endorsement cover?

30) How does the individual named insured endorsement benefit an insured person without a vehicle?

Chapter Review

Table 6.1. Chapter 6 Review: Personal Auto Policies (PAPs)	
Coverage parts	• Part A: Liability Coverages • Part B: Medical Coverages • Part C: Uninsured Motorists • Part D: Damage to Insured's Auto • Part E: Responsibilities After an Accident • Part F: General Provisions
Covered autos	• owned by policyholder • non-owned vehicles being used by or stored on the insured's property • rented or leased by policyholder • loaner vehicles operated by policyholder
Common auto endorsements	• towing and repair • higher coverage for rented vehicle • covers other types of vehicles (e.g., RVs, ATVs, trailers) • covers both individuals if they jointly own a vehicle

Answer Key

1. Personal auto policies (PAPs) provide coverage for the insured's car as well as liability coverage should the insured be held responsible for an accident or loss that caused injury to someone else or damaged someone else's property.

2. Personal auto policy (PAP) coverage includes—but is not limited to—damage from wind, hail, theft, vandalism, or a single- or multiple-vehicle accident.

3. Most states require vehicle owners to meet minimum coverage limits for liability and property damage.

4. The section for definitions helps policyholders avoid any misunderstanding of the terms of the policy.

5. A newly acquired auto (NAC) can include a vehicle that the insured recently purchased either in addition to the one already owned or to replace the one already owned.

6. Collision coverage pays for any damages resulting from an insured vehicle colliding with another object, whereas other-than-collision coverage protects against losses such as weather events, theft, and vandalism.

7. A personal auto policy (PAP) covers vehicles, such as private passenger cars, vans, pickups, trailers, newly acquired cars, and in some circumstances, non-owned vehicles like rental cars.

8. A bodily injury liability claim is a claim for damages made by a person who has sustained some form of injury due to a loss or accident caused by an insured.

9. A property damage liability claim is the claim to pay for repairs caused by the insured to someone else's vehicle.

10. The middle number of the three liability limits represents the total amount of coverage the insured's policy will provide for all injured claimants involved in one loss.

11. Property owned by an insured is excluded from liability coverage.

12. The concept of "other Insurance" states that the insured's policy will pay for its own share of a loss should there be more than one policy that provides coverage for the same loss.

13. The medical payments coverage protects the insured, any member of the insured's family living in the same household, a pedestrian struck by the insured's vehicle, and potentially any other person who is a passenger in the insured's vehicle when the loss occurs.

14. Personal auto policies (PAPs) do not provide coverage occurring during the course of employment if worker's comp benefits are available.

15. Part B does not provide coverage for injuries sustained while occupying a vehicle on a racetrack.

16. Uninsured motor vehicles could include land motor vehicles or trailers that are not insured for liability under any policy, unidentified hit-and-run vehicles, or motor vehicles or trailers that have liability limits that are lower than those of the state's minimum requirements in the state where the insured's vehicle mainly resides.

17. A four-wheeler, like other off-road vehicles, cannot be considered an uninsured vehicle under a personal auto policy (PAP).

18. There is no coverage when both the at-fault vehicle and the damaged vehicle are covered under the same policy.

19. This coverage includes the direct and accidental damage to the insured's vehicle or any vehicle that fits the definition of a non-owned vehicle and the permanently attached equipment of the covered vehicle.

20. Collision coverage involves any loss or accident involving the insured's covered vehicle colliding with another object, regardless of who is liable for the loss, whereas other-than-collision coverage involves a loss that does not include a collision, such as the theft or vandalism of the insured's vehicle.

21. In broad terms, an insured can elect to add transportation coverage to a policy if she would like to have coverage for the rental of a vehicle while her vehicle is being repaired due to a loss that is insured by the policy.

22. If the insured and the insurer disagree about the value of the covered vehicle, each party will select an appraiser; the two appraisers will then choose an umpire to negotiate the coverage.

23. If the covered vehicle is involved in a loss or accident, the insured should notify the insurer as soon as reasonably possible and take all necessary measures to protect the vehicle from further loss or damage.

24. Any person seeking coverage from the policy must cooperate with the insurer during any investigation, settlement, or defense of any claim or suit and provide the insurer with any papers or documents necessary to process the claim in a timely manner.

25. The right to recover payment means that the insurer has the legal right to recover any monies paid out through the policy.

26. A policy can be terminated by cancellation, nonrenewal, or automatic termination.

27. The primary policy would be the one that provides the most coverage to the insured.

28. Transfer of interest is the provision that provides coverage to a surviving spouse/civil partner/domestic partner or legal representative until the end of the policy period.

29. The drive other car (DOC) endorsement covers individuals who use the vehicles listed in the named insured's commercial auto policy or that the named insured borrows. This endorsement is often used to provide coverage for employees and their spouses who use a company car for personal use.

30. If the insured person rents a vehicle or drives a company vehicle, this endorsement will provide coverage for that non-owned vehicle in case of loss or accident.

7. Commercial Property Policies

Commercial Package Policies (CPPs)

The Evolving Coverage of CPPs

Different types of business insurance coverage are sold together as **commercial package policies (CPPs)**. These policies are designed to be customizable. As businesses grow, they face new exposures, and business owners must be able to purchase the proper protections against liability. The most basic businessowner's policy must include liability, commercial property insurance, and business income insurance.

Business owners can purchase a **monoline commercial policy** for each type of coverage they need, or they can purchase the various policies all as one package. Owners can choose whichever coverages they need—all in one insurance product—as their businesses evolve.

For example, Thomas and Susan Lee start a clothing manufacturing business. In the early days of the business, they only have one sewing machine, a small inventory of materials, and no employees. The couple manufactures products in the basement of their home, use their home computer for online marketing, and perform the labor themselves. As for insurance, the couple purchases a commercial package policy that includes commercial property and liability insurance.

Several years later, Thomas and Susan's business has outgrown their basement. Their profits allow them to lease space in a building designed for manufacturing and rent more sewing machines. Since they can no longer be at the business 24/7, they add commercial crime insurance to their commercial package policy. They also add cyber liability and business interruption insurance.

A few years later, the Lees have the funds to purchase their own building and equipment. At this point, they increase the limits of their insurance and add coverage for business equipment and equipment breakdown. As they hire employees to work for them, they also add a workers' compensation policy.

Quick Review Questions

1) How do commercial package policies accommodate different types of businesses?

2) What are the TWO ways in which business owners can purchase commercial insurance to protect their businesses?

Parts of a Commercial Policy

Common Contents of a CPP

Like all insurance policies, commercial package policies have several standard components. Common components include the following:

- insuring agreement: part of an insurance contract that outlines when the insurer will provide coverage in exchange for the premiums
- declarations: a concise summary of the insurance coverage
- common policy conditions: rules about cancellation, coverage changes, audits, premiums, inspections, and assignment of the policy
- coverage parts: separate policies that cover various parts of the business
- additional coverages: additional coverages that give an insured limited protection against certain losses that would otherwise not be provided under the policy
- coverage extensions: refer to coverages listed in the policy that extend the coverages in specific ways
- exclusions: a list that explains which items are not covered
- causes of loss: incidents that trigger insurable losses

Commercial package policies incorporate various types of custom coverages to protect businesses. A commercial property package consists of two or more of the following coverages:

- **commercial general liability coverage:** protects against claims caused by business operations
- **commercial property coverage:** protects the company's physical buildings and assets from covered losses
- **boiler and machinery coverage** (also known as **equipment breakdown insurance**): protects equipment
- **employment practices liability coverage:** protects employers from claims alleging discrimination, wrongful termination, or harassment
- **commercial crime coverage:** protects business owners from crimes
- **commercial auto coverage:** provides vehicle insurance for company cars, trucks, and vans
- **commercial inland marine coverage:** protects a business's products, materials, and equipment while being transported
- **farm coverage:** provides coverage for farming operations as well as the farmer's property
- **builder's risk coverage:** protects buildings during the course of construction
- **business income coverage:** provides funds for a business to continue operations
- **extra expense coverage:** pays for extra expenses needed to resume production (e.g., renting equipment that was damaged)

Quick Review Questions

3) How many coverage types must a commercial package policy have?

4) Which part of an insurance policy describes a commercial policy's coverages and effective dates?

Typical Policy Declarations for CPP

While a full insurance policy outlines all of the details of the policy, the declarations gives the insured and others a snapshot of what the policy contains. In business, vendors, subcontractors, lenders, and others may want to verify that the business owner has a CPP, what the policy contains, and the exact dates of coverage.

Using the previous example of Thomas and Susan Lee's first business policy, a review of the declarations page shows that their names are listed along with the effective dates of the policy. They have $20,000 of coverage for commercial general liability and an additional $20,000 for commercial property. They also have up to $30,000 for equipment breakdown. This is all the coverage they need to start their business, but they will need to add additional coverages as their risk increases during future growth stages.

Table 7.1. Example of CPP Policy Declarations for the Thomas and Susan Lee	
Named Insured(s): Thomas and Susan Lee Policy Period: 01/01/23 to 01/01/24, Time: 12:01am **The policy consists of the following coverage for which a premium is indicated:**	
Commercial general liability	$20,000
Commercial property	$20,000
Inland marine	$______
Commercial auto	$______
Equipment breakdown	$30,000
crime	$______
farm	$______

Quick Review Questions

5) If the Lees have a fire in their home that causes $25,000 in damage to the basement where they work, will the loss be covered?

6) After a customer comes to pick up some shirts she purchased, Susan discovers money missing from the cash drawer. According to the policy declarations, would this loss be covered?

Customary Conditions for CPP

Every commercial package policy contains a "Conditions" section. The "Conditions" section describes limitations on when or how much the insurer will pay in the event of a covered loss. Common policy conditions listed in commercial package policies are described below:

- cancellation: The insurer can cancel the policy before the expiration date as long as the insured is informed in writing about when and why the policy is being cancelled.
- changes: The first named insured is authorized to make changes to the policy.
- examination of books and records: This describes the insurer's right to examine the company's books and records.
- inspections and surveys: This describes the insurer's right to survey and inspect properties to determine their insurability.
- premiums: The named insured is responsible for paying the premiums and is entitled to any return of premiums.
- transfer of duties and rights: The insured must get consent from the insurance company to transfer any part of the policy.

> **Did You Know?**
>
> Commercial insurers can deny a claim if the insured fails to comply with the policy conditions.

Quick Review Questions

7) Thomas realizes he needs to increase his and Susan's contents and inventory coverage to $50,000, so his assistant calls the insurance company to increase the coverage. Why would the insurer NOT comply with this request?

8) If the insurer wants to view the workspace for the Lees's business, do they have to allow the inspection?

9) If the Lees file a claim and the insurer wants to inspect their records, would the Lees be required to make this information available?

Types of Commercial Property Coverage

Building and Business Personal Property Coverage

While all parts of commercial property coverage are important for business owners, the main Commercial Package Form covers building and business personal property because businesses cannot operate at all without this coverage.

Insureds must choose the Cause of Loss Form for building and personal property. The choices are like those for dwelling and homeowner policies: basic, broad, and special. The policyholder chooses the coverage limits and items that are covered. The **Basic Form** for buildings and business personal property covers eleven causes of loss. These include the following:

- fire or lightning
- smoke
- explosion
- riot or civil commotion
- windstorm or hail
- aircraft that strikes the property
- vehicles that strike the property
- glass breakage
- vandalism and malicious mischief
- theft
- volcanic eruption

Helpful Hint

Buildings and structures must be named on the policy declarations in order to be covered.

In addition to the previous perils, the **Broad Form** adds the following six perils:

- falling objects
- the weight of ice, snow, or sleet
- accidental discharge or overflow of water or steam from plumbing systems
- sudden or accidental discharge from HVAC, sprinkler systems, or hot water heaters
- the freezing of plumbing systems
- sudden and accidental damage from an electrical current that is artificially generated

As with dwelling and homeowner insurance forms, the **business property Special Form** covers all risks that are not specifically excluded.

Quick Review Questions

10) Which building and business property form(s) would be BEST to cover a warehouse in Montana?

11) Which building and business property form(s) would BEST suit a manufacturing business located in a high-crime area?

Property Covered and Excluded

The building coverage protects against losses to buildings or structures that are described on the declarations page. Coverage for buildings also includes

- completed additions;
- interior and exterior fixtures;

- machinery and equipment that are permanently installed; and
- personal property owned by the business owner and being used to service or maintain the building, structure, or premises (e.g., fire extinguishers, outdoor furniture).

Building and business property insurance policies also cover alterations and repairs to buildings and additions under construction, as well as repairs and alterations to existing buildings and structures. Similarly, building and business property coverage extends to materials, equipment, and supplies when they are being used to construct an addition or make repairs or alterations to the structure.

The business personal property portion of the policy covers losses for both the structure and its contents.

The following types of business properties are covered:

- furniture and fixtures
- machinery and equipment
- stock
- any personal property owned by the business owner and used in business operations
- others' personal property for whom the insured provides labor, materials, and services
- improvements and betterments on fixtures, installations, additions, and alterations on locations the business owner occupies but does not own
- leased personal property the business owner must insure (unless the business owner has other coverage for it)

Helpful Hint

In general, building and business property coverage policies require that other items (e.g., building supplies, vehicles, or property) be located within 100 feet of these structures in order to be covered.

The personal property of others must be in the business owner's care, custody, or control to be covered. Certain types of property are excluded from business personal property; these include the following:

- accounts, bills, currency, food stamps, debts, money, notes, and securities
- animals (except for those boarding with the insured)
- animals the business owner owns as stock while they are inside buildings
- autos the business owner holds for sale
- bridges, roadways, walkways, paved surfaces, and patios
- contraband and property that is being illegally traded or transported
- the cost of grading, backfilling, filling, or excavations
- the foundations of buildings, structures, boilers, or machinery located below the basement (or surface of the ground if there is no basement)
- land, lawns, water, or crops that are growing
- bulkheads, piers, pilings, docks, or wharves
- retaining walls that are unrelated to the building

- pipes, flues, or drains that are underground
- electronic data, including computer programs
- the cost to replace or restore data on valuable records and papers
- vehicles licensed for use on public roads that are operated primarily away from the described premises, including aircraft and watercraft
- grain, hay, straw, crops outside of buildings
- fences, antennas, and antenna parts

Building and business personal property policies cover the following circumstances as additional coverages:

- debris removal: costs to remove debris that is related to a covered loss
- preservation of property: costs to remove covered property to prevent further loss
- fire department service charge: covers up to $1,000 in fire department services charges that are related to covered losses
- pollutant cleanup and removal: covers up to $10,000 to extract pollutants from land or water
- increased cost of construction: the costs necessary to comply with laws or ordinances
- electronic data: the costs to replace or restore electronic data that was corrupted or destroyed

Quick Review Questions

12) A business owner attaches fixtures and lights to the walls in order to display goods. Are these items insured under the building and personal property policy?

13) Would a chair that is being repaired be covered while it is in the shop, after the customer picks it up, or neither?

14) A storm damages a business owner's roof and signage, causing a heavy sign to fall and damage a walkway. What would be covered under the loss?

15) To protect his art from possible fire damage, a business owner pays $10,000 to relocate it to a safe storage area. Would this be covered under the policy?

Coverage Extensions

Insurance policies commonly include coverage extensions that apply only under certain circumstances, extending beyond what the basic policy covers.

The following coverage extensions are afforded by building and business property policies to provide extra coverage for buildings:

Helpful Hint

The 80 percent coinsurance clause applies to coverage extensions. This means the property must be insured to 80 percent of its value.

- buildings while being constructed on the described premises
- buildings the owner acquires at other locations that are intended for similar business use or are used as warehouses
- Note: The coverage extension for buildings is $250,0oo per building.

The following coverage extensions apply to business owners' property:

- business personal property acquired at any location (excluding fairs, trade shows, and exhibitions)
- business personal property that the owner acquires at a newly acquired or newly constructed building
- Note: The coverage extension for business personal property is up to $100,000.

There are several additional coverage extensions from which business owners may choose:

- **Personal effects and property of others** extends coverage for up to $2,500 for personal effects and the personal property of others in the business owner's care at each described premises.
- **Valuable papers and records** extends coverage up to $2,500 to replace non-electronic lost or damaged papers where there are no duplicates (excluding electronic data).
- **Property off-premises** extends $10,000 of coverage to property away from the business while at a temporary location including at trade shows, fairs, exhibitions, and remote storage.
- **Outdoor property** extends $1,000 ($250 per plant) coverage to fences, satellite dishes, plants, and similar items for covered losses
- **Non-owned detached trailers** extend up to $5,000 of coverage to detached, non-owned trailers being used for business and that are in the business owner's care.
- **Business personal property temporarily in portable storage units** extends coverage for up to ninety days for property being temporarily stored in portable storage units when it is within 100 feet of the building.

Quick Review Questions

16) Because of fire, a business owner moves his undamaged appliances and other merchandise into a trailer until the building can be repaired. Will this property be covered under coverage extensions?

17) Strong winds damaged part of a building and much of its landscaping. Will the loss to the landscaping be covered; if so, how much would the insurer pay?

Conditions

The Building Form and the Business Personal Property Form contain certain conditions that must apply before the insurance company will pay a claim. The conditions on these forms are *in addition to* the common policy and commercial property conditions. They include the following:

- **abandonment:** Business owners may not abandon any property to the insurance company.

- **appraisal:** Either party can demand an appraisal in writing, and then the appraisers choose an umpire who decides the amount of the claim.
- **recovered property:** Business owners must notify the insurer if they recover property after a loss settlement, and they must return the company's money if they get their property back.
- **vacancy:** The insurance company will not pay for losses due to vandalism, sprinkler leakage, building glass breakage, water damage, theft, or attempted theft for buildings left vacant for over sixty consecutive days.
- **coinsurance:** For coverage to apply, property must be insured for at least 80 percent of its value.
- **duties in the event of a loss:** Business owners have a duty to protect their property from further loss, to file a police report if a law has been broken, to notify the insurance company, to provide details of the loss, and to complete a Sworn Claim Form as soon as possible after a loss.
- **valuation:** Insurers will pay the cost to repair or replace property for claims under $2,500. For claims over $2,500, the insurer will cover the actual cash value of property at the time of the loss.
- **loss payment:** The company may settle the loss by agreeing to repair, rebuild, or replace the property with similar kind and quality, and will settle the loss within thirty days of reaching an agreement.

Helpful Hint

The insurer will not pay either the insured or the owner of the property more than the financial interest in the property.

There are additional conditions that apply only to mortgage holders. Each mortgage holder will be paid in the order of appearance, even if a foreclosure is in process. The policy also states that mortgage holders will receive loss payments if they pay the insurance premiums and the business owner fails to comply with his duties.

Did You Know?

To qualify for loss payments, mortgage holders must sign a sworn proof-of-loss statement within sixty days after receiving notice from the company that the insured failed to previously provide this statement.

Mortgage holders are required to notify the insurance company of changes in ownership, occupancy, and substantial changes in risk. If the insured does not comply with the duties and the conditions of the policy, and the mortgage holder receives a loss payment, the mortgage holder's rights will be transferred to the insurance company according to how much is paid out. If the company pays off the entire principal along with interest, the mortgage transfers to the insurance company, and the business owner must pay the insurance company the remaining mortgage debt.

Quick Review Questions

18) Which condition would apply when a business and the insurance company disagree on the value of the property?

19) A business owner discovers that there has been a theft of computers, but she does not file a police report. Is the insurance company obligated to pay for the loss?

20) While a business owner was moving operations to a new location, the old location was vacant for ninety days, during which time vandals broke in and defaced the building's interior and exterior. Would this loss be covered?

21) Would repairs or replacements due to lightning damage be made at replacement cost or actual cash value?

Common Optional Coverages

The Building and Personal Property Form lists optional coverages on the declarations page as they pertain to each item. For example, the declarations page may say "inflation guard" next to the building coverage limit, which means that the inflation guard protection applies only to the building. Some of the common optional coverages are as follows:

- **agreed value:** Insurers pay only the amount stated on the declarations page for costs to repair or replace property.
- **inflation guard:** The coverage amount increases by the percentage stated in the declarations.
- **replacement cost:** This covers the cost to replace the property without considering depreciation.
- **replacement cost to personal property of others:** This covers the replacement cost to personal property of others that may also be listed.

Did You Know?

The formula to figure the inflation guard is the coverage amount times the number of days the coverage has been in force divided by 365.

Quick Review Questions

22) A restaurant owner installs a new fire protection system in his commercial kitchen; it costs $5,500. The market value of the system is $6,000, and the declarations page lists the equipment as having an agreed value of $5,000. If a covered loss damages the system beyond repair, how much would the business owner receive to replace the system?

23) A Building and Business Personal Property Form has $200,000 on a building and inflation guard coverage protection at 5 percent. The building sustains a total loss on the hundredth day of the policy. How much would the business owner receive for the building loss?

Common Commercial Property Conditions

There are other commercial property conditions that may apply to a policy, some of which may be attached to the policy by a separate endorsement. These include the following:

- **concealment, misrepresentation, or fraud:** If the insured commits any of these acts, the coverage is voided.

- **control of property:** If someone other than the insured, who is not under the control or direction of the insured, neglects the property or damages it, it will not affect the insurance coverage.
- **insurance under two or more coverages:** In the case that more than one insurance policy covers the loss, the insurance company will not pay more than the total actual damages.
- **legal action against us:** Insureds may not bring legal action against the insurance company if they have not fully complied with all the terms of the coverage, and any lawsuits must be filed within two years of the date on which the physical loss or damage occurred.
- **liberalization:** This condition states that if the insurance company revises the policy by broadening coverage and does not charge the insured a premium for it during the policy period or within forty-five days before it starts, the broadened coverage applies immediately.
- **no benefit to bailee:** No individuals or organizations—other than the insured—who have custody of the property may benefit from the insurance.
- **other insurance:** If another insurance policy exists, the insurance company will pay its share of the covered loss but will not pay more than the limit of insurance stated on the policy.
- **policy period, coverage territory:** The company will only pay for losses that occur during the policy period and which occur at locations within the coverage territory stated on the policy. The coverage territory includes the United States, Puerto Rico, and Canada.

Quick Review Questions

24) A business that has retail stores in the United States, Puerto Rico, and Jamaica sustains a loss due to high winds and driving rains in all three locations within one year. Would the merchandise being held for sale be covered at all three locations?

25) A commercial insurance company notified a business owner two weeks before the policy's renewal that they would be broadening the business owner's coverage immediately and would not be charging her for the difference in premium. What common commercial property condition is this called?

Causes of Loss Forms

Much like other property insurance policies, such as dwelling and homeowner policies, business owners can choose the causes of loss for which they want to insure their businesses and business personal properties.

Basic Loss Coverage Form

The Basic Loss Coverage Form for building and business personal property only covers the most basic causes of loss as previously discussed in the DP and HO policies. There are eleven causes of loss on the Basic Form, and they include the following:

- fire
- lightning

- explosion
- windstorm or hail
- smoke
- aircraft or vehicles
- riot or civil commotion
- vandalism
- sprinkler leakage
- sinkhole collapse
- volcanic action

Helpful Hint

The three Causes of Loss Forms are similar to those found in the DO- and HO- Forms' basic, broad, and special coverages. Each form lists the specific perils it covers.

Quick Review Questions

26) The ventilation system in a manufacturing facility is not working well and causes smoke to infiltrate the building. Will this be a covered loss under the Basic Form for commercial property?

27) A car was speeding down the road and a passenger in the car threw lit fireworks at a commercially insured building, causing $5,000 in damage to the structure. Would this be a covered loss under the Basic Commercial Form?

28) The water tank of a sprinkler system suddenly collapses, and water damages the interior of the warehouse. Will this be a covered loss under the Basic Commercial Property Form?

29) Shock waves from a volcanic blast damage the exterior and interior of a high-rise office building, making it unsafe for occupancy. Will the repairs to the building be covered under the Basic Form?

Broad Form Loss Coverage

The Commercial Property Form covers all of the named perils as listed in the Basic Form as well as additional perils. The additional perils include the following:

- falling objects
- the weight of ice, sleet, or snow
- water damage

The Broad Form for commercial property insurance includes two additional coverages which include collapse and fungus, wet rot, dry rot, and bacteria.

Collapse refers to the sudden and abrupt collapse of a building that results in not being able to use the building for its intended purpose.

Helpful Hint

This coverage does not apply to a building or a part of a building that is in danger of caving in or falling down. Coverage is also excluded for a building that is already showing evidence of cracking, bulging, bending, leaning, settling, sagging, shrinking, or expanding.

Limited coverage for wet rot, dry rot, fungus, and bacteria is provided if the loss is due to a covered cause other than fire or lightning and/or flood. It is limited to $15,000 within a twelve-month period of time.

Quick Review Questions

30) An airplane hits and damages a manufacturing plant. As a result, the building, property, equipment inside the building, and some outdoor displays are damaged. What would the policy cover under the Broad Form?

31) The sprinkler system in an office building sprung a leak while the building was closed, causing fungus to grow on the walls and floors in addition to the water damage. Would the repairs due to the fungus damage be covered under the Broad Form?

Special Form

Like comparable DO and HO policies, the Special Form for business property coverage is an Open Perils Form, and it is the most comprehensive type of commercial coverage. Unlike the Basic and Broad Forms, which name specific covered perils, the Open Perils Form covers all risks unless they are specifically excluded. The Special Form does, however, set limitations for specific amounts or certain causes of loss. The following limitations apply:

- Steam pipes, steam boilers, steam engines, and steam turbines are not covered when the cause of loss results from an internal failure. An explosion of fuel or gases is covered.
- Hot water boilers and water heating equipment (other than loss due to explosion) are not covered.
- Business personal property and interior damage are not covered for losses due to dust, sand, or the elements unless the elements create an opening in the roof or walls. Loss or damage from the elements is covered if it is due to snow, sleet, or ice thawing on the structure.
- Building materials and supplies that are not attached to the building or structure are not covered for theft.
- Property that is missing where there is no physical evidence to show how it disappeared is not covered.
- Property that was transferred to an individual or place off the premises where the instructions were not authorized is not covered.
- Lawns, trees, shrubs, and plants that are part of a vegetated roof where the damage is caused by changes in temperature, dampness or dryness of the soil, disease, or frost, hail, rain, snow, sleet, or ice is not covered.
- Animals are covered if the loss is covered under specified causes of loss only if they are killed or need to be killed.
- Fragile articles such as statues, marble, and China are not covered for breakage unless the loss is listed under one of the specified causes of loss.

- Builder's machinery, tools, and equipment that are owned by the business owner or that are entrusted to the business owner are not covered unless the cause of the loss is listed under specified causes of loss.
- Damage to fire-extinguishing equipment is covered only if the damage results in a substance discharging from the fire protection system or if the loss is caused by freezing.

Did You Know?

Business income coverage is commonly known as **time element coverage** or **business interruption insurance**.

There are also special limits for certain items; these include the following:

- furs: $2,500
- jewelry, watches, precious and semi-precious stones, bullion, platinum, gold, silver, and other precious metals: $2,500
- patterns, molds, dies, and forms: $2,500
- stamps, tickets, and lottery tickets: $250

The Special Form also offers additional coverage extensions with certain limitations for the following:

- property that is being moved
- water damage, powder, other liquids, or molten material damage
- glass

Quick Review Questions

32) There was a warehouse explosion caused by gas that leaked from a steam boiler. Would this be a covered loss under the Special Form?

33) Does the Special Form cover a theft of $5,000 worth of silver tableware from a business?

34) Would a manufacturing plant's loss of $1,000 for dies and molds be covered under the Special Form?

Business Income

Coverage for lost business income is not included in the Basic, Broad, or Special Forms. Nonetheless, business owners can purchase coverage for the loss of business income. There are three versions of Business Income Forms; they include the following:

- business income with extra expense
- business income without extra expense
- extra expense

The coverage is triggered when a business owner has to suspend business operations because of a covered loss. The following definitions are listed on the Business Income Form:

- **suspension:** business operations that slow down or stop altogether
- **operations:** regular business activities that take place on the described premises
- **period of restoration:** Coverage begins seventy-two hours after a direct physical loss related to business income coverage occurs or immediately after the loss occurs for extra expense coverage.
- **resumption of operations:** Coverage for the period of restoration ends on the date the property should be repaired or the date on which the business can resume at a new permanent location.
- **civil authority:** This covers the loss of business income if the government or any civil authority denies the owner and employees access to the business premises.

The Business Income Coverage Form includes extended business income coverage under additional coverages, and it has specified beginning and ending periods. This item extends coverage for business income to include payment that begins on the date the property is repaired, rebuilt, or replaced, and business operations can resume. The coverage ends on the soonest date the business owner can restore operations within a reasonable time frame where the business once again generates similar business income as before the loss or thirty days after the date on which the business is ready to resume operations. This coverage also applies when business operations must be suspended under a rental value loss.

Coinsurance is an additional condition of the business income and extra expense coverages. To determine the coinsurance figure, the net income and operating expenses should be multiplied for the twelve months after the policy starts, OR the previous anniversary date should be multiplied by the coinsurance percentage listed on the declarations. The limit of insurance is then divided by the figure in the previous step. Finally, the new figure is multiplied by the total amount of the loss: this is the coinsurance amount. The policy will pay the lesser of the coinsurance amount or the limit of the insurance. The insurance company will also deduct certain expenses as outlined in the policy.

Did You Know?

Suspension can apply to any rent revenues that cannot be collected when the property is unusable. If rental value applies to a business property, the business owner would receive income to offset the loss of rent monies.

Optional coverages on the Business Income and Extra Expense Form include maximum periods of indemnity, monthly limits of indemnity, and the agreed value of business income. An explanation of each optional coverage is described below:

- **maximum period of indemnity:** The maximum period the insurance company will pay is either the lesser of the amount of the loss incurred during the 120 days after the period of restoration or the limit of insurance shown on the declarations page. The coinsurance clause does not apply to this coverage.
- **monthly limit of indemnity:** The insurer will pay for business income every thirty consecutive days after restoration begins. The limit of coverage is the **monthly limit factor** (the fraction shown on the declaration pages) multiplied by the limit for this optional coverage. The coinsurance clause does not apply to this coverage.
- **business income agreed value:** For business income agreed value coverage to apply, the business owner must submit a business income worksheet to the insurance company that shows financial data for the business operations. The agreed value should be equal to the coinsurance

percentage multiplied by the amount of net income and operating expenses for the twelve months after the figures that are reported on the worksheet.

Quick Review Questions

35) Which type of incident triggers business income and extra expense coverage?

36) Which clause would provide a business owner with benefits when the business must cease operations because the government closed the road leading to the business?

37) What are the three versions of Business Income Forms?

38) What is the term that refers to the maximum time period the insurance company will cover?

Extra Expense Coverage

Extra expense coverage covers consequential losses. This form is generally used by businesses that are not likely to sustain a business income loss.

Extra expense coverage refers to the necessary expenses a business incurs during the time frame it takes to restore the business to its normal operations after a loss. The expenses must be costs the business would not have incurred unless it had experienced a loss. The coverage does not apply to repairing or replacing property; rather, it reduces the amount of the total loss.

The purpose of extra expense coverage is to compensate businesses with the necessary funds to continue operating at a new or temporary location and to reduce the amount of time a business must suspend operations after a covered loss.

Additional coverages under extra expense coverage include the following:

- civil authority
- alterations and new buildings
- extended business income
- interruption of computer operations

Under "coverage extension," the coverage extends to newly acquired locations (not including fairs or exhibitions) as long as the declarations page shows a coinsurance percentage of at least 50 percent. The most the policy will pay under coverage extensions is $100,000, and the longest the coverage applies is for thirty days after the acquisition. The coverage extension is additional insurance, and the coinsurance clause does not apply to it.

Did You Know?

Extra expense coverage does not apply when a business has to shut down due to electronic data that has been destroyed or corrupted.

Did You Know?

With extra expense coverage, the insured chooses a limit that applies to each loss; that limit determines the amount of time the coverage will pay and the amount of each payment. When the limit is met, no more funds will be paid out.

For example, a restaurant purchased $300,000 in extra expense coverage. A fire broke out causing the restaurant to shut down for three months until the building could be repaired. The declarations page has a maximum limit of $300,00o and limits of 40/80/100. This means the insurer would pay up to 40% of the loss the first month, up to 80% of the loss the following month, and up to 100% of the loss in the final month of the restoration.

Quick Review Questions

39) A café has an extra expense limit of $100,000, and the declarations states percentages of 50/75/100. If a fire damages the kitchen and the café has to shut down for a few months, how much could the business owner expect to receive after the first month of reconstruction?

40) The owner of an insurance agency discovers that hackers stole all his data, and it will cost the business $100,000. He had purchased extra expense coverage in the amount of $250,000. How much can the business owner expect to receive for the loss?

Equipment Breakdown Coverage (Boiler and Machinery Coverage)

Certain businesses rely on expensive equipment to keep their operations running. When that equipment breaks down, it can cause production delays and a loss of profits. **Equipment breakdown** coverage pays for direct losses to covered property from the breakdown of equipment located at the premises listed on the declarations page. The following coverages are included in the Equipment Breakdown Coverage Form:

- property damage
- off-premises property damage
- business income
- extra expense
- service interruption
- contingent business income
- perishable goods
- data restoration
- demolition
- ordinance or law
- expediting expenses
- hazardous substances
- newly acquired locations

The Equipment Breakdown Form requires the insurer to pay for the cost of repairing the equipment or replacing it at the actual replacement cost without considering depreciation. The form allows insurance companies to base payments on the most cost-effective means to replace the equipment, yet the replacement must be of a similar kind and quality as the damaged equipment. Insurers may opt to replace damaged equipment with generic equipment or equipment that has used or reconditioned parts.

Equipment breakdown coverage only applies if machinery breaks down because of an accident. The form defines an accident as an event that causes direct physical damage to covered equipment. An accident must be caused by one of the following:

- mechanical breakdown
- explosion of steam engines, steam piping, steam boilers, or steam turbines (other than combustion explosion)
- an internal problem on steam boilers, steam pipes, steam engines, or steam turbines that causes damage to them
- an internal problem with hot water boilers or other water heating equipment that causes damage to them
- artificially-generated electrical current
- bursting, cracking, or splitting

> **Did You Know?**
>
> The equipment or property must be replaced within twenty-four months for the replacement cost provision to apply; otherwise, the equipment will be replaced on an actual cash-value basis.

The form does not include coverage for normal wear, tear, or deterioration, such as those described in the following conditions:

- depletion, deterioration, corrosion, erosion, settling, or rust
- a gradually developing condition that worsens equipment
- defects in programming errors or limitations, computer viruses, malicious codes, loss of data, loss of access to data, loss of use of data, loss of data functionality, or any other problem with data or media
- contamination by a hazardous substance
- misalignment, miscalibration, tripping offline, or other conditions that can be reset, tightened, adjusted, or cleaned

Multiple deductibles may apply to one accident if this is listed in the declarations. Otherwise, only one deductible applies per loss. The insurer will not pay anything for losses until all applicable deductibles have been applied. The highest deductible applies when more than one type of equipment is damaged by an accident.

Unless the declarations page states otherwise, deductibles for indirect coverages apply to business income and extra expense coverages. Direct-coverage deductibles apply to all other losses, damages, and expenses.

> **Did You Know?**
>
> The declarations page may state a time deductible, which refers to a certain amount of time or days before the company will pay. For example, if a declarations page states a time deductible of three days, the company will only pay after seventy-two hours.

Deductibles may also be expressed as average daily values (ADVs), which refer to the average daily value of business income that would have been earned during the period the business was shut down due to equipment breakdown. To figure the ADV deductible, the amount of business income that would have been earned is divided by the number of days in that period, and then multiplied by the number indicated in the declarations. The insurer will pay for the loss beyond this amount.

> **Helpful Hint**
>
> Business owners are expected to maintain their equipment properly and keep it in good working condition. If the insurance company finds that a piece of equipment was dangerous and not properly maintained, the insurer can suspend coverage immediately.

Commercial losses can be quite complex and large. For that reason, much of the premium that business owners pay goes toward investigations. The "Loss Conditions" section of the form emphasizes the importance of inspections and loss control.

All accidents that were caused by a single accident at one premise will be viewed as a single accident by the insurer. Consequential losses are not always covered in standard Equipment Breakdown Forms, although business owners may purchase an additional policy to cover them.

Quick Review Questions

41) While in transit, a strong wind caused two air conditioning units to be damaged. Is this a covered loss on the Equipment Breakdown Form?

42) A business owner hired a service to tarp the roof in his building until the water damage could be repaired. Would the insurer cover the cost of the tarp installation?

43) A business owner files a claim for damaged equipment, but she wants a new system that is larger and has greater capacity than the original system. Will the insurer pay the cost of the upgraded equipment?

44) A boiler broke down at a manufacturing plant, and the investigation showed that the loss was due to an internal problem within the boiler. Would this be a covered loss under the Equipment Breakdown Form?

45) Two pieces of equipment are damaged in a single accident. One piece of equipment has a $1,000 deductible, and the other has a $3,000 deductible. How will the insurer apply the deductible in this situation?

46) Despite several attempts, a business owner refused to allow the claims adjuster admittance to the building to inspect the damage to his factory. Can the insurer decline the claim or reduce the claim payment for the delay in viewing the property?

Cyber Liability Coverage

Cybercriminals are becoming more and more sophisticated in their strategies to steal confidential information from businesses. Information technology (IT) specialists work hard to fend off cyberattacks, yet it is a race to keep hackers at bay. For this reason, cyber liability insurance is an important coverage for businesses in every industry.

Cybercriminals may use malware, denial-of-service attacks, phishing, spoofing, and more. Criminals are after things like employee records, intellectual property, customer data, and other financial information.

There are two types of insurance coverage that fall under the umbrella of cyber liability: first-party cyber insurance and third-party cyber insurance.

First-party cyber liability insurance pays for losses caused by data breaches on the business's network or systems. A first-party liability insurance policy helps pay for costs that include the following:

- notifying customers that there has been a breach
- purchasing credit monitoring services
- exploring the cause of the data breach
- managing public relations
- paying business interruption and business income costs
- paying ransom costs

An example of a first-party cyber liability loss would be if an employee in a real estate office is working with a client, logs into the computer system, and does not mask his password. The client remembers the password and uses it to steal information from the real estate agency's network.

> **Did You Know?**
>
> Cyber liability claims can originate internally and be caused by employee dishonesty or carelessness.

Another example of a first-party cyber claim is an employee who clicks on a link in an email, which turns out to be a phishing scam. A cybercriminal uses the link to gain access to the business's computer network and shuts it down until the business owner agrees to pay a ransom of a million dollars. Both of these claims would be covered under first-party cyber liability.

Today, it is common for business systems and software programs to interconnect with the systems of vendors, regulatory bodies, and stakeholders, making it easy for one business's computer network and systems to become infected or attacked by a third party. **Third-party cyber liability** insurance policies pay for lawsuits resulting from data breaches on a client's system or network caused by an outside entity.

Quick Review Questions

47) The computer system of a music business was hacked, and the hacker downloaded copyrighted songs and sold them on the internet to make a profit. Would this loss be covered under first-person cyber liability insurance?

48) After a company accountant clicked on an email that was supposedly from the company's payroll office, all employees were locked out of the timeclock page, and a message appeared saying that a hacker had taken control of the program. Would this type of incident be considered a first-party cyber liability claim or a third-party liability claim?

Exclusions

Basic Form Exclusions

The Basic Form carries eight basic exclusions to coverage, and they apply whether the damage is caused directly or indirectly. These causes of loss are excluded even if some other cause or event contributes to the damage at the time of the loss or is connected to the damage in any way. The causes of loss include the following:

- ordinance or law
- movement of the earth
- governmental action
- nuclear hazard
- utility services
- war and military action
- water
- fungus, wet rot, dry rot, and bacteria

> **Did You Know?**
>
> Water damage caused by surface water and above-ground water is never covered under commercial policies. Separately purchased flood insurance would cover this loss.

The Basic Form contains additional exclusions, and they are attached to the package's "Property" section. Business income, extra expense, and legal liability are described as exclusions under the "Special Exclusions" section.

Quick Review Questions

49) Lightning strikes a utility pole, causing a power surge to a manufacturing plant and badly damaging the electrical system. Would this loss be covered under the Basic Form?

50) If a civil war unexpectedly breaks out, and a business's building is damaged in the skirmish, will the damage to the building be covered under the Basic Form?

Broad Form Exclusions

The exclusions for the Broad Form are the same as for the Basic Form, and there are additional special exclusions for certain coverages. The following special exclusions apply to Broad Forms:

- extra expense
- business income
- leasehold interest
- legal liability

Quick Review Question

51) A flower shop is insured by the Broad Commercial Property Form. Workers left the back doors wide open, and a wind came gusting through, damaging all 100 floral arrangements that were set for delivery that day. Would this be a covered loss under the policy?

Special Form Exclusions

While the Special Form covers all perils (including those listed on the basic and Broad Forms), it lists several specific exclusions. The covered causes of loss on the Special Form refer to direct physical losses, except those that are excluded or limited by the policy. The Special Form includes the exclusions found on the Basic Form.

The Special Form also excludes the following:

- losses by artificially generated electrical, magnetic, or electromagnetic energy that interferes with devices
- delay, loss of market, or loss of use
- smoke, vapor, or gas from industrial operations or agricultural smudging
- wear and tear, rust, smog, settling/cracking/shrinking/expansion
- nesting, infestation, discharge, or release of waste by insects, birds, rodents, or other animals
- mechanical breakdown
- changes in the atmosphere
- the explosion of steam boilers, steam pipes, steam engines, or steam turbines
- continuous or repeated seepage/leakage of water that occurs for fourteen days or longer
- water that leaks or stems from plumbing systems
- dishonest or criminal acts
- voluntary parting with property by fraud or false pretense
- rain, snow, ice, or sleet to personal property out in the open
- collapse
- discharge or the seepage of pollutants
- failure to take steps to prevent further damage

Did You Know?

Commercial property policies do not pay for the extra expenses involved in rebuilding or reconstructing properties according to current laws or regulations.

The Special Form will pay for the following causes of loss if they result in a covered cause of loss:

- weather conditions
- acts or decisions, including the failure of any part to act

- faulty, inadequate, or defective planning or development; design and construction; faulty materials; or faulty maintenance

In addition to the general exclusions, the Special Form also has special exclusions in the Extra Expense, Business Income, Leasehold Interest, and Legal Liability Forms. Exclusions for these losses only apply to specific property that is outlined within the policy.

Quick Review Questions

52) A major mudslide occurs that damages several office buildings in a strip mall. Will this type of loss fall under exclusions on the Special Form?

53) An exterminator found that squirrels had nested in the attic of a business's building. Would the cost to remove the squirrels and clean up the attic be covered under the Special Form?

54) An auto repair business has a satellite system installed for the television in their customers' waiting room. The satellite gets damaged in an electrical storm. Would the business owner be able to claim the repairs on the Special Form?

55) A volcano erupts near a dental office, and ashes from the volcano cover the parking area. Will the business owner have coverage under the Special Form to remove the ash?

56) The local government plans to seize a fireworks warehouse because a wildfire is spreading dangerously near it. The authorities move the merchandise and destroy the building to prevent the fire from spreading. Will the business owner be able to have the building replaced under the Special Form?

Equipment Breakdown Coverage Exclusions

As with all other commercial forms, the **Equipment Breakdown Form** carries a host of exclusions. The exclusions that apply to this form are not covered even if another cause or event contributes to a loss or follows a loss, damage, or expense.

The same exclusions in the Basic Form apply to the equipment breakdown coverage. There are additional exclusions that apply to the Equipment Breakdown Coverage Form whether a loss, damage, or expense is a direct or indirect loss, and regardless of whether the loss is due to an accident:

- failure to protect property: Coverage is excluded in any case where an insured does not leverage all reasonable means to protect covered equipment and property from further damage after an accident.
- fines: The insurance company will not pay for fines, penalties, or punitive damages in connection with covered or uncovered losses.
- deliberate acts: Losses caused by any person who deliberately causes damage or harm to the equipment or property are excluded from this coverage form. This includes acts of vandalism, malicious mischief, and sabotage.
- lightning: Damage caused by lighting is excluded from this coverage form.

- windstorm or hail: This exclusion applies unless the covered building or structure sustains an accident that is caused by windstorm or hail. The exclusion also does not apply when wind or hail causes a hole in the roof or walls of the structure.
- vehicle collision: Damage caused by a vehicle hitting a structure or objects falling from an aircraft are not covered. The exclusion does not apply to unlicensed vehicles owned by the business and used for business purposes.
- leakage or discharge from automatic sprinklers: This exclusion includes the collapse of sprinkler system tanks.
- diagnostic tests: Tests (e.g., electrical insulation breakdown test, hydrostatic pressure test, pneumatic pressure test, gas pressure tests) are not covered.
- water to extinguish a fire: Water damage due to attempts to extinguish a fire is not covered, even if the attempt is not successful.
- elevator collision: Damage because of an elevator collision is excluded from coverage.

As it pertains to business income and extra expense, extra expense only, and utility interruption coverage, coverage does not apply to any business that could have been conducted if the accident and breakdown had not taken place.

The Equipment Breakdown Form does not afford coverage for losses that extend beyond the period of restoration. This exclusion also applies to business income that would have been earned after the business got back up and running, even if the loss was a result of a suspension, lapse, or cancellation of a contract during the period of restoration. The insurer will also not pay for extra expenses for the insured to continue operating the business after the period of restoration, even if the loss is contracted and paid for while the business was being restored. Certain exclusions do NOT apply when all of the following circumstances are true:

- The excluded peril occurs away from the premises and causes an electrical surge or disturbance.
- An electrical disturbance or surge is transmitted through the utility lines.
- An electrical disturbance or surge causes an accident to covered equipment owned by the business owner or a landlord and is in the business owner's control.
- The loss, damage, or expense caused by an electrical surge or disturbance is not covered by other insurance coverage.

Quick Review Questions

57) A new regulation has been instituted since the equipment was installed; it requires that older equipment be upgraded if it was replaced. Will the Equipment Breakdown Form support the extra expense required to support this regulation?

58) A business owner sustained a loss to the business due to a mudslide, so he hired a contractor to build a retaining wall to prevent mud from damaging the building in the future. If damage occurred anyway, would the entire loss be covered?

59) A forklift owned by the company crashed into a warehouse, knocking down part of a wall and destroying equipment inside the building. Would this loss be covered under the Equipment Breakdown Form?

60) An elevator broke down and dropped to the basement. Would this loss be covered under equipment breakdown coverage?

61) A small fire damages part of a storeroom in a manufacturing plant. Firefighters quickly extinguished the fire, but business equipment was damaged by water during the process of extinguishing the fire. Would the Equipment Breakdown Form cover the lost equipment?

Chapter Review

Table 7.2. Chapter 7 Review: Commercial Property Policies	
Commercial Package Policies (CPP)	
Policy types	• packages (single contract) • monoline (single coverage that is chosen separately)
Coverage parts	• general liability • commercial property • commercial auto • equipment breakdown • crime
Possible parts	• policy coverage • policy declarations and conditions • Cause of Loss forms • endorsements
Property policy declarations	• covered property, its location, its owner, and the amount of coverage • usually cover anything located at the mailing address of the insured
Commercial Property Conditions	
CPP conditions	• *cancellation:* Only the first named can cancel policy. • *changes:* The term changes have to be made by endorsement. • *examination of books and records:* This allows insurers to audit insureds' records for up to three years after the policy ends. • *inspections and surveys:* Insurers may conduct surveys and inspections, and make recommendations. • *premiums:* The first named insured is responsible for paying premiums. • *transfer of rights and duties:* The policyholder's rights and duties may be transferred to another owner with the written consent of both.
Other common CPP conditions	• *concealment, misrepresentation, or fraud coverage:* Coverage is voided if insurers discover that the policyholder committed fraud. • *control of property:* This covers any act of negligence by individuals who are not under the direction of the policyholder. • *legal action against the insurer:* The insured cannot bring a case against the insurance provider until all policy claims have been completed, and the legal action must be brought within two years of the claim's resolution.

Table 7.2. Chapter 7 Review: Commercial Property Policies	
	• *no benefit to bailee:* With the exception of the actual policy owner, no individual who has custody of covered property can receive a claims payout. • *subrogation:* The insurer takes over any rights to recover damages from a third party after the claim is paid.

Answer Key

1. Business owners can add or delete coverages to commercial package policies in order to protect their businesses as their needs evolve.

2.Business owners can choose coverage for specific losses, or they can choose a package that bundles everything into one policy.

3. Commercial package policies must have two or more types of coverage.

4. The declarations page lists the policy's coverages, limits, deductibles, and effective dates.

5. The policy would pay the limit of $20,000, and the Lees would have to pay the remaining $5,000.

6. This type of loss would not be covered until the Lees added crime coverage.

7. The insurer would not comply with such a request because only named insureds can change policy coverage.

8. The insurer has the right to survey or inspect a business to affirm that the operations are actually as the insured describes them.

9. This condition falls under the examination of books and records, so the Lees would have to comply with the request.

10. Properties in Montana have a high risk of frozen pipes and complications from the weight of ice, snow, or sleet. These would not be covered under the Basic Form, so the owner should buy the Broad Form.

11. All policy forms include coverage for theft, vandalism, and malicious mischief, which are important risks to cover for properties located in high-crime areas.

12. All fixtures inside the building are covered in a building and personal property policy.

13. A chair that is being repaired will only be covered while it is in the care, custody, and control of the business that is repairing it.

14. Wind is a covered peril, but the walkway is an exclusion under the policy, so repairs to it would not be covered.

15. Relocating a piece of art to prevent it from sustaining possible fire damage would fall under the category of additional coverages: preservation of property.

16. Coverage extensions cover property while in temporary storage within 100 feet of the building.

17. Trees, shrubs, and plants are covered for up to $250 each under the outdoor property extension.

18. In the event that a business and the insurance company disagree on the value of the property, either party can request an appraisal, and then each chooses and pays for an appraiser. The appraisers will choose an umpire to help determine the proper value.

19. No. One of the conditions for coverage is that the insured must notify the police if a law has been broken.

20. As a condition of the policy, a vacant building is only covered for sixty days.

21. Appliances and equipment used to service the building are paid at actual cash value.

22. The policy would only pay the value of $5,000 that is listed on the declarations page.

23. The formula to figure the inflation guard is the coverage amount times the number of days the coverage has been in force divided by 365: $\$200{,}000 \times .05 \times 100\ days \div 365 = \$2{,}739.73$.

24. The merchandise would be covered for the locations in the United States and Puerto Rico, but the merchandise at the Jamaica location would not be covered because Jamaica is not a covered territory.

25. In liberalization, the insurance company liberally applies broadened coverage without the insured having to pay an additional premium.

26. Losses caused by industrial operations are not covered under Building and Business Personal Property Forms.

27. Objects thrown out of a vehicle are covered under the "Aircraft and Vehicles" section of the policy.

28. Damage caused by a collapsed water tank for a sprinkler system is covered under the "Sprinkler Leakage" section.

29. Under the Basic Form, the repairs would be covered under the "Volcanic Action" section.

30. The Broad Form covers everything except items that are/were out in the open.

31. Yes; sprinkler leakage is a covered loss under the policy.

32. Steam boilers are only covered if the explosion is due to a gas or fuel leakage; therefore, the event described in this question would be covered.

33. The Special Form only covers up to $2,500 for the loss of silver, so the policyholder would lose the other $2,500.

34. If a covered loss results in the destruction of dies and molds, they would be covered for up to $2,500.

35. Business income and extra expense coverage is triggered by the suspension of business operations due to a covered loss.

36. If the government closes the road leading to a business and the business must cease operations as a result, the civil authority clause would provide the business owner with benefits.

37. The three versions of Business Income Forms include business income with extra expense, business income without extra expense, and extra expense.

38. *Maximum period of indemnity* is the term used to describe the maximum time period the insurance company will cover; it is usually the lesser of 120 days after the loss or the limit of insurance shown on the declarations page.

39. The business owner would receive half the $100,000 limit within the first month of repairing the damage.

40. Extra expense coverage does not apply to electronic data that has been corrupted or destroyed; however, the business owner can be compensated if he has cyber liability coverage.

41. Yes, because the Equipment Breakdown Form covers property located off site.

42. Equipment breakdown coverage will pay the costs needed to reduce the amount of the total loss, such as tarping the roof.

43. The business owner is only entitled to the cost to replace damaged equipment of like kind and quality, so any upgrades will have to be out of pocket.

44. Yes. This type of incident is considered a covered loss because it was due to an accident.

45. In a single accident, only the larger deductible applies when more than one piece of equipment is damaged.

46. Under the "loss conditions" provision, business owners are obligated to allow insurers to conduct an investigation; their claims may be denied if they do not cooperate.

47. This is considered a data breach by copyright infringement, and it is covered because the loss impacted the business's entire computer system.

48. Because the incident occurred after an employee clicked on a fake email, it falls under the cyber first-party coverage.

49. Since the cause of loss occurred away from the described premises, the loss would not be covered.

50. Damage caused by any act of war is not covered, even if it is an undeclared act of war.

51. No. The Broad Form does not cover the costs of replacing finished stock.

52. No. Damage due to a mudslide or mudflow is always excluded on the Special Form.

53. No. Damage due to animal infestation is excluded from the Special Form.

54. No. Damage to satellite dishes and systems is excluded from the Special Form.

55. No. The cost to remove volcanic ash is not covered under the Special Form.

56. Yes. Actions that a government takes to prevent a fire is covered under the Special Form.

57. No. The ordinance and law exclusion states the policy will not pay for increased costs due to changes in laws or regulations.

58. The insurer would recognize that the business owner took all reasonable steps to prevent damage to his property, so the claim would be paid.

59. Collisions caused by business-owned vehicles that are unlicensed are covered under the Equipment Breakdown Form.

60. Losses due to an elevator collision are excluded under the Equipment Breakdown Form.

61. The Commercial Property Form would likely cover the fire damage, but the Equipment Breakdown Form excludes coverage for water damage caused by extinguishing a fire.

8. Commercial General Liability Insurance (CGL)

Basic CGL Concepts

Regardless of the type of industry, every business carries risks, and **commercial general liability (CGL)** insurance protects businesses from lawsuits resulting from bodily injuries or property damages that may occur in the course of normal business operations.

For example, a customer could allege that a company's product malfunctioned, causing an injury, or that an injury was sustained on the business's premises. In either of these cases, a business could be held legally liable.

A CGL policy protects commercial businesses by covering medical services, hospital fees, ambulance charges, professional nursing services, or funeral expenses. Commercial general liability insurance also pays for court costs and legal fees to defend covered businesses against lawsuits.

> **Did You Know?**
>
> Some policies require that the insured avoid doing certain things in order for the coverage to apply. To be certain of coverage, applicants must double-check the requirements outlined in their policies.

This coverage provides another advantage for businesses that use contractors and subcontractors regularly because it allows them to extend coverage to other people under certain work-related circumstances. Contractors and subcontractors who are covered under the business owner's policy do not have to pay the premiums or meet other requirements of the policy.

CGL coverage is triggered by an occurrence where property damage, bodily injury, or personal injury is involved. Not all types of claims are covered by a CGL policy. Coverage only applies in situations in which the business owner has a legal duty to act or not act.

Also, the policy applies only when the business owner's or an employee's actions have caused an injury that resulted in actual damage to property, personal injury, or bodily injury. There are three main coverage sections of a CGL policy:

- **Bodily injury and property damage** protects against an injury or damage caused by normal operations or damage to property caused by the business.
- **Personal and advertising injuries**, which infringe on the personal or intellectual rights of an individual or business.
- **Medical payments** coverage reimburses an individual for medical or funeral expenses that occurred because of a covered bodily injury or death.

> **Did You Know?**
>
> Medical payments coverage pays without regard to the insured's liability.

CGL policies can be structured as claims-made policies or as occurrence policies. A claims-made policy pays for claims regardless of when an incident occurs. In contrast, an occurrence policy only pays for incidents that occur during a specified period, even if that period extends past when the CGL policy has expired.

Quick Review Questions

1) The business owner of a construction company brought a food truck onto a construction site and asked his family members to work in the food truck to serve the workers coffee and doughnuts in the morning. The business owner failed to notify the insurance company that the food truck was on the construction site and that family members were working as employees. A couple of carpenters got burned after spilling hot coffee on themselves. Would this be a covered loss under a CGL policy?

2) A plumbing business is sued by a competitor who alleges that the company's logo design and colors are very similar to their own logo. The owner of the plumbing business decides to fight the issue in court. Will the business owner be able to recoup the defense costs for this type of case?

3) A large corporation hosted a festival for its employees during which one of the guests tripped over an electrical line and got electrocuted. She was taken to the hospital by ambulance and died several days later. Which of the coverages of a CGL policy would respond in this type of scenario?

Definitions Found in CGL

Insurance terms are very important when it comes to settling a claim. For that reason, insurance companies define common insurance terms so there is no confusion about what they mean.

A CGL policy will define the following terms:

- **occurrence:** the accident itself or continuous/repeated exposure to harmful conditions that led to the occurrence
- **bodily injury:** any bodily injury including disease, sickness, or death
- **property damage:** any type of physical damage to property, including consequential losses of use of the damaged or undamaged property; excludes the loss of use of electronic data
- **coverage territory:** applies to losses that occur in the United States of America (including its territories and possessions), Puerto Rico, and Canada due to damaged goods manufactured or sold in the described coverage territories; covers the activities of a business owner who has a home located in one of the coverage territories while the business owner is away from the business premises for a short time for business purposes

> **Did You Know?**
>
> Unlike some other insurance policies, the definitions in a CGL policy are listed at the end of the policy.

- **premises and operations:** covers losses that occur on the business premises or because of business operations
- **products and completed operations:** covers bodily injury and property damage occurring away from the business but that arises from the company's work or products; applies to products or

items for repair that are still in the business's possession; excludes tools, uninstalled equipment, and abandoned or unused materials

- **employee:** coverage for people who are employed by the company, including leased workers; excludes temporary workers
- **auto:** covers land motor vehicles, trailers, or semitrailers being used on public roads, including any permanently attached equipment (covered under the definition of the term *autos*)

The coverage also protects **mobile equipment**, which includes the following land vehicles and machinery and any equipment attached to them:

- bulldozers, farm machinery, forklifts, and similar off-road vehicles
- vehicles used to move power cranes, shovels, loaders, diggers, drills, and grading and road construction equipment
- non-self-propelled vehicles used to move air compressors, pumps, generators, and other equipment used for cherry picking, spraying, welding, building cleaning, service equipment, and geophysical exploration equipment

The CGL policy also includes coverage for **insured contracts** that may be the business owner's legal responsibility if the owner does not have protection under other policies. The following types of contracts also apply to this definition:

- leases for the property
- sidetrack agreements
- easement or licensing agreements
- obligations required by ordinances to indemnify a municipality unless the work is for a municipality
- elevator maintenance agreements
- agreements where the business owner assumes the tort liability of a third party to a third person or organization for bodily injury or property damage
- contractual liability (except in situations that are listed in the exclusions)

Did You Know?

Tort liability refers to liabilities imposed by the law in the absence of contracts or agreements.

Quick Review Questions

4) An employee of a plumbing company was upset to learn that she was the subject of a customer complaint, which she then posted on her personal social media account. The customer saw the posts online and sued the plumbing company for libel. Would the business owner's CGL policy cover this loss?

5) Scaffolding falls on a customer inside a home improvement store, causing the customer to be taken by ambulance to the hospital for emergency treatment. Will the CGL policy pay for any of the customer's medical bills?

6) A carpenter's tools mysteriously disappeared on a jobsite. Would this type of loss be covered under products and completed operations?

7) A contractor hires a temporary employee to fill in for a carpenter who is injured. Would the temporary worker be considered an employee according to the CGL policy's definition of the term *employee?*

8) A tractor with a permanently attached cherry picker on it malfunctions and damages a client's trees. Will this loss be covered under the definition of mobile equipment or autos?

9) A reputable company that manufactures lawnmowers sold a lawnmower that had a faulty blade; the blade snapped, causing the purchaser to lose a toe. Will the cost of the purchaser's surgeries fall under the definition of bodily injury or the definition of products and completed operations?

Section I - Types of Coverages

Bodily Injury and Property Damage Liability (Coverage A)

Insurance policies have different coverage parts. Part A of a CGL is the core coverage, and it covers bodily injury and property damage under the same heading.

Accidents that cause injuries can happen even in the safest of business environments. Bodily injury coverage pays for medical expenses and lost income for individuals who sustain injuries on the company premises or as a result of something caused by the business.

When someone alleges a bodily injury caused by a business, the insurance company will investigate the claim for legitimacy. If the injuries are accidental, the insurance company will pay for the injured person's medical expenses related to the injury. This can include emergency services, hospitalization, and recovery expenses. Coverage A may also pay for the injured person's lost wages and income.

The property damage coverage pays for losses where a business owner or employee damages someone else's property. Property damage coverage also pays for the loss of use due to property damage. For example, if a semitruck driver hits a building and damages it while backing into the loading dock, the business owner's CGL policy would cover the damage to the building.

The insuring agreement is the first section of a commercial general liability coverage form, and it outlines the exact circumstances under which an insurance company will provide coverage. Further, it states that the insurer will pay claims for occurrences in which the insured is legally obligated to pay as a result of bodily injury or property damage that occurs in the coverage territory during the policy period.

The insurance company will only pay up to the limit of liability as stated on the declarations page or under the section on supplementary payments; it has no responsibility to defend the insured over damages that exceed the limit of liability.

Some of the most important exclusions in Coverage A are as follows:

- **contractual liability:** excludes coverage for bodily injury and liability in connection with a contract or agreement; does not apply to liability the insured has in the absence of an agreement and does not apply to an insured contract where bodily injury or property damage happens after the execution of the contract or agreement

- **workers' compensation:** excludes bodily injury where employees get injured on the job; available as separate coverage
- **pollution:** excludes losses due to actual, alleged, or threatened dispersal, seepage, discharge, migration, release, or escape of pollutants; excludes losses related to testing, monitoring, and cleaning up pollutants
- **damage to property:** excludes damage to property the insured owns, rents, or occupies, abandoned property, property received on loan, and property that is in the care, custody, and control of the insured

> **Helpful Hint**
>
> A CGL policy is defined not by the perils it covers, but by the list of exclusions stated in the policy. If an incident is not excluded, that means that it is covered.

- **recall of products, work, or impaired property:** excludes damages for losses related to product recalls, work recalls, or impaired property if the defect or deficiency must be withdrawn from the market because it is unsafe for public use or consumption
- **electronic data:** excludes damages to electronic data, corrupted data, or the inability to access or manipulate data
- **personal and advertising injury:** excludes bodily injuries that originate from personal and advertising injuries
- **damage to your work:** excludes property damage to the insured's work that arises from the work or any part of it
- **damage to your product:** excludes property damage to the insured's products

> **Did You Know?**
>
> Supplementary payments do not reduce the limits of insurance coverage stated on the policy.

- **recording and distributing material or information in violation of law:** excludes bodily injury and property damage when the act violates laws such as the Telephone Consumer Protection Act (1991), CAN-SPAM Act (2003), and the Fair Credit Reporting Act (1970)
- **supplementary payments:** may apply to both Coverage A (bodily injury and property damage) and Coverage B (personal injury and advertising injury); covers the expenses incurred by the insurer to investigate or settle a claim (e.g., bail bonds, prejudgment interest, post-judgment interest, certain defense costs)

Quick Review Questions

10) Which part of a CGL policy outlines the exact circumstances under which the insurance company will provide coverage?

11) How does the insured know which perils are covered under a CGL policy?

12) A company decides to recall the candy it sells after several customers report becoming ill after consuming it. Will CGL cover the costs of having the products returned and reimbursing the customers?

13) One of the containers used by a landscaping firm sprang a leak, and chemicals spilled around the worksite. The spill damaged part of the building and threatened to cause many people to become ill. Would the damages from this type of loss be covered by a CGL policy?

Personal Injury and Advertising Injury (Coverage B)

In addition to bodily injury and property damage, CGL policies cover personal injury and advertising injury. **Personal injury** refers to acts by an insured that violate the rights of an individual or business. Specific acts of personal injury that are covered under a CGL policy include the following:

- **libel:** a business owner or employee who makes false statements in writing about another individual or business
- **slander:** a business owner or employee who makes false statements orally about another individual or business
- **copyright infringement:** a company that uses work or other intellectual property that is protected by copyright without the owner or creator's permission
- **invasion of privacy:** concerns a person's right to privacy, which is protected by law, and violations for invading that privacy; applies to anyone who commits intrusive or unwanted actions that violate another person's or business's rights
- **false arrest, detention, or imprisonment:** when a person holds someone against that person's will or takes someone into custody unwillingly; may be charged with false arrest, detention, or imprisonment
- **wrongful eviction:** when business tenants may violate their lease or fail to pay their rent, causing a landlord to bring eviction proceedings against them; wrongful eviction examples: turning off the utilities or changing the locks on a building

Business owners or their employees who commit any of these crimes would be protected under Coverage B.

As is the case with Coverage A, the insuring agreement is the first section under Coverage B. This section states the circumstances under which the insurance company will cover a loss. Specifically, the insurance company will pay for personal injury and advertising claims for which the insured is legally liable and which are covered under the policy. As with other insurance policies, coverage is available up to the policy limits and may also make supplementary payments where appropriate. Offenses must arise out of the business and must have occurred within the coverage territories and during the policy period.

Did You Know?

Insurance companies may also make supplementary payments for personal injury and advertising injury.

The "Personal Injury and Advertising Injury" section also lists sixteen exclusions. A few of the most common of these are as follows:

- knowingly violating the rights of another
- publishing materials that are knowingly false
- criminal acts
- infringing on copyrights, patents, trademarks, or trade secrets
- insureds in media and internet-type businesses
- electronic chatrooms or bulletin boards

Quick Review Questions

14) An employee at one business posted negative, critical posts on social media about an employee at a competitor's business. That person, in turn, alleged libel and threatened to sue. Would this type of loss be covered under personal and advertising injury?

15) An author used the lyrics of a published song in a fiction novel without first getting permission from the songwriter. If the songwriter sues the author, will the loss be covered under personal injury and advertising coverage?

16) A restaurant owner decides to retaliate against his competitor by posting criminal information on the competitor's website. Which type of crime might the competitor allege against the restaurant owner?

17) A business tenant had a few slow months and could not pay his lease, so the landlord locked the doors after the business owner closed up shop for the day. Which part of personal and advertising injury coverage would protect the landlord if she got sued?

Medical Payments (Coverage C)

Coverage C protects the insured from expenses for bodily injuries caused by an accident. With this in mind, medical payments are considered **goodwill coverage** that is paid regardless of fault. As with all insurance, the company will pay up to the limit listed under medical payments for any one loss.

As with other types of coverage, there are exclusions under the medical payments coverage:

- **any insured:** Medical payments will not be paid to any insureds, except volunteer workers.
- **hired person:** Insurers will not pay for injuries to any person hired to do work for the company or any tenants of the insured.
- **injury on normally occupied premises:** No coverage applies for medical payments to any person who gets injured on premises owned or rented by the business owner for people who normally occupy that space.

Did You Know?

The accident causing bodily injury must occur within the coverage territory and during the policy period for coverage to apply. Also, the medical expenses must be incurred within one year from the time the accident occurred.

- **workers' compensation and similar laws:** Medical payments will not be paid to employees or others if those individuals are entitled to benefits under workers' compensation, disability benefits, or benefits under similar laws.
- **athletic activities:** Injuries sustained by any person when instructing or participating in physical exercise, sports, athletic contests, or games are excluded from medical payments coverage.
- **products-completed operations hazard:** Medical payments as a result of products or completed operations are excluded under medical payments coverage (but they are included in another part of the policy).
- **Coverage A exclusions:** All exclusions under Coverage A apply to medical payments coverage.

Quick Review Questions

18) A corporation scheduled an annual picnic and carnival for its employees, and there was a minor incident where a booth fell on an employee and a volunteer. Would medical payments coverage apply here?

19) A visitor to an office building slips and falls on an icy sidewalk, sustaining minor scrapes and bruises. Will the trip to the ER be covered under medical payments coverage?

Table 8.1. CGL Section I Coverages

Coverage A	
Bodily injury	covers any medical conditions caused by the insured's business activities
Property damage	covers any loss, damage, or destruction of others' property caused by the insured's business activities
Coverage B	
Personal injury	protects against damages from mental anguish caused by false arrest or imprisonment, wrongful detention or conviction, malicious prosecution, slander, libel, etc.
Advertising injury	protects against slander, libel, defamation, or invasion of privacy caused by the business owner's advertising
Coverage C	
Medical payments	covers necessary medical care for people injured because of the insured's business operations

Section II - The Insured

When setting up a business, business owners can choose from several different types of business structures. The type of business structure determines who is considered an insured person on a CGL policy. The type of business structure covered will be listed on the declarations page.

The following list describes various types of businesses and people who are considered insured persons according to a CGL policy:

> **Did You Know?**
>
> Most businesses can get a CGL policy regardless of how the business is legally structured, but the actual type of coverage purchased will vary depending on the structure.

- **individual or sole proprietor:** The business owner and that person's spouse are insureds only with respect to their conduct involving the business.
- **partnership or joint venture:** The partners and their spouses are insureds only with respect to their conduct involving the business.
- **limited liability company (LLC):** The business owner and members of the LLC are insureds as far as their behavior relates to the business. Managers are also considered insureds but only as their behavior relates to their duties as managers.
- **organization other than a partnership, joint venture, or LLC:** The business owner is an insured; executive officers, directors, and stockholders are covered only while performing their official duties.
- **a trust:** The business owner is an insured; trustees are also covered but only regarding their official duties.

Quick Review Questions

20) A small warehouse is set up as a partnership. One of the partners had to go on temporary disability in order to recuperate at home from an illness. His wife took over his duties in his absence, and while touring the facility with a customer, a heavy box toppled off a shelf and fell on the visitor's foot. Would the wife be considered an insured in this situation?

21) A trustee was alleged to have mismanaged funds. If a lawsuit were to be brought against the trustee, would the trustee be considered an insured under a CGL policy?

Section III - Limits of Liability

Unlike personal home and auto insurance policies, which pay for claims per person or per incident, CGL insurance policies have an aggregate limit. Section III of a CGL policy states the **aggregate limit**, which is the total limit of coverage the insured chooses at the time of the policy inception. Once the maximum amount has been paid out on a CGL policy during a policy term, the insurance company will not pay any additional funds until the next term.

The aggregate limit stated on a CGL policy applies to Coverage A (bodily injury and property damage), Coverage B (personal and advertising injury), and Coverage C (medical expenses). There is a separate limit for each occurrence that is the maximum for medical payments shown on the declarations for any one person.

The aggregate limit excludes claims for the products-completed operations hazard under Coverage A. CGL policies state a separate aggregate limit for products-completed operations, and policies have a maximum limit for personal and advertising injury claims. There is also a specified limit for damage to premises rented to the insured (or rented or temporarily occupied with the owner's permission for fire damage).

Did You Know?

There is no limit to how many claims an insured can file as long as the total amount requested is not more than the aggregate limit stated on the policy.

For example, if a business owner purchases coverage with an aggregate limit of $1 million and files two claims of $600,000 during the policy period, the insurer would only pay $1 million. The business owner would have to pay the rest out of pocket.

Quick Review Questions

22) Three visitors to a business slipped and fell on a wet floor, resulting in injuries. The limit for medical payments is $5,000. All of the visitors sue for their injuries. One visitor has $6,000 in medical expenses; one has $2,000; and the other has $5,000. How much will the insurance company have to pay out in total?

23) A business owner has a $1 million aggregate limit on a CGL and was sued in a class action lawsuit for the injuries of twelve customers. How many of the customers would be entitled to payments under the policy?

Section IV - Conditions

Conditions are one of the basic elements of an insurance contract along with the declarations page, insuring agreement, and exclusions. Policies that have multiple parts, such as CGL policies, generally have specific exclusions and conditions for each type of coverage. The "Conditions" section in a CGL policy describes the conditions that apply for an insurance company to pay for a covered loss.

CGL policies also have certain conditions that apply to all coverages on the policy. In order to understand what is and is not covered, insureds need to know which conditions apply to all losses as well as which conditions apply to certain types of losses. Some of the common conditions for a CGL policy are as follows:

- **bankruptcy:** The insurance company agrees to fulfill its obligations under the policy even if the insured is bankrupt or insolvent.
- **duties of the insured:** Insureds are required to notify the insurance company as soon as it is practical for any situation that may result in a claim and provide as many details as possible. Insureds must also record all details in the event of an actual claim, cooperate fully with investigations, and provide copies of documents as requested.
- **legal action against the insurance company:** Individuals or organizations may not join the insurance company in a lawsuit or sue the insurance company unless the insurance company fails to comply with the terms of the policy.

- **other insurance:** Where another insurance policy applies to a loss, the CGL policy is the primary insurance contract. If another policy is also primary, the companies share the loss equally. The CGL policy may be considered an excess policy in certain circumstances.

> **Did You Know?**
>
> Unlike personal insurance premiums, where the premium does not change throughout the life of the policy, the premiums for a CGL policy may fluctuate up or down.

- **premium audit:** This condition states that the premiums paid are only considered as deposits. The insurance company will conduct periodic audits and send advance notice of audits to the insured. If the audit shows that the insured overpaid for the policy, the insurance company will refund the difference. If the audit shows that the insurance owes a higher premium based on the audit, the insured must pay the difference.
- **representations:** An insured who accepts a CGL policy is agreeing that the statements presented on the declarations are complete and accurate. This condition also states that the insurance company has issued the policy based on representations made by the insured.
- **separation of insureds:** All individuals who are described in the definition of the term *insured* are covered under the CGL policy. Except for the rules listed under the limits of insurance and the rights of the first named insured, all insureds are covered as if they are the only named insured and the insurance applies separately to them.
- **transfer of rights of recovery against others to the insurance company:** Any rights the insured has to recover payments made in connection with a claim are automatically transferred to the insurance company. Insureds agree to transfer rights of recovery to the insurance company and help the insurance company enforce them.
- **nonrenewal:** The insurance company may opt to terminate the policy at the end of its coverage period. In making that decision, the insurance company must mail or deliver written notice of the nonrenewal within thirty days of the policy's expiration.

In addition to the conditions listed on the policy, the insured must pay the premiums on time for the policy to continue to be in effect. Insureds must also notify the insurance company any time there are changes in insureds or risks.

Quick Review Questions

24) A landscaping business files a claim for property damage for $100,000. During the course of the investigation, the insurance company learns that the landscaping business filed for bankruptcy. Would the insurance company be legally required to pay the claim and bear the expenses of defending the insured?

25) A boutique owner grows its product line significantly over the second quarter of the year. After an audit, the owner is surprised to learn that he owes an additional premium to the insurance company. Does the boutique owner have to pay the additional amount?

26) The owner of an auto mechanic shop told the insurance company that customers would not be allowed into the garage area. The insurance company later found out that the mechanics regularly brought customers into the garage area. Would the insurance company be required to pay a claim if a customer got hurt in the garage?

27) An insurance company decided not to renew a CGL policy; however, the company mailed the nonrenewal notice forty-five days after the policy's expiration date. Would the insurance company have to renew the policy if the business owner requests it?

Liability and Damage Coverage Exposures

A commercial exposure is any situation or condition that could cause a business or its owner to become legally liable for damage or injury to another person or company.

The types of exposures are different for companies based on the unique risks that are prevalent in their industries. Exposures common to many businesses include those that occur on the premises due to manufactured or completed products, or the risk of fire to rented properties.

Premises and operations coverage pays for bodily injury or property damage losses that occur as a result of business operations on the business premises. For example, a slip-and-fall injury of a nonemployee would fall under premises and operations coverage.

Products and completed operations hazard coverage covers bodily injury and property damage losses when damage occurs off the business premises and is due to the company's products or completed work. For example, a customer who becomes ill after ingesting a company's food product would be covered for medical expenses under the products and completed operations coverage.

Fire damage legal liability coverage is part of a CGL policy, and it comes into play when a business owner rents a property from a landlord. In such cases, it can be difficult to determine whose policy covers the fire loss. For fire damage legal liability to cover, the investigation must show that the insured was directly at fault for the loss.

Did You Know?

When a fire occurs at a location rented by a business, it can be difficult to determine whose policy covers the fire loss. It is not always clear whether the fire was caused by the business owner's actions or the landlord's actions.

Quick Review Questions

28) A visitor is touring a warehouse when he accidentally steps on a chemical spill, damaging his shoes and burning his legs. Under which coverage type would this loss be classified?

29) Several children become injured as a result of playing with a new toy, and their parents sue the company. Would this type of loss be covered under the company's CGL?

30) A retailer rented a storefront to sell clothing, and an employee accidentally left the space heater on after leaving for the day, causing $25,000 of fire damage. Who would be responsible for the loss: the landlord or the business owner?

31) A CGL policy shows an aggregate limit of $1 million and a per-occurrence limit of $300,000. The insurance company had already paid a previous claim of $300,000 in damages. If the business filed another claim for $400,000, how much would the policy pay, and how would this loss impact the aggregate limit?

Chapter Review

Table 8.2. Chapter 8 Review: Commercial General Liability Insurance (CGL)	
Who may be insured?	• sole proprietorships • partnerships/joint ventures • LLCs or trusts
Coverages	• things related to the building and property • injuries caused by the manufacture or performance of the job • damages incurred after the insured has left the jobsite or handed over the product
CGL coverage forms	• Coverage A—bodily injury or property damage • Coverage B—personal and advertising injury protection • Coverage C—medical bills • supplementary payments

ANSWER KEY

1. This loss would not be covered for two reasons: the food truck was not a regular part of normal operations, and the business owner failed to inform the insurance company about the food truck.

2. This would be a claim for advertising injury, which covers attorney fees, court costs, and other legal defense fees.

3. The bodily injury coverage would pay for the ambulance fees, emergency room fees, and hospital bills. Medical payments coverage may also come into play to pay for funeral and burial expenses.

4. Yes; it would be covered under the definition of advertising injury.

5. The commercial general liability (CGL) policy will cover the ambulance bill, hospital bills, and recovery bills under the definition of bodily injury.

6. Tools are excluded from coverage under the definition of products and completed operations, but a contractor may be able to purchase additional coverage for tools.

7. Temporary employees are not considered employees under the "Definitions" section in a commercial general liability (CGL) policy.

8. The definition of autos includes equipment that is permanently attached to the vehicle, so it would be covered. (If the cherry picker was removable, it would be covered under the definition of mobile equipment.)

9. Even though the occurrence did not happen on the business premises, the customer's injuries are covered under the definition of products and completed operations.

10. The insuring agreement is listed at the beginning of each section of a commercial general liability (CGL) policy, and it describes in detail what must be in place for the insurance coverage to apply.

11. The specific perils are not described in a commercial general liability (CGL) policy, so the insured must check the policy to see which losses are excluded.

12. Costs associated with product recalls are excluded under commercial general liability (CGL) policies, but business owners may be able to purchase additional coverage to protect against product recalls.

13. Bodily injury and property damages caused by pollution are not covered under commercial general liability (CGL) policies.

14. The loss must have arisen from the business itself to be covered; in this case, it was not.

15. This type of loss would be covered under copyright infringement.

16. The type of crime described would be considered an invasion of the competitor's privacy.

17. This would be considered wrongful eviction.

18. Medical payments coverage would cover for the medical expenses of the volunteer only; the employee's medical expenses would be covered by workers' compensation.

19. Slip-and-fall accidents are covered losses under commercial general liability (CGL) policies; medical payments coverage applies regardless of who is at fault for the accident.

20. Spouses of partners in a partnership are considered insureds.

21. Trustees are considered trustees in relation to their duties; managing trust funds is part of their duties.

22. The insurance company have to pay out $12,000: $5,000 for two visitors and the full $2,000 for the third visitor. The business will have to pay the remaining $1,000 for the visitor with the $6,000 bill.

23. Each plaintiff would be entitled to claim payments, but the policy would discontinue paying after the $1 million aggregate limit had been reached.

24. As a condition of the policy, the insurance company must pay the claim despite the bankruptcy filing.

25. Yes. The initial premium the insured paid is only a deposit. As the boutique owner's inventory grows, the additional stock must be insured accurately.

26. No. As a condition of the policy, insureds must make accurate representations about increased risks and notify the insurance company if the risks change. Failure to notify the company that customers are now allowed in the garage means that those people are not covered.

27. Yes. A notice of the insurance company's intent to not renew must be mailed or delivered within thirty days of the policy's expiration date. Since the insurer failed to give adequate notice, coverage would have to continue.

28. Yes. Because the loss occurred on the business premises and was a result of business operations, premises and operations coverage would apply.

29. Yes. It would be covered under products and completed operations coverage.

30. The employee, and therefore the business owner, is responsible for the loss, which would be covered under fire damage legal liability coverage.

31. The insurance company would only pay $300,000 for the loss as it is the per-occurrence limit. There would still be $400,000 left from the aggregate limit ($\$1,000,000 - \$600,000 = \$400,000$).

9. Commercial Inland Marine Policies

The Purpose of Inland Marine Policies

Personal Articles Floaters

Societies have engaged in trading since ancient times, and transporting goods by sea was the most viable form of transportation at the time. **Ocean marine** insurance was created to compensate shippers for goods that failed to make it to their final destinations due to circumstances beyond the shipper's control. Ocean marine insurance is often called a **floater** because goods were essentially floating as they were being transported by ships.

With time, shippers expanded their operations inland. **Inland marine** (IM) insurance was developed as an offshoot of ocean marine insurance to protect shippers against the risks of transporting goods over land. The term *floater* continues to be associated with inland marine insurance because the coverage "floats" with the goods.

Today, inland marine insurance covers products, equipment, and materials while being transported via trucks, airplanes, and trains. Inland marine floater policies are offered to cover all named risks or perils. Common types of personal articles floaters include the following:

- furs
- cameras and camera equipment
- fine jewelry
- silverware
- musical instruments
- China and crystal
- electronic equipment
- personal computers
- fine arts (e.g., valuable paintings, books, antiques, rugs)
- coins
- postage stamps

Quick Review Questions

1) Why is inland marine insurance different than ocean marine insurance?

2) Which type of insurance would be appropriate for a shipper who needs to transport goods across the ocean and to inland parts of a country?

Commercial Property Floaters

A **commercial property floater** covers business property that is not stored at a fixed location. Construction companies commonly purchase commercial property floaters to cover heavy equipment such as cranes, bulldozers, graders, tractors, and more. Such equipment may be temporarily stored at a company's location and is often transported to jobsites for construction projects. Commercial floaters are also used to protect company cars, cellular phones, and laptop computers for sales operations.

Helpful Hint

Commercial property floaters are added to commercial business policies as riders; additional premiums apply.

Commercial property floaters may be scheduled or unscheduled. **Scheduled property** is itemized on the insurance policy, whereas **unscheduled property** broadly protects various classes of business assets.

Insurance riders amend the terms of the policy; for that reason, commercial inland marine conditions are added to the common policy conditions. The conditions apply to specific coverage forms and are similar to the common policy conditions discussed previously. There are two groups of conditions: loss conditions and general conditions. The following common loss conditions apply to inland marine policies:

- abandonment
- appraisal
- duties in the event of a loss
- insurance under two or more coverages
- other insurance
- pairs, sets, or parts
- the transfer of rights of recovery against others to us (i.e., the insurer)

There are additional inland marine conditions that also apply to the IM rider:

- **recovered property:** The insured and the insurer must promptly tell the other if they have recovered the property. The insurance company may return the property to the insured at the insured's option. The insurer will also pay the recovery expenses and expenses to repair the recovered property up to the policy limit.
- **reinstatement of limit after loss:** The limit of insurance will not be reduced by the amount of the claim except for the total loss of a scheduled item.
- **loss payment:** The insurer will provide proof of its intentions within thirty days, after receiving a sworn proof of loss, and they will not pay more than the insured's financial interest in the property. Insurers may adjust losses of property owned by others and may defend the insured against such suits at the insurer's expense. The insurer will not pay for losses that were paid by others.

The IM rider also contains the following common general conditions:

- concealment, misrepresentation, or fraud
- control of property
- legal action against us
- no benefit to bailee
- policy period, coverage territory
- valuation

Quick Review Questions

3) Where would an insured find the condition that concerns repairing damage to a piece of equipment that has many parts?

4) Where would the insured find the conditions in the event of a disagreement with the insurer on the amount of a loss?

5) Under which circumstances may insureds bring legal action against an insurance company?

Inland Marine Coverage Forms

Unfiled versus Filed Coverage Forms

Inland marine coverage forms may be part of a commercial package policy (CPP) or they can be purchased as stand-alone policies.

Because inland marine policies cover several different kinds of losses, the insurance industry has separated inland marine policies into two categories: filed and unfiled. **Filed forms** are reviewed and approved by state insurance departments. These forms generally cover the risks of direct physical loss to property.

However, the bulk of inland marine policies are **unfiled**, meaning the range of coverages is virtually limitless. Because each insurance company creates its own unfiled forms, the policies and rates vary, sometimes significantly. Unfiled policies may cover direct loss or physical damage, or they may only cover specified causes of loss.

Each type of form requires a separate declarations page that specifically describes the covered property, which means there may be more than one inland marine declaration attached to a business policy.

Just as other policies do, both filed and unfiled inland marine policies list several exclusions. Some of the common exclusions one can expect to find on inland marine policies are as follows:

> **Did You Know?**
>
> Insurance companies may also use unfiled forms so they can market policies to their customers; the state insurance department may eventually review the forms for official approval.

- property that is stationary and stored long-term on the business property

- vehicles used in the course of business
- earthquake damage
- flood damage
- property being shipped by sea or air
- damage to property before shipping

Table 9.1. lists common types of coverages that insurance companies offer under unfiled and filed forms.

Table 9.1. Inland Marine Coverage: Filed versus Unfiled Forms		
Unfiled		
fine arts dealers	contractors equipment	stamp and coin dealers
processors' legal liabilities	electronic data processing	cold storage locker
builders' risks—installation	laundries and dry cleaners	installations
furriers block	garment contractors	radio and TV towers
exhibition floater	bridges and tunnels	processing risk
motor truck cargo	air cargo	parcel post
annual transit	trip transit	air transit
bailee's customer	warehouseman	pattern and die
salesperson samples		
Filed		
valuable papers and records	commercial articles	accounts receivable
equipment dealers	signs	theatrical property
camera dealers	film	mail coverage
fine arts	floor plans	jeweler's block
medical equipment	musical instruments dealers	

Quick Review Questions

6) A business purchased several forklifts to be used on the business property, where they are stored in a utility building all year long. Would an inland marine policy be the right way to insure the forklifts?

7) A business purchased several inland marine policies to cover business equipment it was going to ship. An earthquake damaged several pieces of the heavy equipment before they were about to be shipped. If the specific pieces of equipment were covered under an inland marine policy, would the insured be covered for the loss?

Common Inland Marine Forms

The following examples of common inland marine forms aim to clarify how the coverage works in a real sense.

First, **accounts receivable coverage** (also known as **trade credit insurance**) protects business owners against losses when customers fail to pay them. This type of coverage may also pay for indirect costs, such as interest payments for loans that are secured by the property. Additionally, accounts receivable coverage pays for money that was lost because records were damaged or destroyed due to covered perils, extra costs to reestablish accounting records, and unusual fees to aid in data recovery.

Some IM policies may only pay for claims and operating costs that stem from covered property damage claims. Accounts receivable coverage usually excludes the following situations:

- a client's inability to pay
- misunderstandings
- defective products
- erroneous advice
- government or military action
- nuclear hazard
- dishonesty or false pretense
- concealment
- movement of the earth

Before paying a claim, adjusters may make deductions for payments being held due to disputes or earned deductions (e.g., promotional discounts given to customers). The totals for deductions will be subtracted from the total claim payment.

Next, a **bailee** is a business that possesses someone else's property for a short period. **Bailee's customer insurance** provides protection for property a business holds for a customer. It also provides coverage for the customer's property while it is in transit to or from the customer. The coverage becomes effective when the business issues a receipt to a customer. For example, bailee's customer coverage protects the following types of businesses:

- furriers
- cleaners and laundry services
- warehouses

Next, **commercial articles coverage** protects cameras, fine arts, and musical instruments belonging to the business. This coverage may even include worldwide coverage, and it may be written on a named-perils or open-perils basis.

Another type of IM coverage, **contractor's equipment floaters**, protects portable equipment used in business. It is sometimes known as **contractor's tools and equipment insurance** since maintenance businesses, repair services, and construction trades often take tools with them to various jobsites.

Another IM rider is the **additionally acquired property** floater that extends coverage to certain types of property a business acquires during the policy term. Generally, the insured must have coverage with an 80 percent coinsurance clause for coverage to apply. This extension of coverage may apply for 30 – 180 days, depending on the policy. Coverage is generally available for up to $250,000 per building, and the limit may be increased by endorsement.

Another IM floater, **electronic data processing coverage**, is designed to protect against losses involving equipment that processes data, such as computers and backup systems due to losses caused by fire, power surges, and various other perils. This floater typically covers the following types of electronic equipment:

- hardware
- data and software
- media
- smartphones and tablets

Inland marine floaters can also protect other types of property. **Equipment dealers coverage** protects mobile equipment such as generators, elevated work platforms, lighting equipment, equipment used in construction, and more to be sold by dealers. This type of coverage usually covers all risks, although there are certain exclusions. This form does not cover autos that are leased or rented to others, portable audio equipment, or losses caused by racing, demolition contests, and stunt racing.

Even more expensive items can be protected under the **jeweler's block** floater, which protects against losses or damage to high-valued jewelry and precious metals and stones owned by retailers, manufacturers, wholesalers, and pawnbrokers. Coverage is usually provided on an all-risk basis. The coverage does not apply to jewelry when it leaves the business premises, although coverage for jewelry in transit may be added by endorsement. Certain limits may apply depending on how jewelry is shipped (e.g., USPS, UPS, registered mail, priority mail).

Coverage for signs under an inland marine form includes fluorescent, neon, and automatic and mechanical electric signs. Coverage applies to signs that are at or near the place of business. A 100 percent coinsurance provision applies to sign coverage, which means that the insureds must cover signs for their full values.

The next floater, **valuable papers and records**, covers the cost to reconstruct valuable papers and records that have been damaged or destroyed due to a covered loss. Insureds must list the premise locations where they keep valuable papers and records. Covered documents are protected both while located at the scheduled premises or while they are away from there. Coverage for valuable papers and records does not include losses due to electrical or magnetic disturbances or electronic recordings that have been erased. Errors or omissions in processing, duplicating, or copying records are also not covered under this policy form. Inland marine policies include exclusions commonly seen in other policies:

- government action
- nuclear hazard
- war
- dishonest or criminal acts
- fraud, trickery, or false pretense
- unauthorized instructions to transfer property to any person or place
- weather conditions
- faulty, inadequate, or defective planning, zoning, development, design, craftsmanship, building materials, repairs, or construction
- collapse, other than as provided in the additional coverage
- wear and tear, gradual deterioration
- insects, vermin, or rodents

Quick Review Questions

8) A customer dropped off three furs at a furrier to be cleaned and repaired, and they were stolen from the furrier. Which inland marine coverage form would cover the loss of the furs?

9) A tornado hit a pawnbroker's shop, and much of the jewelry was lost in the rubble. Which inland marine coverage would reimburse the store owner for the loss of the jewelry?

10) A music store insured a variety of musical instruments on an open perils inland marine form without worldwide coverage. The store owner took a violin to a music convention in Europe, and the violin went missing at the close of the trade show. Would this loss be covered under the commercial articles floater?

11) An RV dealer insured one hundred RVs that are for sale and sitting on his lot. The owner decided to offer a short-term lease to a preferred customer who wanted to take a road trip with it. While on the trip, the RV sustained wind damage. Would this loss be covered under equipment dealer's coverage?

12) A real estate office had a power outage. When the power came back on, she found none of the computers were working due to a power surge. Which type of inland marine form would cover this type of loss?

13) A construction foreman allowed an employee to borrow a portable generator for temporary use; however, the foreman had not cleared this request with the business owner, and the generator sustained water damage. Would this loss be covered under a contractor's equipment floater?

Additional Coverages for the Transport of Goods

Who Is Who in Inland Marine

The oldest form of inland marine coverage protects for loss of property in transit. The logistics of moving cargo from one point to another involves specific procedures and parties. There are three parties involved in transporting goods, and each has their own obligations:

- The **shipper** is the sender of the goods.
- The **carrier** is the party that actually moves the cargo.
- The **consignee**, or recipient, is the person to whom the carrier is transporting the goods.
    - For example, UPS, FedEx, and DHL are carriers.
    - These carriers may transport goods via steamship, truck, or airline.

Another term that is important in the shipping industry is **free on board (FOB)**. Goods may be shipped **FOB origin**, which means the buyer takes ownership of the goods at the origin where the goods were shipped. **FOB destination** refers to a process in which the buyer takes ownership of the goods only when they have reached the destination.

For example, the Gorgeous Home company buys 10,000 cans of paint from the Pretty Walls company:

- Pretty Walls sends the freight FOB destination.
- The Pretty Walls company loads the cargo onto a semitruck; at this point, they retain ownership of the goods.
- Gorgeous Home will take ownership of the freight once it receives the shipment.

Quick Review Questions

14) What are the three parties involved in a shipping transaction?

15) What are the two forms of FOB shipping?

Important Concepts in Inland Marine Liability

Carrier liability refers to how and when the carrier is responsible for goods that are damaged, lost, or delayed. There are two types of carriers: common carriers and contract carriers.

Busses, trolleys, trains, planes, and ships transport people for a profit. Shipping goods on a common carrier works much the same way. **Common carriers** accept shipments from anyone and deliver them to any address. In contrast, **contract carriers** have exclusive contracts with specific companies.

Inland marine liability insurance provides coverage to loads while they are being transported and while they are being loaded or unloaded. Coverage generally applies to property being held at a premises for up to thirty-one days, as long as no storage fee applies. These are typically all-risk types of policies—except for the listed exclusions.

Carriers cannot be held liable for losses when they have taken the necessary precautions to prevent damage and delays. The reason for this is that carriers have limited control over perishable products that require temperature-controlled environments.

For a carrier to be held liable for a damaged shipment, the shipper must be able to prove that the cargo was undamaged when the carrier received it. Shippers must also prove that the goods arrived at the destination damaged or that they did not arrive at all. Additionally, shippers must be able to substantiate the amount of damage they are claiming. Carrier liability will pay up to the policy limit provided that the damage occurred during shipping, the damage was the direct fault of the carrier, and the shipper has met all of the conditions of the policy.

A **bill of lading (BOL)** is a legal document issued by a carrier to acknowledge that they have received the cargo; it is an important term in transporting goods over land. Once the goods reach the final destination, the BOL serves as the document of title, which proves who ultimately has the goods.

A BOL contains all of the information necessary to successfully ship cargo and get it to its final destination. The type and quantity of the goods are described on the BOL. The cargo's destination is also listed on the BOL. Since the BOL determines who has responsibility for cargo at specific points of the shipping process, the party that has responsibility for the cargo under the BOL is financially responsible for any damage caused.

Contract carriers exist in addition to common carriers, and there are differences in the legal liabilities each of them has. Common carriers have a duty of care, which means they must act in ways that a reasonably careful person would under similar circumstances. By contrast, contracts used by contract carriers outline the specific responsibilities of the carriers. A contract carrier's liability is subject to the terms of the contract. While common carriers are generally responsible for the loads they carry, there are certain situations where they have no liability. For example, common carriers would have no liability in the following situations:

- acts of nature (e.g., tornadoes, hurricanes, falling trees)
- war or military action
- fraud committed by the shipper
- inherent defects in goods
- nuclear hazards
- wear and tear
- wetness or dampness on uncovered loads
- losses caused by delay

As concerns damage or loss caused by carrier negligence, contract carriers are more responsible for damaged cargo than common carriers. Various types of damage claims can be made for goods being transported. The following types of claims that can be made against a shipper or carrier include the following:

- visible damage
- missing part of shipment

- concealed damage
- loss

Motor truck cargo insurance is an insurance policy that protects goods (i.e., freight) that are hauled by for-hire trucking companies. Such policies cover both common carriers and contract carriers. The purpose of motor truck cargo is to protect the property being transported until it reaches its final destination. Motor truck cargo insurance is appropriate for box trucks, flatbeds, cargo vans, car haulers, tractor-trailers, and other long-haul or local shipping trucks and vehicles.

This type of insurance pays for losses to goods when a truck accidentally drops them on a road waterway due to a crash or rollover. A motor truck cargo policy also pays for losses due to fire, theft, and hijacking. Depending on the policy, coverage may also include equipment failures, equipment breakdowns, and the breakdown of refrigeration systems. The coverage applies to cargo while it is being loaded and unloaded and while it is being held at docks or terminals.

Motor truck cargo insurance pays for the costs needed to prevent further damage to cargo as well as legal expenses for defense costs and settlements. Motor truck cargo insurance may also pay to remove the debris and clean up pollutants caused by the debris.

Helpful Hint

Over the life of the policy, motor truck cargo insurance may cover specific shipments or a series of shipments.

Quick Review Questions

16) A truck was carrying a large load of sugar to a warehouse where it sat for one day before the warehouse workers unloaded it. A gas spill suddenly ignited, causing about half the load of sugar to be engulfed in flames. Would this loss be covered under an inland marine policy?

17) A boat from a contract carrier transported a large load of clothing from Canada to the United States. The crew on the boat failed to adjust the humidity levels on the ship during the voyage, and the clothing became damaged by mold. Would the carrier be held liable for this type of loss?

18) What is the PRIMARY purpose of a BOL?

19) A contract carrier accepted a shipment of laptop computers that were to be transported over land from New York to Los Angeles. Upon arrival, the receiving party noticed several of the boxes storing the computers were damaged, but the larger boxes they were stored in were undamaged. Would the carrier be held liable for the damaged goods?

20) A business owner started a van line company to transport office supplies between store locations. Would the business owner be able to purchase inland marine insurance to cover the merchandise during transit?

21) A train carrying a load of paper goods when derailed, and the wreck strewed paper all over a farmer's field. After being repaired, the train continued the transport; however, the shipment was short several cases of paper. Would an inland marine policy cover the shortage?

22) A common carrier transported produce from Illinois to Nebraska by train; a tornado struck and destroyed the load. Would this loss be covered by an inland marine policy?

23) A customer ordered a shipment of cell phones. When the shipment was received and the box was opened, the customer discovered that half of the phones do not turn on. An investigation reveals that there is an inherent flaw in the phones that occurred during the manufacturing process, and it was not detected by quality control. Would this loss be covered by inland marine insurance?

Various Transit Coverage Forms

Annual versus Trip Transit Coverage Forms

There are two ways to insure goods being transported from one place to another: shippers may use an annual transit policy or a trip transit policy.

An **annual transit policy** is used by shippers who regularly ship goods. In exchange for a flat premium, this policy offers protection for numerous shipments over the life of the policy. Large shippers that use a reporting form and make reports monthly, quarterly, or annually benefit from an annual transit policy. Annual transit policies may be made on an open-perils or named-perils basis, and they can apply to incoming or outgoing shipments.

By contrast, a **trip transit policy** is designed to protect single shipments of specifically described property. Coverage applies from the departure location to the destination location and while it is in temporary storage along the way. This type of policy may also be written on an open-perils or named-perils basis.

As mentioned, common carriers include FedEx, UPS, and other small shippers. Common carriers usually ship smaller items, and the cargo is measured by volume which, in part, determines the rates. Shippers of large items or large volumes of items (e.g., heavy equipment and store deliveries) may use several carriers to move their goods. In such cases, the freight may be more than several tons, which will affect inland marine insurance rates.

Quick Review Questions

24) A real estate brokerage firm decided to ship equipment and materials to a trade fair in a distant city. Would an annual trip transit policy or a trip transit policy be an appropriate policy for this purpose?

25) A trucking company has contracts with several retail stores locally and nationally. Would the company benefit more from annual trip transit insurance or trip transit insurance?

Cameras and Musical Equipment

Dealers of cameras and musical instruments often provide repair, restoration, and cleaning services. Customers may leave their cameras or instruments with dealers for weeks or months at a time, so dealers need insurance protection for the property of others while the property is in the shop. Inland marine insurance for cameras and musical equipment is designed for this purpose since these goods typically have a high value and can be easily damaged.

The policy does not cover cameras or musical instruments that are permanently kept on the dealer's property; it is only intended to cover property that is transported from place to place. Inland marine policies also do not cover cameras or musical instruments that are shipped over water; this requires ocean marine insurance. An inland marine policy will also not cover cameras or musical instruments that are in poor condition since they are susceptible to further damage.

There may not be coverage for items that are being exhibited for public display unless the premises are also covered by the policy. If there is a loss to a part of a camera or musical instrument, only the damaged part may be covered.

Inland marine policies for cameras and musical instruments typically cover all risks except for the exclusions listed on the policy. Common exclusions include the following:

- wear and tear
- earthquake
- mysterious disappearance
- flood
- theft from an unlocked and unattended vehicle

Certain conditions may apply to this coverage. For example, policies are generally valued at a reasonable cost of repair of the item at the time of the loss or a replacement of an item of similar kind and quality up to the policy limit.

Inland marine policies may also have a coinsurance listed that is usually from 80 percent to 100 percent of the property's value. If the coinsurance clause is not met, the insurer may only pay a portion of the claim. In the event of a loss, insureds must do what they can to preserve and recover the items listed on the policy.

Quick Review Questions

26) A musical instrument dealer decided to register for an exhibition of various harps in Europe. The dealer planned to display the harps, give a presentation about them, and allow the public to try them out. Due to the size and weight of the instruments, the dealer decides to ship the harps by boat. Would an inland marine policy cover the harps if the dealer has a loss on one or more of them?

27) A musical instrument dealer works out an agreement with the local grade school to offer private lessons for band instruments. The dealer keeps various instruments on the property for the students to use so that they do not have to bring their own instruments in for lessons. Will the musical instruments reserved for the students be covered under the owner's inland marine policy?

28) A camera dealer arrived at the shop one morning to find that heavy rains had caused the shop to flood. Several camera items the dealer had been repairing and cleaning were damaged in the flood. Would this type of loss be covered by an inland marine policy?

29) A camera dealer is holding an expensive camera to repair for a client. The camera and its correct value are listed on the dealer's records. The dealer has an inland marine policy with a 100 percent coinsurance clause. If a fire breaks out in the dealer's shop, will the expensive camera be covered?

Medical Equipment Floater

The inland marine **medical equipment floater** covers the transport of specific types of mobile medical equipment, tools, cameras, laptop computers, and other equipment used by vendors or medical equipment technicians.

For example, a medical equipment vendor might deliver and install medical equipment in a facility or someone's home. Medical technicians may need to take medical equipment somewhere to calibrate it or upgrade it off-site.

> **Helpful Hint**
>
> Medical equipment can be quite costly, and it is not usually included in coverage for commercial property.

The following coverages do not apply under a medical equipment floater:

- items that are considered stationary property at the business location
- business vehicles
- damage from earthquakes or floods
- property shipped by air or sea
- property damage that occurred before shipping

Quick Review Questions

30) A medical equipment vendor has an order to deliver ten portable oxygen tanks to customers' homes. The vendor dispatches a medical equipment technician to deliver the oxygen tanks, set them up for customers, and ensure that they are all working properly. Will the oxygen tanks be covered under a medical equipment floater while they are in transit to the customers' homes?

31) A medical equipment company employs technicians to service medical equipment to make sure it works properly. A call comes into the company from a nursing home that is requesting a medical equipment specialist to come out to service and calibrate various types of medical equipment that are normally kept at the residential facility. If a loss occurs to the medical equipment at the nursing home, will it be covered under an inland marine policy?

Commercial Fine Arts Floater

Companies commonly decorate their spaces with expensive art items (e.g., statues, tapestries, paintings, Persian rugs). Under a CPP, these items are considered business personal property.

While these items are covered, they are subject to certain limitations or exclusions, meaning that business owners may not get the full value of these items in the event of a loss. For example, the replacement cost coverage does not apply to antiques, works of art, or rare articles—even if the policy includes replacement cost coverage. Also, coverage is void for issues such as extreme changes in temperature or humidity levels, fungus, or animal infestations.

A **commercial fine arts floater** covers these items on an all-risk basis; although, as with any policy, there are exclusions. While commercial fine arts policies from various insurers may differ slightly, they commonly carry the following exclusions:

- mysterious disappearance
- pollution
- wear and tear
- flood and earthquake
- repairing, retouching, or restoring
- war, government action, or nuclear hazard
- employee dishonesty
- fraud
- the breakage of fragile items (unless caused by a named peril)

Did You Know?

A commercial fine arts floater contains a pair-and-set clause, which means that the insurance company can restore or pay for both items in the pair when only one part of the pair or set has been destroyed or damaged.

Quick Review Questions

32) A business owner has several expensive paintings hanging in the office. They are not covered under a commercial fine arts inland marine policy. A fire breaks out in the office, and the paintings are destroyed along with other items in the office. Will these paintings be covered to their full market value at the time of the loss?

33) An antique lamp that is part of a set of lamps is insured under a commercial fine arts floater. The lamp, which is rare and cannot be replaced, is stolen from an office building. How will the business owner be compensated for this loss?

Floor Plan Merchandise

The **floor plan merchandise** rider is a type of insurance policy for retailers. It covers merchandise that has been financed by a lender and is designed to protect either the lender, the business owner, or both. This policy covers financed merchandise until it gets sold.

While this type of policy is intended to insure merchandise before it can be sold, it can also cover items while in transit over land. Inland marine insurance policies for floor plan merchandise cover goods for all risks except those that are specifically excluded.

Of course, an inland marine policy for floor plan merchandise will not cover items being transferred by ship or airplane. While the policy will not cover repairs for a crash involving a business vehicle, it will cover the contents inside the vehicle. As for property damage that occurs once it has been loaded, an inland marine policy for floor plan merchandise will cover items that get damaged while being transported.

As with other types of inland marine policies, business owners should be aware of the exclusions listed on the policy. Exclusions typically include the following:

- earthquake damage
- flooding damage
- stationary property
- property transported by sea or air
- property damaged before the shipment

There are additional conditions for floor plan coverage; they include the following:

- If the policy is cancelled while the property is being transported, it will be covered until it has been delivered.
- Property will be valued according to the cost of reasonably restoring it to its condition before the loss, the cost to replace it with similar property, or the cost to the dealer (including shipping charges). The insurance company will value the sold property at the net sales prices after accounting for allowances and discounts.
- Where there is a single interest, the insurer will only pay the part of the loss that the party's interest bears as it pertains to the total value of the property.
- Where there is a dual interest and a party does not comply with the provisions of the policy, the payment will not affect the interest of a secured lender as long as the lender has done everything possible to comply with the provisions.
- The insured must take a physical inventory of the merchandise at least every twelve months and must keep accurate records of inventory, purchases, payments, and sales. The insured must also keep a record of property they are holding for others, if applicable.

Quick Review Questions

34) A clothing retailer took out a loan for $50,000 to cover merchandise purchased by a wholesaler to put into a store. Some of the merchandise was transferred to the store and some was being held in a warehouse. Would a loss to the merchandise in the store be covered by a floor plan merchandise policy if one was in force?

35) An earthquake caused damage to electronic devices that a dealer was planning to sell. The items had a loan on them, and the dealer had floor plan merchandise coverage on them. Would this type of loss be covered under a floor plan merchandise policy?

36)An employee at an office supply retailer accidentally set fire to his desk. The fire spread and damaged other office supplies that were being held for transport to retail stores in the area. Would this loss be covered by floor plan merchandise coverage?

37) A business owner purchased a floor plan merchandise policy for party supplies to protect them while they were being shipped to various party stores. The business changed ownership while the merchandise was in transit and the new owner cancelled the floor plan merchandise policy. At what point would the coverage cease to be valid?

Mail

Insurance companies, banks, fiduciaries, trust companies, security brokers, and other transfer agents often need to transfer property via a mail service. Inland marine coverage for mail is necessary for these types of services.

Covered property is divided into classifications. The first classification is for the following types of property when sent by first-class mail:

- bonds
- stock certificates
- certificates of deposit
- other securities
- coupons attached to bonds
- money orders
- drafts or checks
- postage and revenue stamps
- notes
- bills of lading
- warehouse receipts
- other documents of value

The second classification pertains to the following items only as long as they are sent by registered mail:

- gold bullion
- platinum and precious metals
- currency
- unsold travelers' checks
- jewelry
- watches
- precious and semi-precious stones

This type of property is only covered while it is in the care, custody, and control of a postal service run by the government and while it is in transit by a messenger or common carrier taking it to or from a government post office. Property will continue to be covered until it arrives to the recipient or is returned to the sender if it was unable to be delivered.

Policies may include separate limits depending on the type of mail service, and there may also be separate limits for any single recipient on one day. Items will be valued at their actual value and will not be less than the market value on the day of the loss.

Helpful Hint

Contraband and property being illegally transported or traded are excluded from coverage.

There is one extension of coverage that pertains to errors and oversight. For example, if the value of any mailing is not accurately recorded, the insurance company will pay the actual value of the property as long as the sender promptly notifies the insurance company of the error or oversight. The payment will be limited to the limit of insurance as shown on the declarations page. For a situation where the total value of property in a single shipment is more than the limit of insurance, the insurance company will only pay the part of the loss the limit of insurance bears to the actual value.

Exclusions on the mail inland marine form include government action, weapons (including atomic weapons, mines, and torpedoes), and war and military action.

Quick Review Questions

38) A jewelry broker sent a shipment of precious and semi-precious stones to a small jewelry store in a rural area via standard postal mail. The broker purchased a mail inland marine policy for the shipment. Would the stones be covered by mail inland marine coverage?

39) A bank sent a certified check to a customer for $10,000 by registered mail but insured it under mail inland marine coverage for $1,000. After discovering the oversight, the bank called the insurance company and told them of the error. In the event of a loss, would the insurance company reimburse the bank for $10,000 or $1,000?

Chapter Review

Table 9.2. Chapter 9 Review: Commercial Inland Marine	
Features	• Policies are filed (standardized) or unfiled (unique exposure) with state regulatory authorities. • Coverage is available on any portable property. • Policies are called "floaters" because the coverage floats with the insured property anywhere in the world.

Nationwide marine definition	• Coverage is written on inland marine and ocean Marine forms.
	• The coverage defines four classes of risk:
	  • domestic shi0pments and transportation risks
	  • tunnels, bridges, and other instrumentalities of transportation and communication
	  • commercial property floater risks
	  • personal property floater risks

Answer Key

1. Inland marine insurance differs from ocean marine insurance because each type of operation carries different types of risks. For example, goods being transported inland are not typically subject to being stolen by ocean pirates or lost on a sinking ship.

2. A shipper who needs to transport goods across the ocean and to inland parts of a country would need to purchase ocean marine coverage for the goods' transport by sea and inland marine insurance while the goods are being transported by truck or train.

3. This "pairs, sets, or parts" loss condition concerns repairing damage to a piece of equipment that has many parts.

4. Conditions in the event of a disagreement with the insurer on the amount of a loss can be found under the "Appraisal" section.

5. Insureds must fully comply with the policy terms and can bring suit within two years from the time they learned of the loss.

6. Inland marine policies protect property or equipment that is regularly transported over land to be used at other locations, so it would not cover property stored on the premises.

7. No. Inland marine (IM) policies exclude damage from earthquakes.

8. Bailee's customer coverage pays for losses that take place when business owners have a customers' property in their custody and care.

9. Jeweler's block coverage protects pawnbrokers against all perils.

10. This type of loss would apply because it is an open perils policy; however, in this case, the coverage would be voided because the loss occurred outside the coverage territory.

11. No. Inland marine (IM) coverage excludes loaned or leased vehicles.

12. Under the electronic data processing floater, the business owner would be entitled to the costs to repair or replace the computer equipment.

13. This loss would be excluded since it would be considered a dishonest act that involved an employee entrusting another employee with company property without first getting approval from the business owner.

14. The three parties involved in a shipping transaction are the shipper (sends the goods), the carrier (transports the goods), and the consignee (receives the goods).

15. The two forms of free on board (FOB) shipping are FOB origin and FOB destination. With FOB origin, he recipient legally owns the property once the company sends the product. With FOB destination, the consignee does not legally own the merchandise until it is has reached the destination.

16. Inland marine insurance covers shipments for fire damage while they are being loaded or unloaded.

17. Yes; contract carriers must not be negligent when handling cargo.

18. A bill of lading (BOL) legally proves that the carrier has received the merchandise; once the goods reach the final destination, the document serves as proof of who ultimately received the goods.

19. Contract carriers generally only have to show that *they* were not negligent. In this case, the cause of loss was probably due to goods that were damaged before they were loaded onto the truck, in which case the carrier would likely not be held liable.

20. Yes; inland marine insurance would be appropriate in this situation.

21. The accident was no fault of the carrier; however, inland marine policies cover shortages as well as total losses, so the loss would be covered.

22. A tornado that destroys goods is considered an act of God and would therefore not be covered by an inland marine policy.

23. Since the damage occurred before the shipper received the goods, the shipper would be responsible for the loss—not the carrier.

24. Trip transit insurance is designed for single trips for specified goods, so it would be the most appropriate policy in this situation.

25. Annual trip transit insurance is designed to cover numerous loads of unspecified goods to various locations over a year, so this would be the most appropriate policy in this type of situation.

26. Shipping items listed on an inland marine policy over the water would require an ocean marine policy.

27. No. An inland marine policy cannot be used for items that are normally kept on the property.

28. No. The cause of loss of flooding is excluded from inland marine policies.

29. Yes, since the cause of loss of fire would be included in the policy, and the dealer kept an accurate record of the item's value.

30. Since the oxygen units are mobile property and are being transported across the land, they will be covered under an inland marine policy.

31. No; only portable medical equipment is covered.

32. No. While fire is a covered cause of loss, a business personal property policy would not cover the increased value of the paintings. If the business owner had gotten a commercial inland marine policy, the full market value of the paintings would be covered.

33. Under the pair-and-set clause, the insurer can decide to offer compensation for the set of lamps, rather than offering funds to replace one of them.

34. Merchandise stored at both locations—the store and the warehouse—would be covered under a floor plan merchandise rider.

35. Earthquakes are excluded under floor plan merchandise coverage.

36. Only the merchandise being held for sale would be covered.

37. Even though the policy was cancelled mid-transit, the coverage would remain in force until it was delivered.

38. Precious and semi-precious stones are not covered unless they are shipped via registered mail.

39. Mail inland marine policies have an extension of coverage for errors and oversights; since the bank promptly notified the insurance carrier of the oversight, the loss would be covered.

10. Workers' Compensation, Employers' Liability, and Other Business Policies

Workers' Compensation

General Workers' Compensation Concepts

Workers' compensation is a type of insurance that pays for medical expenses and replaces the income for workers who get injured or become ill due to a work-related incident. Employers may purchase workers' compensation even if they are not required to have it in order to avoid being sued for large amounts due to an employee's work injury. Certain employers in all fifty states must purchase workers' compensation. In the state of Texas, workers' compensation is optional except for private employers who contract with government entities. Some contractors also may require independent contractors and subcontractors to have workers' compensation.

> **Helpful Hint**
>
> Workers who are covered under workers' compensation cannot sue their employers for negligence.

State rules for workers' compensation vary depending on the number of employees an employer has. States also require certain types of jobs to provide workers' compensation insurance. Large companies may qualify as self-insured employers as defined by each state's Department of Insurance, and they must provide workers' compensation under that program if the state requires them to carry it. Employers may have to pay a penalty if they are required to carry workers' compensation and do not do so.

Workers' compensation pays for claims over workers' injuries regardless of fault. This means the insurance will pay the claim even if the worker or the employer was fully or partially responsible for the accident. Employers and employees who were involved in the incident do not have to provide proof that they were not at fault. There are some exceptions to this rule (e.g., if gross negligence or misconduct is involved).

The **Occupational Safety and Health Administration (OSHA)** is the federal agency that ensures employees have safe and healthy working conditions. It was established in 1971 when the **Occupational Safety and Health Act of 1970** went into effect. OSHA sets the standards for safe working conditions, enforces them, and provides training, education, and outreach for employers and their employees.

OSHA has created six programs to work cooperatively with labor groups, businesses, and other organizations to help prevent illnesses, injuries, and fatalities in workplaces:

- **Alliance Program:** a program for trades, labor unions, professional associations, educational institutions, and faith-based organizations to learn more about health and safety in the workplace

- **OSHA Strategic Partnership Program:** a partnership program to improve health and safety in government agencies, major corporations, private industries, and large construction projects
- **Voluntary Protection Programs:** recognition programs to honor employers that have implemented health and safety systems and have injury and illness rates below the national averages listed for various industries on the Bureau of Labor Statistics
- **OSHA Challenge Program:** a program that works with employers to help them develop safety and health management programs or assist with improving existing programs
- **On-Site Consultation Program:** a program that provides free and confidential consultations on site for small- and medium-sized businesses to learn how to identify and address safety hazards
- **Safety and Health Achievement Recognition Program (SHARP):** a program that honors small businesses that have used the On-Site Consultation Program and stand as a model of safety for other businesses

The definitions of the terms *employee* and *employer* are important because the relationship determines whether an employee is covered under a workers' compensation policy. In simple terms, an **employee** is defined as a person who works for wages or a salary. From a legal perspective, the courts may use a test to determine whether a worker is an employee or an independent contractor. The **common law test** states that an employment relationship exists when an employer has the right to control the work process. The **economic realities test** states that an employment relationship exists if the worker is economically dependent on the employer for continued employment. Courts may also use a hybrid test, which is a combination of the common-law and economic realities tests.

Did You Know?

Even though certain types of workers fit the definition of employer-employee relationships, they are exempt from workers' compensation insurance. For example, domestic servants and farm workers are exempt from workers' compensation insurance in most states.

Quick Review Questions

1) A construction company contracted a plumber for their housing development. One of the plumbers fell down the stairs of one of the homes and was seriously injured. Would this type of incident be covered under workers' compensation?

2) A farmer hires hundreds of seasonal workers each July to detassel her corn crop, and the workers complete the job by the end of the month. If any of the workers must be hospitalized because of heat stroke, would the farmer's workers' compensation cover the claim?

3) Which of OSHA's programs recognizes employers who maintain OSHA's health and safety protocols?

4) What options do employers have if their state regulations require them to have a workers' compensation policy and they do not want to purchase one?

Workers' Compensation Regulations

Some states have monopolistic state funds for workers' compensation, which means that employers must purchase workers' compensation from the state rather than a private insurance company. In other states, workers' compensation may not be required for certain types of employees, including domestic employees, farm workers, or family members. Employers must cover the expenses for workers' compensation policies at no expense to employees.

The number of employees also has a bearing on whether employers must carry a workers' compensation policy. For example, in Florida and Alabama, employers with four or more employees must carry workers' compensation. Part-time employees may or may not be covered depending on the state laws.

> **Did You Know?**
>
> States commonly exclude casual employees who do not have set schedules or minimum required working hours. Examples of casual employees are entertainers, taxi drivers, commercial fishermen, real estate agents, and product demonstrators.

In some states, workers' compensation is quite comprehensive. For example, in those states, employers must cover all employees, even if they are working illegally. In other states, there may be exemptions from workers' compensation for sole proprietors, partners, or executive officers in nonprofit organizations.

In every state, insurance companies must pay for medical services for workers who are covered under workers' compensation policies. This is done at no cost to the employee. Copays and coinsurance clauses do not apply. Employees who become ill or injured on the job can continue to receive payments for as long as their treating physicians deem necessary so long as the treatment is connected to a work-related injury.

When a worker reports an injury, the employer is required to ensure that the ill or injured employee gets medical care immediately. Shortly thereafter, the employer must notify the insurance company according to the terms of the policy. In some states, employers must also notify a workers' compensation board run by the state.

Once the claim has been filed, the insurance company will assign a claims adjuster who will review the claim and approve or decline benefits. If the insurer declines benefits, a reason that is backed by the policy wording must be provided. The insurer will begin paying the medical bills and lost wages once the claim has been approved. Workers' compensation policies pay for the following medical expenses:

- emergency care
- medical bills
- ambulance fees
- hospitalization costs
- rehabilitation costs
- ongoing care
- disability benefits
- funeral costs

Employees who get injured at work may be classified as being temporarily or permanently disabled depending on the severity of their injuries. Workers who are expected to make full recoveries and return to work are typically classified as temporarily disabled. Temporarily disabled employees may return to work with restricted duties and lower pay while they are recuperating.

Workers who have severe impairments may not be able to return to work. Such workers are classified as permanently disabled. Within this classification, workers may be further classified as having **permanent total disabilities**, which means they can no longer work at all. Workers who can return to some form of work other than their previous employment may be classified as having **permanent partial disabilities**.

> **Helpful Hint**
>
> Workers' compensation policies will also pay for the wages an employee loses until the employee is approved to return to work. Workers may not receive all of their lost income under disability; they typically receive approximately two-thirds of their wages if they are on any kind of disability.

As noted in the bullets above, workers' compensation policies include a death benefit for workers who die as a result of work-related injuries. Coverages vary based on the insurer and state laws. The death benefit can pay for funeral and burial expenses or provide financial support for the worker's family members.

OSHA defines a **work-related injury** as any event or exposure in a work environment that contributes to or causes a health condition or significantly aggravates one. Not all injuries are included under workers' compensation policies. For example, workers' compensation does not cover the following:

- injuries sustained as a result of a natural disaster
- injuries resulting from horseplay or fights
- injuries sustained during off-duty recreational duties
- injuries due to conduct that violates company policy
- injuries sustained while committing a serious crime
- injuries in conjunction with drugs or alcohol
- self-inflicted injuries
- one-time illnesses or ordinary diseases
- preexisting conditions

Quick Review Questions

5) An individual accepts a job with an employer who covers the employee under a workers' compensation policy. Is it legal for the employer to take funds out of the employee's paycheck to pay for the cost of the workers' compensation policy?

6) An employee was injured when a ceiling fan fell on her; she is expected to recover and return to work within a few weeks. Which type of disability would this be classified as?

7) An employee acquires a long-term illness because of a work-related situation. His physician determines that they employee can return to some type of meaningful employment, yet the employee will never be able to return to his previous employment. How would such a disability be classified under workers' compensation?

8) A covered employee broke her leg after falling off a building, and the injury required many months of physical therapy. Would the workers' compensation policy cover the cost of physical therapy and lost wages?

Structure of a Workers' Compensation Policy

Every workers' compensation policy is based on a form from the National Council on Compensation Insurance (NCCI). Policies may have slight differences based on state laws and the actual form provided by the insurer.

There are two parts to a workers' compensation policy: workers' compensation and employers' liability insurance.

As stated earlier, the workers' compensation portion applies to accidental bodily injury or disease that caused or aggravated by conditions within the work environment. The insurer is only obligated to pay for injuries or illnesses that have occurred during the policy period. The insurer has the right to investigate and settle claims and the right and duty to defend the insured against claims. Likewise, insurance companies are not required to defend claims or suits that are not covered by the insurance policy.

Employers' liability is the second part of a workers' compensation policy, and it covers claims by ill or injured workers that the workers' compensation portion of the policy does not cover. Workers may sue their employers if they do not feel as though the benefits they received under a workers' compensation policy adequately compensated them for their illness or injury. This is the type of situation where employers' liability comes into play. Employers' liability covers the following four types of claims:

- third-party lawsuits due to an employee's work-related injury or illness
- loss of consortium lawsuits where a spouse sues due to loss of marital benefits
- consequential lawsuits over bodily injury filed by nonemployees who are affected by an employee's work-related illness or injury
- dual-capacity lawsuits where an employer has a secondary relationship to the employee

> **Helpful Hint**
>
> Most of the time, workers' compensation and employers' liability are combined into one policy. In states where employers must purchase workers' compensation from a state fund, employers can purchase employers' liability as a standalone policy or as an endorsement of the workers' compensation policy.

Quick Review Questions

9) The spouse of an employee files a lawsuit against his employer because of a work-related fatality. The surviving spouse had just given birth, and the loss of income created a financial hardship. Would this type of loss be covered under workers' compensation or employers' liability?

10) An employer files a claim against her workers' compensation policy after an employee is injured on the job. The insurance company denies the claim, causing the injured employee to file a lawsuit against the employer. Would the employer be responsible for the defense costs of the lawsuit?

Employers' Liability

Workers' compensation insurance has its origins in the Federal Employers' Liability Act of 1908 (FELA), which was passed to compensate railroad workers who were subject to injuries or death when the railroad system was being expanded across the nation. The purpose of FELA is two-fold: to discourage negligence in the industry and to compensate railroad workers as they are exposed to dangerous conditions in building the railway.

FELA is like workers' compensation in some ways. It differs insofar as FELA is a federal law while workers' compensation is regulated at the state level. Another difference is that FELA applies to railroad workers and other workers who engage in interstate commerce. Workers under FELA have the right to sue their employers if they are injured on the job due to the employer's negligence.

Generally, employees who collect benefits under a workers' compensation policy cannot sue their employers for negligence. Nonetheless, there are certain situations where a worker does have the grounds to sue an employer.

For example, a worker may believe the employer's insurance company was incorrect in their assessment of denying the claim. An employee may also feel that the employer acted in bad faith or was negligent in some way, which caused the employee to become ill or injured.

In these types of situations, an employee may sue the employer. If any of these things were to occur, the workers' compensation policy would not cover the cost to defend the company against such allegations. The employer would have to pay for the defense and court costs out of pocket unless the employer also has employers' liability coverage.

Employers' liability insurance is usually covered under Section II of a workers' compensation policy, but it can also be purchased as a standalone policy to cover the gap in coverage that workers' compensation does not cover.

Workers' compensation premiums are calculated based on a standard formula that includes the following components:

- employee classification rate
- employer payroll
- experience modification rate (EMR)

First, employees are assigned a **four-digit class code** that refers to the type of work they do. Rates for workers' compensation are based in part on the class code. The **National Council on Compensation Insurance (NCCI)**, the regulatory agency that oversees workers' compensation, sets the codes and classification rates. The code correlates to the amount of risk that is associated with a particular job. Employers may have many different class codes based on the types of jobs their employees do.

Did You Know?

The rates for workers' compensation are the same in all states, regardless of the state's cost of living.

The next step in the formula is to figure out the employer payroll. Employers pay premiums based on every $100 of payroll for each employee class code.

The **experience modification rate (EMR)** shows how a business compares to other employers in the same industry that have similar employee class codes. The age of the business and the frequency, severity, and number of workers' compensation claims determines the rate. All three components are involved in the formula. The formula for workers' compensation is as follows:

$$employee\ classification\ rate \times employer\ payroll\ per\ \$100 \times EMR = workers'\ compensation\ premium$$

Large employers may be able to take advantage of a premium discount based on a high volume of employees. The discount takes into account the administrative cost savings that are present when insuring large numbers of employees.

Did You Know?

Certain workers' compensation plans provide dividends at the end of the policy period to those employers who have few or no claims during that period.

Employers may also benefit from **retrospective rating** which is essentially a safety incentive program that rewards companies that successfully reduce workplace injuries. Rates are based on assessing workers' compensation risks based on the previous twelve months. If the risk is higher at the end of the term, the employer may have to pay an additional premium; however, if the risk is lower than expected, the employer may be due a refund.

Quick Review Questions

11) A railroad worker loses his arm in an accident while working on a railroad construction site. Will this worker be able to submit a workers' compensation claim?

12) A fire broke out at a factory, and employees were exposed to the smoke before quickly being evacuated from the building according to the company's fire escape plan. One worker with asthma had medical complications causing her to take a few weeks off of work. Would this employee be entitled to workers' compensation?

13) What is the formula for workers' compensation premiums?

14) Are there any situations wherein an employer can get all or part of her workers' compensation premiums back?

Commercial Flood Insurance

The National Flood Insurance Program (NFIP) covers commercial buildings in addition to residential dwellings. Unlike other types of commercial insurance, commercial flood insurance covers only one peril: loss by flooding. Loss due to flooding is not covered under standard commercial insurance policies.

Did You Know?

The only way to purchase flood insurance is through an insurance agent.

Business owners can purchase flood insurance from the federal government through the NFIP or from private insurers.

The definition of what constitutes a flood is the same for both residential and commercial properties. Commercial flood coverage also protects owners from damage to the business property and its contents.

In most cases, business owners have to wait thirty days from the date they purchase flood insurance before the policy goes into effect.

As is the case with residential properties, mortgage lenders generally require business owners to purchase flood insurance if the building is located in a high-risk flood area; otherwise, purchasing flood insurance is optional. While flood insurance is not mandatory in some cases, business owners may opt to purchase it anyway to protect their businesses. Flood insurance can prevent the problems of having to pay for a flood-damaged property without having to withdraw funds from savings or take on additional debt.

Did You Know?

According to FloodSmart.gov, one inch of water can cause over $25,000 in damage.

The payouts for commercial flood insurance work differently than they do for commercial property policies. Commercial flood insurance covers direct physical damage to the building structures based on the actual cash value (ACV) of the damages or the limit stated on the policy—whichever is less. Contents are also covered at actual cash value, including inventory and stock. In addition to the structure, coverage for buildings includes the following:

- foundation
- systems used to service the building (e.g., water heaters, plumbing and electrical systems, heating and air conditioning systems)
- permanently installed carpeting over unfinished floors

- permanently installed bookcases, wallboard, paneling, and cabinets
- awnings and canopies
- walk-in freezers
- outdoor antennas and aerials attached to the structure
- fire extinguishing equipment and sprinkler systems

The contents coverage includes the following:

- furniture, fixtures, machinery, and equipment owned by the business
- stock
- portable air conditioners, dishwashers, and microwave ovens
- carpets and rugs that are not covered under the building coverage
- washing machines and dryers
- food freezers (other than walk-in freezers) and the food in them
- certain valuable items up to $2,500 (e.g., original artwork, furs)
- self-propelled vehicles that are not licensed and are used to service the location as long as they are stored inside the insured building
- up to 10 percent of contents coverage for improvements made by an occupying tenant to a building
- outdoor antennas and aerials attached to buildings
- fire extinguishing equipment and sprinkler systems

The NFIP offers up to $500,000 for commercial building coverage and up to $500,000 for its contents. There are separate deductibles for the building and contents coverages, and the claims are separate for the structure and the contents.

Did You Know?

Commercial flood insurance has separate deductibles for the structure and contents.

Not everything is included under commercial flood insurance. The following items are excluded from flood coverage:

- damage caused by mildew, mold, or moisture that the property owner could have prevented
- damage caused by a backup of sewers or drains (unless there is a flood in the vicinity of the building that caused the backup)
- precious metals, currency, recorded data, and valuable papers (e.g., scrip, stock certificates)
- property outside the building or in another structure (e.g., trees, plants, septic and well systems); walkways, patios, decks, hot tubs, fences, seawalls, and swimming pools
- financial losses due to an interruption in business or the loss of use of the insured's property
- most self-propelled vehicles, including their parts
- damage to business vehicles (Note: Business owners may be able to get coverage under a commercial auto policy.)

Quick Review Questions

15) A warehouse floods with water, and an adjuster determines that the cause of the loss is due to flooding. The business owner immediately files a claim with the NFIP for the loss. When the waters recede, the business owner does nothing to dry the property out, causing mold and mildew to grow on the walls. Will this be a covered loss under a commercial flood policy?

16) A manufacturer of wood furniture sustains a flood due to unusually heavy rains. The business owner is storing lumber and products in various stages of completion in the building. Will the building, materials, and finished products be covered under one claim?

17) A 75-year-old, one-story office building was damaged by a flood and deemed a total loss. The cost to rebuild the office building is $200,000 but the depreciation on the building is $25,000. The deductible for the building is $1,000. How much will the NFIP pay for the claim?

18) There was a flood in a restaurant, and the business owner had a flood insurance policy but only carried insurance on the building. A walk-in freezer and two freestanding freezers were damaged in the flood. Would all the freezers be covered under an NFIP policy?

Crime

Additional Coverage for Crime

Crime coverage (fidelity insurance) covers financial losses due to crimes or dishonest acts committed by employees, volunteers, and contractors. This type of coverage can be added to a commercial package policy or it can be purchased as a standalone policy.

Crime coverage includes theft, robbery, forgery, and electronic crimes. Coverage also pays for losses for the damage or destruction of money, securities, and other property while on the insured's premises and at other places (e.g., while money or property is being transported). Losses due to an employee or someone else fraudulently manipulating a company's computer system to transfer funds to an external account are also covered under crime coverage. Other covered losses include an insured receiving counterfeit currency and an employee fraudulently sending transfer instructions to the insured's bank under the name of the insured.

Did You Know?

There are two forms of crime coverage: one for commercial entities (CR DS 01) and one for government entities (CR DS 03). Each has different triggers that are similar to the General Liability Form.

With a Commercial Crime Form (CR DS 01), the coverage applies per loss. With a Government Crime Form (CR DS 03), the coverage is provided on a per-employee basis or a per-loss basis. The **per-employee basis** means that the full limit of coverage is available for each employee who commits a crime under this coverage. For example, if a policy has a limit of $100,000 for crime insurance, and three employees commit a crime, the amount of coverage that could be paid out is $300,000. Some other unique characteristics of government forms are as follows:

- The coverage territory does not include Canada.

- They contain a clause that provides indemnification to public officials who must give individual bonds for loss if their subordinates commit dishonest acts.
- The definition of the term *employee* does not include references to directors, trustees, limited liability company managers, brokers, consignees, or commissioned merchants; it adds references to public officials.
- Dishonesty exclusions do not include references to partners, officers, directors, and limited liability company managers, but they do add references to public officials.
- Cancellation regarding conditions that apply to employees refers to officials and other employees who are authorized to manage employees as opposed to partners, officers, directors, and limited liability company managers.

Business owners who purchase crime insurance may choose their own limits of coverage for various types of crimes. Each type of crime has its own insuring agreement, conditions, and exclusions. The declarations page lists the specifications and limits for each type of coverage separately. Table 10.1. provides a sample of a crime declarations page.

Table 10.1. Sample Crime Declarations Page	
Employee Theft (Employee Dishonesty)	$ ________
Alteration and Forgery	$ ________
Inside-Theft of Money and Securities	$ ________
Inside-Robbery or Safe Burglary of Other Property	$ ________
Outside the Premises	$ ________
Computer Fraud	$ ________
Fund Transfer Fraud	$ ________
Counterfeit Paper Currency and Money Order	$ ________

The Commercial Crime Form lists the following exclusions:

- legal expenses: attorney fees and court costs
- losses after the insured knows an employee committed a crime
- losses that are indirect or consequential (e.g., due to business interruption or loss of potential income)
- data theft, including theft of a business's data, trade secrets, client lists, or intellectual property

- fines and penalties
- losses based only on inventory records
- salaries, bonuses, commissions, fees, and associated lost income
- expenses incurred while putting a proof of loss together (unless coverage is included in the policy for this)

Quick Review Questions

19) An employee is contacting current clients to determine how satisfied they are with their insurance coverages. She decides to download the customer list and sell it to a competitor. Would this type of crime be covered under crime coverage if the employee gets caught?

20) An audit reveals that a cashier has been stealing small amounts of money from the cash register over a period of several months. Will this type of loss be covered under crime coverage?

21) An employee posing as her boss transferred a large sum of money from the business account to her own personal account. Will this type of loss be covered by a crime policy?

22) An employee forged the business owner's name on company checks and deposited the money into his own bank account. The owner discovered the theft but failed to take action with the employee until the employee had forged checks ten more times. Would this be a covered loss under the policy?

Employee Dishonesty and Theft

Employee dishonesty and theft insurance protects businesses from financial harm caused by criminal acts committed by their employees and certain other individuals. The coverage includes theft of business property, including office equipment, inventory, cash, securities, and money orders. Employee theft and fraud insurance also cover credit card fraud, forgeries of business checks, drafts or promissory notes, and embezzlement.

There are two types of employee dishonesty and theft insurance coverages: a discovery-based policy and a loss sustained policy. The difference is that a discovery-based policy (Discovery Form) reimburses business owners for losses that are *discovered* during the policy period; a loss sustained policy (Loss Sustained Form) pays for losses that *occur* during the policy period.

A theft of money or securities is covered as long as it occurs inside the business premises or the premises of a bank. The policy also pays for loss from damage to the premises and damage to a vault, locked safe, cash drawer, cash register, or cash box due to unlawful entry or attempted theft. The policy will also cover loss or damage to property inside the premises that results from the actual or attempted burglary of a safe or the robbery of a custodian. Outside the business premises, the policy will pay for the loss of money, securities, and other property stolen while in the care of a messenger or armored car.

Did You Know?

A discovery-based policy pays for losses that are discovered during the policy period.

Damage to the building and other property is covered at replacement value without depreciation. Items may only be replaced with materials of like kind and quality.

Employee dishonesty and theft coverage extends to computer fraud, funds transfer fraud, and the acceptance of fraudulent money orders and counterfeit money by employees. Forgery includes fraudulent instruction, such as someone sending a request for money via electronic devices, telegraphs, cable, teletype, or telephone, as well as written instructions.

Exclusions on the Employee Dishonesty and Theft Form include acts committed by the insured and their partners and members even if they colluded with a covered person. The policy also does not include acts of theft or dishonesty where the insured had knowledge of them before the policy period began. Other exclusions include the following:

Did You Know?

A discovery-based policy pays for losses that are discovered during the policy period.

- losses from the unauthorized disclosure of confidential information (e.g., trade secrets, patents, customer lists, processing methods)
- unauthorized disclosure of confidential information (e.g., financial or personal information) that the company holds for other people or entities (e.g., customers, vendors, contractors)
- governmental action
- indirect loss
- legal fees, costs, and expenses
- nuclear hazard
- pollution
- war and military action
- inventory shortages
- trading
- warehouse receipts

The normal conditions apply (e.g., cancellation, changes, liberalization, other insurance, concealment/misrepresentation/fraud, cooperation, and duties in the event of a loss). The insurance company has the right to make inspections and examine books and records. Insureds may not bring legal action against the insurer unless they have complied with all of the terms of the policy and bring a suit within two years.

Quick Review Questions

23) A business owner purchased a discovery-based dishonesty and theft policy which started on May 1st. On April 30th of the following year, the owner discovered that an employee had taken a large sum of money from the cash register. The claim was not settled until May 15th of the new term. Would this claim apply to the old term, the new term, or not at all?

24) An employee stole securities from his employer, and the business owner filed a claim. How would the value of the securities be calculated?

25) An employee used a company computer to fraudulently transfer business funds to a friend's bank account. Would this be a covered loss under a dishonesty and theft policy?

26) An employee stole €1,000 from the business owner's desk. Would this loss be covered under dishonesty and theft?

Bonds

Insurance bonds are legal contracts between parties to ensure that a party fulfills its obligations or to protect against theft. Whereas insurance policies involve two parties—the insurer and the policyholder—insurance bonds involve three parties.

A **surety bond** is an agreement between the three parties to cover losses or damages if the principal fails to meet the responsibilities stated in the agreement. The **surety** is the insurer of the bond, which the **obligee** requires the **principal** to purchase in order to guarantee that the principal will fulfill his obligations. Often, local municipalities, other government agencies, individuals, or companies may be the obligees in a three-party agreement. The surety bond protects the obligee if the principal does not uphold his part of the agreement. Bonds include an **indemnity agreement** that states that the principal will pay for potential losses or damages caused by any claims or legal costs that may arise.

For example, Jessica Smith is a contractor. She needs to complete a housing development with twenty homes within two years in order to comply with local regulations. In this example, Jessica is the principal, the insurance company is the surety, and the obligee is the local government. If Jessica fails to complete the work according to the timeline, the insurance company can step in and secure a new contractor or financially compensate the obligee (the local government) to fulfill the agreement.

The party that requires the principal to be bonded generally sets the amount of the bond, which is also the penalty amount. If the obligee makes a claim on the bond, the surety must pay a sum up to a maximum of the penalty amount.

A **fidelity bond**, also known as an **honesty bond**, has a different purpose than a surety bond. Fidelity bonds are designed to protect businesses against losses resulting from employees who are dishonest or display fraudulent actions.

The insuring agreement describes the specific situations where the bond will make a payment. The typical agreements include the following:

- employee dishonesty
- trading loss
- Employee Retirement Income Security Act (ERISA)
- restoration expenses

> **Helpful Hint**
>
> While insurance bonds provide protection, they are not insurance policies. Whereas insurance policies pay for losses on behalf of the insured, surety bonds provide a guarantee that one party will compensate another party even if the principal does not fulfill the expectations as stated in the agreement.

Another way that bonds differ from insurance policies is the period of time for which the bond is active. For example, surety bonds are generally effective for a period of one, two, or three years. Continuous bonds are continuously effective until the surety company cancels them.

Quick Review Questions

27) The owners of a huge corporation with thousands of employees want to protect themselves from employee theft and dishonesty. While the company has a sufficient number of managers supervising employees and adequate security measures in place, the owners are aware of the risks of employee theft with so many employees. Which type of bond would the owners need to purchase to protect the company from financial loss in this situation?

28) An employee falsified timesheets for other employees so that they would qualify for health care and other voluntary benefits to which they are not actually entitled. Under which type of coverage would this loss fall?

29) A computer repair technician responded to a call for the repair of a desktop computer in a client's home that was being used for business. While at the client's home, the technician stole a laptop computer and a cell phone. Which type of bond would this small company need to cover this type of loss?

30) A hospital made plans to add a new wing to its campus. Which type of bond would the hospital need to ensure that the contractors will complete the job in the time frame agreed upon by the parties?

Professional Liability Insurance

Explanation of Professional Liability Coverage

Professional liability insurance (errors and omissions insurance) is liability insurance for professionals to protect their businesses against claims of mistakes. Claims are paid even when they are baseless.

Any professional who engages in giving people advice or consultations should have the protection of professional liability insurance. The following types of professions (and many more) benefit from professional liability coverage:

- accountants and tax preparers
- consultants
- content writers and marketers
- counselors
- engineers
- graphic designers
- health care professionals

- insurance agents
- investment professionals
- realtors
- stockbrokers
- technology professionals

With most insurance policies, the insurance company has the right to settle losses without the insured's consent. It is important to keep in mind that professional liability insurance policies often have a **consent to settle clause**, which means that the insured has the right to fight settlements she does not believe are reasonable. Professional liability insurance pays for legal fees, court judgments, settlements, licensing fees, and other costs associated with professional mistakes. Professional liability insurance covers the following acts:

- inaccurate or incorrect advice
- misrepresentation
- negligence
- violation of good faith and fair dealing
- copyright infringement

State regulations mandate which professionals must have professional liability and how much they must carry in order to keep their licenses. For example, insurance agents in Rhode Island must have professional liability with a minimum limit of $250,000 per occurrence and a $500,000 aggregate limit. Most often, states require professional liability for health care professionals, lawyers, insurance agents, and real estate agents; nonetheless, professional liability coverage is recommended for anyone who engages in giving advice or consultations to clients.

Quick Review Questions

31) After being audited, a taxpayer discovers that she owes a significant sum to the IRS due to the tax preparer's mistake, and she sues the accountant over the mistake. Will this claim be approved if the tax preparer has adequate professional liability insurance?

32) An attorney failed to file a lawsuit within the statute of limitations, which caused the client's case to be dropped. The client sues for negligence. Will the lawyer's professional liability policy pay for the legal fees and settlement expenses in this case?

Medical Malpractice

Standards in the health care field are designed to ensure that patients receive the proper medical care. It is considered **malpractice** any time medical professionals fail to meet the standards of care in their fields. Medical malpractice coverage can be tailored to almost any medical professional working in any field of medicine. Many things can go wrong in hospitals, clinics, dental offices, and physicians' offices. For example, a medical provider can misdiagnose a patient or provide a delayed diagnosis, causing more

> **Did You Know?**
>
> Most medical malpractice insurance policies are written on a claims-made basis, which means that the coverage applies whenever a claim is made and reported within the policy period.

significant health issues or even death. A health care professional can forget to obtain signed informed consent forms or can make a mistake during treatment or surgery.

How is medical practice (a type of professional liability) different from general liability? Both types of insurance protect the business. Both types of insurance can also be purchased to satisfy the insurance requirements for a certain occupation or industry. Unlike general liability insurance, which covers bodily injuries and property damage, professional liability insurance covers mistakes and negligence that are related to making errors or leaving out important information.

Quick Review Questions

33) A lab technician misread laboratory results for a patient, causing the patient to miss a diagnosis of HIV/AIDS. This mistake resulted in a delay of several years of getting the patient the appropriate treatment and caused the patient's spouse to also become infected. Would the lab technician be covered if she has medical malpractice insurance?

34) A surgeon operated on a patient to remove a tumor, but he failed to remove all of the cancer, causing the patient to need a second surgery. Would the surgeon be covered if the patient sued for this type of mistake?

Directors and Officers (D&O) and Employment Practices Liability (EPL)

Directors and officers (D&O) liability insurance and employment practices liability insurance (EPL or EPLI) both protect companies from lawsuits, although they protect in different ways.

Directors and officers play an important role in businesses, and **D&O insurance** is designed to protect companies against lawsuits from decisions these people make when companies cannot indemnify them. D&O insurance also protects the personal assets of board directors and officers and their spouses if they get sued in connection with their duties. Lawsuits can stem from employees, customers, vendors, or third parties.

> **Helpful Hint**
>
> Directors and officers may be sued for both actual and alleged acts; D&O insurance covers both.

D&O insurance also covers breaches of fiduciary duties that cause financial losses, the misuse of company funds, fraud, misrepresentation in a prospectus, theft of intellectual property, and poor governance.

> **Did You Know?**
>
> EPLI insurance can be added to a business owners policy (BOP).

While D&O insurance covers legal fees, financial losses, and settlements, it does not cover fines, penalties, or punitive damages. Illegal entities and illegal acts are also excluded from D&O coverage.

Employment practices liability insurance (EPLI) protects businesses against claims made by employees over acts or allegations of discrimination, wrongful termination, failure to promote, and harassment. It also covers allegations of physical, sexual, and emotional abuse.

EPLI insurance may be added to a business owner's policy (BOP) by endorsement, or purchased as a standalone policy. This type of policy is typically a claims-made policy, which means that claims are valid only when the incident occurs during the policy term. The reason for this is that claims by employees may come months or years later.

Quick Review Questions

35) A shareholder of a company alleges that the directors and officers of a company misrepresented financial information before and after a merger took place. Several other shareholders join the suit, which ultimately becomes a class-action lawsuit. Which type of insurance will cover this type of loss?

36) Several employees file a lawsuit against their employer over alleged discrimination concerning promotions. Which type of insurance will cover this type of loss?

37) An employee working for a factory alleged that several employees were bullying and harassing him. Rumors began been circulating among other employees about the employee who filed the complaint, and the stress of the situation caused the employee to quit. Would this be a covered loss if the employee decides to sue his former employer?

Cyber Liability and Data Breach

People commonly post things on the internet and on social media that could harm others. **Internet liability insurance** protects businesses from claims or allegations of defamation of character, infringement of intellectual property, and privacy rights. This type of insurance also protects against incidents where someone spreads a virus or malicious code on business computers.

New data protection laws have been enacted around the globe to protect consumer privacy, forcing companies to notify customers when a data breach threatens personally identifiable information. **Data breach insurance** is also known as **cyber liability** or **network security and privacy liability insurance**. This can be a costly expense for business owners; data breach insurance provides the funds for business owners to respond to data breaches expeditiously.

Cyber liability coverage is typically a claims-made policy, which means that claims must be filed during the policy period. Various types of coverage may be included in a cyber liability policy. Some of the more common coverages include the following:

- website publishing liability
- network security liability
- the replacement or restoration of data coverage
- cyber extortion coverage
- business income and extra expense

> **Did You Know?**
>
> Businesses can be sued over what they publish on their websites; cyber liability will pay to defend such lawsuits.

Depending on the policy, other coverages may also apply. Each type of coverage shows an individual aggregate limit which is subject to an overall policy limit.

Quick Review Questions

38) A company sustains a data breach that exposes the credit card information of thousands of customers. Which coverage would pay the expenses to notify the customers of the breach and inform them how to further protect their information?

39) A business owner received an electronic message that a hacker locked the company's computer system and is asking for a ransom of a million dollars to unlock it. Which type of insurance coverage would protect against this type of claim?

Umbrella and Excess Liability

Sometimes, business owners may find that the maximum limits available for purchase are not enough to fully protect their companies, so they may take out **umbrella and excess liability** policies to cover these shortfalls. Such policies pay only for third-party liability claims up to the policy limit when the underlying limits have been exhausted. Umbrella policies may cover multiple policies.

For example, The Castillo Brothers' Tortilla Company has $1 million of liability coverage through their CPP. The masa for their tortillas was contaminated, and the company accidentally distributed tainted tortillas. Several people became ill from consuming their product and required $1,200,000 in medical care. The company was found liable, but since they only have $1 million in liability coverage, they had to turn to their commercial umbrella policy to make up for the $200,000 shortfall.

People commonly use the terms *umbrella insurance* and *excess insurance* interchangeably, yet there are significant differences between them. The concept behind excess liability policies is to simplify coverage by keeping it consistent with the underlying policies. An excess policy is a follow-form policy, which means that it covers the same perils, conditions, additions, and exclusions as the underlying policies. Follow-form policies cannot be changed by adding endorsements.

> **Helpful Hint**
>
> Excess liability policies generally have a minimum limit of $1 million in coverage. Coverage amounts are available in increments of $1 million and may be available for up to $25 million.

Umbrella policies differ from excess liability policies in two important ways. First, unlike excess liability policies, umbrella policies are not follow-form policies, which means that the coverage may be broader than the underlying policies. For instance, umbrella policies often cover losses globally, while the underlying policies may limit the coverage territory to certain countries. In this way, umbrella policies can effectively close insurance gaps. By contrast, excess policies only cover the exact perils, terms, and conditions of the underlying policies. Umbrella policies also require a minimum out-of-pocket amount, such as a deductible or self-insured retention before claims are paid; excess liability policies do not have these requirements.

Quick Review Questions

40) A construction company has a general liability limit of $1 million and an umbrella policy with a $2 million limit. The self-retention limit on the umbrella is $10,000. A customer was seriously injured when a building collapsed on a jobsite and the medical bills amounted to $1.5 million. How much will the commercial policy or the umbrella pay?

41) A business purchased an excess liability policy with a $1 million limit. The underlying policies limit coverage to the United States and Canada. The business owner filed a liability claim for $1.2 million for an incident that occurred in Mexico. How much would the excess liability policy pay?

42) A general contractor bid on a project, and the client requires a general liability policy with a $5 million limit per occurrence. How can the contractor satisfy this requirement if he only has a $2 million general liability policy?

43) A business has a general liability policy with a $300,000 limit. The company also purchased a commercial auto policy and an umbrella policy with a $1 million limit that covers the business for liability. While driving a personal car, the business owner gets into a multi-vehicle crash, which is the business owner's fault. How much will the umbrella pay if the claim is $500,000?

Chapter Review

Table 10.2. Chapter 10 Review: Workers' compensation, Employers' liability, and Other Policies	
Workers' Compensation	
Standard policy concepts	• *the insured:* the employer or named insured • *locations:* policy coverage for all places listed on the declarations page • *work-related:* any injury or illness occurring at the place of employment • *non-work-related:* any condition not related to the work or the workplace
Employers' liability	• Federal Employers' Liability Act (FELA) originally applied to railway workers; it outlines regulations in addition to workers' compensation. • Coverage is in Section II - Liability. • Actions must begin within three years from the cause of action.
How premiums are calculated	• The insurer must apply a rating bureau classification to each $100 of an employer's payroll. • The company's expense modification factor must be calculated from a combination of payroll, losses, and premiums. • Discounts on premiums are available to employers who have a high volume of employees.
Crime	

Program coverage	• covers both business and government entities
	• events that trigger coverage and their related forms:
	    • *Discovery Form:* coverage for the discovery of a covered occurrence taking place at any time but discovered during the policy or reporting period
	    • *Loss Sustained Form:* coverage of any loss the policyholder discovers during the coverage or reporting periods

Bonds	
What is a bond?	• *principal (obligor):* the person who promises to fulfill an obligation and must purchase the bond; goes through the underwriting process • *obligee (or insured):* the person who receives the payment in place of a failed promise • *guarantor (or surety):* the company providing coverage; paid only if the principal defaults on his promise

Table 10.2. Chapter 10 Review: Workers' compensation, Employers' liability, and Other Policies	
Surety	• *surety:* someone who guarantees the performance of another • *surety bond:* the three-party contract that creates the bond • *penalty:* a set time limit for which the surety is valid

Fidelity	• coverages:
	    • *individual:* one employee
	    • *named schedule:* group of named employees
	    • *position schedule:* anyone holding a position on that schedule
	    • *commercial blanket:* all employees/limits of liability involved in the promise

Professional Liability	
Purpose and characteristics	• protects professionals against legal liability • typically written on a claims-made basis rather than for a specific time period
Errors and omissions	• protects brokers and agents from financial loss due to a lawsuit with the insured • protects against losses resulting from not placing correct coverage, giving incorrect advice, or failing to inform the policyholder of potential issues • typically written on a claims-made basis rather than for a specific time period
Medical malpractice	• written for medical care providers • protects policyholders from lawsuits over injuries they may have caused
Directors and officers (D & O)	• covers any mistakes made by executives working in an official capacity • triggered by a wrongful act • does not cover penalties, fines, or punitive damages
Employment practice liability (EPL)	• covers the employer for any HR violations caused by discrimination, sexual harassment, or physical or emotional abuse
Cyber liability and data breach	• covers any cyber risks • protects from internet-related publishing perils (e.g., slander) • protects from failing to keep a business network secure • covers the cost of restoring/replacing data

Table 10.2. Chapter 10 Review: Workers' compensation, Employers' liability, and Other Policies	
	• covers expenses incurred from extortion threats
Umbrella and Excess Liability	
Business owner may choose:	• a primary liability policy (underlying policy) • a standalone policy (umbrella policy) • a policy with increased limits of liability (Excess Form)
Personal umbrella	• offers a minimum of $1,000,000 in additional coverage • protects insureds against financial catastrophe • retains limits that policyholders must pay before the umbrella policy covers certain losses • requires policyholders to have primary liability policies
Commercial	• provides businesses with higher limits of liability coverage than regular CPPs • requires policyholders to pay the self-insured retention (similar to a deductible in other types of insurance) before the umbrella pays out

ANSWER KEY

1. Independent contractors are not considered employees and are therefore not covered by the construction company's workers' compensation policy.

2. Since seasonal workers only work for a few weeks, they are not considered employees of the farmer and as such, they are not entitled to coverage under the farmer's workers' compensation policy.

3. The Voluntary Protection Programs and the Safety and Health Achievement Recognition Program (SHARP) recognize employers' efforts.

4. In most states, self-insurance is an acceptable form of workers' compensation.

5. No. Employers who provide workers' compensation benefits must provide them to their employees at no cost.

6. In this scenario, the classification would be that of a temporary total disability.

7. This is a partial total disability. This classification is reserved for individuals who must change occupations because of a work-related injury or illness.

8. The policy would cover all medical expenses and lost wages until the employee can safely return to work.

9. The spouse would have grounds to sue under employers' liability and, depending on the circumstances surrounding the death, may or may not be successful in getting damages awarded by the court.

10. Yes. It is the insurer's right and responsibility to defend the employer.

11. While the employee would not be able to be compensated under a workers' compensation policy, he would be entitled to have his medical payments paid for and his wages replaced under the Federal Employers' Liability Act (FELA).

12. The worker would be entitled to compensation under workers' compensation; however, the employee could not sue the employer since the fire was sudden and unexpected, and an evacuation plan had been established.

13. To calculate the workers' compensation premiums, multiply the employee classification rate by the employer payroll rate per $100 times the experience modification rate (EMR):

$$employee\ classification\ rate \times employer\ payroll\ per\ \$100 \times EMR$$
$$= workers'\ compensation\ premium$$

14. Employers may be able to get a return on their premiums if they have a workers' compensation dividend policy or a retrospective rating policy.

15. The policy would cover damage to the structure and the contents, but it would not cover the cost to clean up mold or mildew because the owner could have prevented it from growing.

16. Because there are separate deductibles, the building and materials claims would have to be made separately.

17. The payout will be $\$200{,}000 - \$25{,}000 = \$175{,}000$. The final payout minus the $1,000 deductible equals $174,000.

18. Only the walk-in freezer would be covered because it is permanently installed in the building.

19. No. Losses due to data theft are not covered by crime coverage.

20. Crime coverage pays for losses of currency due to employee theft.

21. Crime coverage pays for losses where an employee intentionally moves funds from the company's bank account to an external account.

22. No. Losses are not covered when a crime has been committed after the insured became aware of it.

23. Since the theft was discovered during the old term, the claim would apply to that term.

24. The claim would be paid according to the market value at the close of business on the day the loss was discovered.

25. The theft of funds using a computer is covered under this type of policy.

26. Yes. The funds would be replaced at the face value of euros, and the deductible would apply.

27. A fidelity bond protects employers from fraudulent or dishonest acts by employees.

28. The Employee Retirement Income Security Act (ERISA) is a federal act that sets the minimum standards for voluntary retirement and health plans. Coverage under ERISA refers to the loss of or damage to property that is contained within an employee benefits plan.

29. This situation describes a theft of customer property; a fidelity bond is the proper bond to cover this type of loss.

30. The hospital would need a surety bond. In this case, the contractors are the principals and the hospital is the obligee.

31. This type of claim will be covered under the mistakes, errors, and oversights clause.

32. This type of claim would be covered under professional negligence.

33. A mistake in reading lab results is a covered loss.

34. A professional liability policy would pay for any judgments or settlements in this type of case.

35. In this case, the directors and officers insurance protects the board from misrepresentation lawsuits.

36. This type of lawsuit would concern the employer's practices, so employment practices liability insurance (EPLI) would pay to defend such a lawsuit.

37. If the employer has employment practices liability insurance (EPLI), this loss will fall under the harassment coverage of such a policy.

38. Cyber liability would cover this type of loss. Most policies state that the loss must have been reported within the policy period for coverage to apply.

39. This type of threat is considered cyber extortion coverage, and it would be covered by cyber liability coverage.

40. The total amount paid out will be $1,490,000: the general liability policy will pay $1 million, and the umbrella policy will pay $500,000. The construction company will only have to pay the $10,000 self-insured retention limit.

41. Neither policy would pay in this case because Mexico is not a covered territory under the policy, and since the excess policy is a follow-form policy, it would not pay for this loss either.

42. The contractor could add a $3 million umbrella policy, and then the $2 million general liability policy along with the additional $3 million umbrella would be sufficient to satisfy the $5 million liability requirement.

43. In this scenario, none of the claims will be paid because the commercial auto policy and umbrella policy only cover the business. The loss would have to be paid by the business owner's personal auto policy.

11. Business Auto Policies (BAPs)

Introduction to Business Auto Coverage

Covered Autos (Section I)

The BAP Form is separated into five sections:

- **Covered Autos (Section I)** defines covered autos according to their descriptions, which are further designated by symbols in the BAP.
- **Liability Coverage (Section II)** provides a list of coverages, extensions, exclusions, and limitations for liability within the insurance agreement; it also defines who is considered an insured.
- **Physical Damage Coverage (Section III)** lists coverages, extensions, exclusions, and limitations for claims that deal with physical damages.
- **Business Auto Conditions (Section IV)** lists the loss conditions and general conditions that are applied to claims.
- **Business Definitions (Section V)** clarifies the terms used throughout the BAP.

> **Helpful Hint**
>
> The language and clauses used to describe responsibilities for each covered peril establish a contract between the insurer and the insured when it comes to insurance payouts or denied payouts.

Each section delineates the insurer's and the insured's responsibilities for responding to claims.

Section I on the BAP Form lists ten coverage symbols on the declarations page that describe the type and coverage for each auto. If a coverage symbol is shown beside the coverage name, it means that the coverage applies. The coverage symbols comprise numerals ranging from one through ten.

Table 11.1. Coverage Symbols Found on the BAP Form	
1	any auto (used only for liability coverage)
2	owned autos
3	owned private passenger autos
4	owned autos other than private passenger autos
5	owned autos subject to no fault

Table 11.1. Coverage Symbols Found on the BAP Form	
6	owned autos subject to uninsured motorists law
7	specially described autos
8	hired autos
9	non-owned autos
10	mobile equipment subject to financial responsibility or other insurance laws

The general definitions on a BAP differ from those on a personal auto policy (PAP). For example, the BAP Form defines the term *accident* as "continuous or repeated exposure to the same conditions resulting in bodily injury or property damage," but a PAP Form does not define the term *accident* at all. Additionally, a PAP Form offers detailed explanations for the definition of a trailer, while the BAP Form only includes one short definition: "includes a semitrailer."

Did You Know?

The disparities between the general definitions offered on a PAP and a BAP often confuse insureds, as the vast majority of insureds typically fail to understand the nuanced differences between the two policies.

Symbol 7 is a unique designation because it refers to "specifically described automobiles." This means that Symbol 7 covers only those autos that are listed in Item Three of the Declarations Form, and each Symbol 7 vehicle has a separate premium. Also, the coverage for Symbol 7 extends to non-owned trailers that are attached to those autos listed in Item Three on the Declarations Form. Thus, if Symbol 7 is used, there must be an attached vehicle schedule. If an auto is not listed on said schedule, it will not be covered in the BAP.

Section I of the BAP describes a vehicle as either "owned" or "newly acquired." The definition of the term *newly acquired* is a somewhat gray area because it is not defined in the BAP. Does it mean that the insurer obtains the auto by *buying it* or by merely *taking possession of it*? The BAP allows the insured to make a valid case for both. It is therefore best practice for an insured to notify the insurer immediately upon buying or taking possession of a new covered auto to see which description will provide the best coverage.

Symbol 10 refers to all mobile equipment subject to compulsory responsibility, financial responsibility, or motor vehicle insurance laws. In contrast, **Symbol 19** refers to land vehicles that are not directly subject to compulsory responsibility, financial responsibility, or motor vehicle insurance laws. Symbol 19 is the auto designation for mobile equipment vehicles that might be considered as "covered autos" according to the BAP and therefore qualify for liability coverage. Consequently, if Symbol 19 is entered next to a coverage item, the insured will have coverage for that particular piece of mobile equipment.

There are basic exclusions that exist in the BAP that deny liability coverage for certain covered autos. The insurer agrees to pay damages for incidents that are described as "accidents," which must be unforeseen events. Liability coverage will therefore not be offered to incidents in which the property damage and bodily injury is deemed as planned or foreseen. Coverage may be offered in certain cases, but it will not be unlimited.

For instance, when an insured vehicle is transporting fuel or waste and has an accident, the clause concerning covered pollution costs or expenses will not apply. Coverage might be extended to the general cleanup of waste or fuel spills that occur before or after a covered auto arrives at its final destination, although these coverages are rare. The criteria for this coverage are as follows:

- The accident occurred on property that was not rented or owned by the insured.
- The waste was not directly in or a part of the covered auto.
- The spill occurred as a result of the maintenance or use of the covered auto (i.e., cleanup costs are covered because property damage occurred to the customer's tank before the spillage).

Quick Review Questions

1) What are the FIVE sections listed on the BAP Form?

2) Under which item is Symbol 7 listed on a Declarations Form?

3) What does Symbol 19 designate on the BAP Form?

4) What are the three criteria for an insurer that covers pollution spills?

Liability Coverage (Section II)

A BAP liability insuring agreement, which is the main contract between the insurer and the insured, consists of three parts:

- the insurer's promise to pay for covered perils
- pollution coverage
- duty to defend

There are several entities who may be considered insureds for liability coverage. The named insured on the BAP policy is, first and foremost, considered an insured driver for any covered auto; likewise, the named insured will be considered an insured under liability coverage whether the auto is considered owned or non-owned. Although there are some exceptions, any individual who uses a covered auto that is borrowed, hired, or owned by the named insured will also be considered an insured.

Likewise, if the named insured borrows or hires a covered auto from another entity or owner, that entity or owner will not be considered an insured. Insurers are focused on liability coverage for the named insureds, so those who are hired or borrow a covered auto should secure their own auto insurance for liability coverage. Nevertheless, this exception does not include borrowed or hired trailers that are connected to covered autos: if a trailer that is borrowed or hired is

> **Did You Know?**
>
> Named insureds will not be considered as insureds under their own BAPs if the auto is not designated on the policy.

deemed a covered auto in its own right, the owner or responsible entity for that trailer will be considered an insured under liability coverage.

Coverage under the BAP varies from the coverage provided on the BOP. On the BAP, individuals who are members of an LLC, partners of the business, or employees of the business will not be considered as insureds while removing property from or moving property to a covered auto—only the named insured or the employee driving the vehicle is covered. For instance, if the named insured is transporting goods to another business, and that said business's members, partners, or employees injure a third party, those members, partners, or employees will not be considered as named insureds if an insurance claim is filed by the third party (or other). Additionally, if a partner or member owns a covered auto, that person will not be considered an insured, nor will any member of that person's household be considered an insured. While Symbol 1 or Symbol 9 can technically define these autos as "covered autos," they will not be considered as insured, nor will any member of the named insured's households be considered as insured. The other LLC owner(s) must rely on their own insurance policies for coverage unless the BAP offers a contrary endorsement.

Did You Know?

In the BAP, there is an omnibus clause that protects managers who assign employees to transport goods, services, or harmful substances. The clause helps protect the supervisor, who might be considered liable for giving the direct order to the employee.

The "Coverage Extensions" section for liability coverage on the BAP Form include both supplementary payments and out-of-state coverage extensions. Supplementary payments will be made for the following:

- all incurred legal expenses
- the loss of earnings for up to $250 per day due to any of the following:
  - time off from work
  - court costs
  - all interest accrued in a suit against the insured

Any payouts will not, however, reduce the overall limit of insurance. Out-of-state coverage extensions protect against auto accidents occurring in a state other than the one in which the auto is licensed. Insurers are responsible for increasing the limit of insurance in order to match out-of-state compulsory or financial responsibility laws.

For instance, if an auto licensed in Pennsylvania gets into an accident in Michigan, the coverage guarantee must match the state coverage limits in Michigan. Additionally, this section of the BAP states that insurers are also responsible for meeting both minimum coverage requirements and maximum limits.

Although liability coverage for BAPs is relatively extensive, liability coverage exclusions exist for most auto-related insurance claims. As is the case with all coverage exclusions, the BAP excludes the following:

- claims that are not insurable under any other insurance policy or endorsement
- claims better covered under other kinds of insurance policies

- exposures covered by endorsements for additional premiums

Additionally, thirteen major coverage exclusions exist for BAPs. Some will be familiar from this book's previous discussion of property liability coverage, but they are slightly different in a business policy. These inclusions include the following:

Table 11.2. The Thirteen Major Coverage Exclusions for a BAP	
Name of Exclusion	**Description**
Expected or intended injury	• denies coverage for any bodily injury or property damage resulting from an act that was planned, anticipated, and/or intended
Contractual	• states that if a previous insurance contract or agreement exists with delineated liability, the liability will not be covered by the BAP
Workers compensation and **employee injury**	• denies coverage for any injury that is already covered under workers compensation, disability, or unemployment compensation law
Fellow employee	• denies coverage in cases where one employee lays a claim against another employee in response to an injury sustained during employment
Care, custody, or control	• denies coverage for property damage or pollution costs/expenses connected to accidents involving owned or transported property that is deemed to be in the care, custody, or control of the insured
Handling of property	• denies coverage for any bodily injury or property damage that occurs before an insured begins loading property onto a covered auto or after the property has been unloaded by the insured
Movement of property	• denies coverage for any incident that occurs as a result of the movement, loading, or unloading of property by a mechanical device that is not attached to the covered auto
Operations	• denies coverage for any claim that arises from incidents of operations that are not directly addressed in the BAP
Completed operations	• denies coverage for faulty workmanship that is discovered after work that has already been completed or abandoned
Pollution	• denies coverage for any pollution that occurs when hazardous materials are exposed to the environment while moving the hazardous materials

Table 11.2. The Thirteen Major Coverage Exclusions for a BAP	
Name of Exclusion	**Description**
	onto a covered auto prior to transport, transporting the hazardous materials, and after the hazardous materials reach their final destinations • Note: If the pollution stems from any malfunctioning parts, the insurer will cover the claim.
War	• denies all claims in the event of a war or war-like/military action
Racing	• denies coverage for damages or losses resulting from activities such as professional racing, organized racing, demolition contests, and/or stunting activities
Limits of insurance	• limits the policy's liability in order to counter endless payouts and stacking issues; limits listed on declarations page

Quick Review Questions

5) Which of the following exclusions is listed on Section II of the BAP Form: wear and tear, sound equipment, diminution in value, or operations?

6) What is ONE exception to the pollution exclusion on Section II of the BAP Form?

Physical Damage Coverage (Section III)

The **"Physical Damage Coverage" section (Section III)** discusses three major types of coverage for physical damage. These types of coverage are as follows:

- **Comprehensive coverage** protects the insured from any loss resulting from anything other than a collision or overturn of the vehicle.
- The **specified causes of loss** coverage includes such events as damage to a conveyance transporting a covered auto, mischief or vandalism, fire, lightning, windstorm, hail, earthquake, explosion, theft, or flood.
- The **collision coverage** protects against losses incurred by a covered auto's collision with another vehicle or object or an auto overturn.

> **Helpful Hint**
>
> While some of these exclusions are absolute, others might be partial or limited. The declarations page should always be double checked when determining coverage.

There are six main exclusions that are listed on the "Physical Damage Coverage" section (Section III) of the BAP. Two, **nuclear hazard or war** and **racing** are familiar; however, there are several that are new:

- The **wear and tear** exclusion denies payments for losses that result from the following factors: wear and tear, freezing, mechanical breakdowns, electrical breakdowns, blowouts to tires, punctures to tires, and road damages to tires.
- The **sound equipment** exclusion does not cover any loss of or damage to sound reproducing or receiving equipment that is permanently installed in the vehicle.
- The **auto electrical system** exclusion clarifies that any equipment connected to and drawing power from the covered auto's electrical system that can be deemed as permanently installed, integral to the housing of permanently installed electrical equipment, or necessary for standard operation of a covered auto will be covered.
- The **diminution in value** exclusion states that the insured will not receive coverage for a decrease in value of the covered auto due either to age or an accident.

> **Did You Know?**
>
> The BAP provides coverage extensions for temporary transportation or the loss of use of a covered auto due to theft. Expenses incurred as a result of renting, borrowing, or hiring another covered auto are also covered under this extension.

Section II of the BAP provides options for how an insurer can choose to pay for a documented loss to a covered auto. There are two options:

- The insurer can pay the actual cash value of any damaged or stolen property.
- The insurer can pay for the damaged or stolen property to be replaced with something that is comparable in price or quality.

For example, if an insured bought her auto for $45,000 in September 2023, and an incident causes a loss in December 2024, the amount paid will be according to the valuation on December 2024 rather than the initial cost of the vehicle.

On the other hand, if the insurer chooses to replace or repair the property, the insurer must guarantee that the items are of similar—but not necessarily identical—kind or quality.

> **Helpful Hint**
>
> When an insurer chooses to pay the actual cash value, the cash value will be valuated at the time of the documented loss.

For instance, if the actual cash value of a damaged radio is $800, but the insurer finds a comparable radio for $650—one that is perhaps a different brand—the insurer has the right to purchase the other brand for the lesser amount.

Quick Review Questions

7) Which of the following events would be excluded according to Section III of the BAP Form: electrical breakdowns, lightning, windstorm, auto overturn?

8) According to Section III of the BAP, what is ONE type of physical damage coverage from which an insured can choose?

Coverage Conditions (Section IV)

In the **"Coverage Conditions" (Section IV)** of the BAP, there are five loss conditions and eight general conditions. The loss conditions, which are similar to those discussed earlier, include the following:

- appraisal
- duties of the insured in the event of a loss
- legal action against the insurer
- loss payment
- transfer of the rights of recovery

The following general conditions also resemble those discussed earlier:

- bankruptcy
- concealment, misrepresentation, or fraud
- liberalization
- no benefit to bailee for physical damage coverages
- other insurance
- premium audit
- policy period and coverage territory
- two or more coverage forms

Quick Review Questions

9) What are TWO loss conditions in Section IV of the BAP?

10) According to the general conditions, can an insured receive coverage for Mexico?

Garage Liability Coverage versus Garage-keepers Liability Coverage

Coverage for Vehicles While in Garages

The **Garage Coverage Form** is similar to the BAP except that it has specified clauses for losses or damages to covered autos that occur while in the care, custody, or control of franchised and non-franchised businesses that sell, stored, and/or service covered autos.

While both coverages are on the same form, they are two different types of coverage that contain distinct specifications and clauses. The major difference between the two policies is that the Garage Liability Form deals with the insured's liability for operations; the "Garage-keepers" section deals with coverages for damages to the insured's customers' vehicles.

Covered risks for garage liability insurance include the following:

- autos damaged by on-site equipment
- damages resulting from products sold or manufactured
- third-party injuries
- discrimination or dishonesty claims
- accidental collisions

Covered risks for garage-keepers insurance include the following:

- weather-related events
- fires
- collisions
- theft/vandalism

Helpful Hint

Franchised and non-franchised businesses that sell, store, or service covered autos do not qualify under other ISO forms, so these businesses will need to arrange the Garage Liability Coverage Form in order to receive specified coverage for losses or damages.

For both types of garage coverage, the exclusions applicable to each of these risks are discussed in a different section of the BAP.

Quick Review Questions

11) Which ISO form MUST be used by all businesses that work with cars?

12) Which of the following risks would NOT be covered by a garage-keepers policy: weather-related events, fires, theft/vandalism, or third-party injuries?

Autos Covered Under Garage Insurance (Section I)

Section I of the Garage Coverage Form lists designation symbols, many of which are similar to those listed on the BAP Form, but they have the number *2* in front of them. Symbols 21 through 29 on the Garage Coverage Form are the same as Symbols 1 through 9 on the Business Auto Policy Form. These designations are listed fully in Table 11.3.

Table 11.3. Auto Designation Symbols Found in the Garage Coverage Form	
21	any auto
22	owned autos only
23	owned private passenger autos only
24	owned autos other than private passenger autos only
25	owned autos subject to no-fault
26	owned autos subject to compulsory uninsured motorists law

Table 11.3. Auto Designation Symbols Found in the Garage Coverage Form	
27	specifically described autos
28	hired autos only (rented, leased, borrowed, or hired by the policy owner, but not autos owned by partners, employees, or members of an LLC)
29	non-owned autos used in a garage business (for vehicles not owned, rented, leased, borrowed, of hired by the policyholder; also applies to vehicles owned by partners, employees, and member of an LLC)
30	autos left for safekeeping, storage, repair, or service (used to provide garage-keepers with coverage for employees or customers their household members who pay for services)
31	dealer's autos (physical damage coverage)

While Symbols 9 and 29, both focus on non-owned autos, the emphasis for Symbol 29 is on non-owned autos used in a garage business. Symbol 30 does not have a comparable symbol on the BAP Form; it is for customers (including employees and members of households) who leave an auto with a garage for service, repair, storage, or safekeeping. Symbol 31 is for a dealer's auto that experiences physical damage while in the garage.

Coverage for newly acquired autos is dependent upon the symbols entered next to a coverage on the Garage Coverage Form. Symbols 21 through 26 indicate that an insured will be granted coverage for all newly acquired autos, so long as those autos are acquired during the policy period; however, Symbol 27 is different. If it is listed on the Garage Coverage Form, insureds will only receive coverage for newly acquired autos if one condition is met: in order to obtain coverage, insureds must tell their insurers within thirty days that they possess newly acquired autos.

According to Section I of the Garage Coverage Form, liability coverage will be extended to trailers designed to travel on public roads. In order for these trailers to be considered covered autos, they must have a load capacity that is less than 2,000 pounds. Additionally, temporary substitutes for covered autos will be covered if the named covered auto on the policy has broken down, is destroyed, or is considered a loss. If the named covered auto on the policy is being repaired or serviced, a temporary substitute will also be eligible for coverage.

Quick Review Questions

13) Are any symbols on the Garage Coverage Form similar to those on the BAP Form?

14) How does the Garage Coverage Form define Symbol 30?

15) Which symbol, if it is listed on the Garage Coverage Form, allows the insured to receive coverage for newly acquired autos?

16) What requirement must a trailer meet in order to qualify as a covered auto under the BAP?

Garage Liability Coverage (Section II)

Garage liability insurance is an umbrella policy, meaning that it provides additional coverage for the daily operations of companies with garage services, particularly those in the automotive industries. Coverage for garage liability insurance is traditionally divided into two parts: commercial auto liability coverage and general liability coverage. On most standard coverage forms, these two divisions will be listed as "garage operations—covered autos" and "garage operations—other than covered autos."

Garage operations—covered autos will pay for bodily injuries or property damages incurred by accidents that result directly from garage operations that involve the use, maintenance, or ownership of covered autos. Garage liability insurance also provides automotive service businesses with coverage against property damages to third-party personal possessions, such as a customer's smartphone.

For example, if an employee at a detailing business was moving a car and accidentally drove over a customer's smartphone, the broken smartphone would likely be covered under garage liability insurance. Likewise, if the employee ran over a customer's toes and the customer needed medical attention, the customer would likely receive a payout under this section of a policy.

The second type of liability coverage, **garage operations—other than covered autos**, on the other hand, will pay for bodily injuries or property damages incurred by accidents that result from garage operations other than the use, maintenance, or ownership of covered autos.

An example of this coverage would be a payout for a customer who breaks his ankle by slipping on unmarked, neglected tools within a garage and has to go to the ER. This coverage will pay for all of the necessary medical costs.

The following entities are typically considered insured under the "Garage Operations—Covered Autos" section of a garage liability policy:

- the primary insured
- any person who is permitted to use a covered auto that is owned, hired, or borrowed
- the owner from whom someone hires or borrows a covered auto
- an employee if the covered auto is owned by that employee or a member of that employee's household
- an employee while using a covered auto not owned, hired, or borrowed by the automotive service business
- someone using a covered auto being worked on in the business of repairing, servicing or selling the covered auto, unless that business falls under "garage operations"
- customers of the automotive service business (only if the customer has no other available insurance)

The following entities are also typically considered insured under the "Garage Operations—Other than Covered Autos" section of a garage liability policy:

- the organization named in the declarations
- directors, officers, or shareholders (but only while acting within the scope of their duties)

- members (if a limited liability company) or partners (if a partnership)
- employees

All automotive service businesses—specifically those that interact often with the public (e.g., dealerships, car repair shops, towing companies, car washes, car detailing businesses, parking garages)—should consider obtaining garage liability insurance.

Supplementary payments and out-of-state coverage extensions for garage liability coverage are handled in the same way as in the BAP. For instance, a policyholder will receive a certain, limited payout for the cost of bail bonds, court proceedings, expenses, or fees resulting from a suit without reducing the limit of the insurance.

The following information is taken from the Insurance Services Office, Inc. (ISO) Standard Forms for BAP and garage coverages. For more details, the original forms should be reviewed. The Garage Coverage Form has seventeen exclusions. Exclusions on the Garage Coverage Form differ slightly from those on the BAP Form. The exclusions may be the same, are mostly the same, or do not appear in either form.

Helpful Hint

Garage liability insurance typically differs according to the specific type of business. For instance, a car wash has different types of exposures than a traditional car detailing business.

Table 11.4. Similarities between Exclusions on BAPs and Garage Liability Policy Forms

Degree of Similarity	Exclusion
Identical wording	• contractual • workers' Compensation • fellow employee • racing • war
Similar wording	• expected or intended injury • employee indemnification • employer's liability • care, custody, or control
Not defined under the BAP	• leased auto • pollution • watercraft or aircraft • defective products • work performed

Table 11.4. Similarities between Exclusions on BAPs and Garage Liability Policy Forms	
Degree of Similarity	**Exclusion**
	• loss of use • products recall • distribution of material
Not defined in the Garage Liability Form	• handling of property • movement of property by mechanical device • operations • completed operations

Generally speaking, the Garage Liability Form's definitions for these exclusions are more detailed in order to account for business-specific scenarios.

The "Limits" portion of Section II is broken up into two categories: garage operations and covered autos.

According to the first category, the following liability coverages will be provided if selected by endorsement:

- personal injury
- personal and advertising injury
- liquor liability
- damage to rented premises
- incidental medical malpractice liability coverage
- non-owned watercraft coverage
- Broad Form products coverage

> **Helpful Hint**
>
> Besides these omissions, perhaps the biggest discrepancy between the two forms is how they each deal with pollution. The BAP Form details the pollution exclusion under a single clause; the Garage Coverage Form separates it into protection for "covered autos" and "other than covered autos."

Any bodily injuries or property damage stemming from one of the incidents listed above will be deemed singular accidents instead of multiple accidents.

The deductible listed on this section of the Garage Coverage Form is also different from the one listed on the BAP Form. Work performed on any auto may have a $100 deduction for any property damage.

Quick Review Questions

17) Name three of the five exclusions that are defined the same way on both the Garage Coverage Form and BAP Form?

18) Are supplementary statements payments and out-of-state coverage extensions for garage liability coverage the same as in the BAP?

19) Which of the following exclusions is not found on the BAP Form: products recall, completed operations, operations, pollution?

20) How does Section II divide up the limits on the form?

Garage-Keepers Coverage (Section III)

Found under Item Five of the garage-keepers Declarations Form and designated by Symbol 30, garage-keepers insurance covers damages or losses to covered autos that are left in the care of another entity for storage, safekeeping, service, or repair purposes. The garage-keepers policy will cover any land motor vehicle that is deemed "auto"; therefore, most garage-keepers policies will also include semi-trailers and trailers.

According to Section III, the insurer bears the right and duty to defend the insured against any legal suit seeking compensation for a covered accident that results in bodily injury or property damage. The accident can only be compensated if it occurs in the coverage territory and the accident occurs during the policy period. The insurer's duty to defend and make payouts ends when the limits of insurance are finally exhausted.

Insureds should be aware that garage-keepers coverage is usually triggered when the designated insured on the policy is found to be legally liable for an incident. In some instances, however, garage-keepers coverage will also be triggered to cover defense costs that accrue in order to disprove a charge.

The Garage-Keepers Coverage Form comes with a list of extensions in which supplementary payments will be offered to the insured. These payments are offered for the following:

- legal expenses
- loss of earnings for up to $250 per day
- court costs
- all interest accrued in a suit against the insured.

Any payouts for legal expenses will not reduce the overall limit of insurance.

The Garage-Keepers Coverage Form has a list of exclusions in which insurance payouts will not be applied. They are similar to those found in the BAP and include the following:

- liability by agreement or contract
- theft or conversion by an insider
- defective parts/materials and faulty work
- sound equipment
- radar
- war

Quick Review Questions

21) What is the definition of the theft or conversion by an insider exclusion?

22) Which type of fees do NOT affect the aggregate limits of the garage-keepers policy?

Coverage Against Physical Damage (Section IV)

The coverage for physical damage on the Garage Coverage Form closely mirrors the coverage for physical damage on the BAP Form, except that Symbol 31 on the Garage Coverage Form extends coverage to "Dealers Autos." Additionally, the BAP Form has a section discussing towing coverages; this section is absent from the Garage Coverage Form. The language is otherwise essentially the same.

The insurer agrees to pay for losses to covered autos or a covered auto's equipment for the following events:

- fire
- lightning
- explosion
- theft
- windstorm
- hail
- earthquake
- mischief
- vandalism
- sinking, burning, collision, or derailment of any conveyance transporting the auto

The insured is required to attach a supplemental schedule to the policy in order to extend coverage for certain risks. For instance, if an insured wants additional glass breakage coverage for an auto dealership, the insured is required to attach a supplementary physical damage schedule to the policy.

Physical damage coverage, which has a deductible, is applied to each of the policyholder's vehicles. Symbol 31 is applied to a declarations page for physical damage coverage for autos held at car dealerships, including those autos that are consigned to certain dealerships. These types of autos are listed on Item Eight of the declarations page.

In Section IV, the insuring agreements for physical damage coverage are the same as those found in the BAP Form.

Additionally, physical damage coverage is offered for glass breakage. This provision is the same as the one detailed in the Business Auto Policy Form. The insurer agrees to pay for the following losses under this provision:

- glass breakage
- losses that result from striking a bird or animal

- losses from falling objects or projectiles

Although many of these losses can technically be defined as collision losses, insurers offer this provision so these incidents can be considered as comprehensive losses. As a result, the insured might have the opportunity for a lower deductible for covered incidents. In most instances, this provision will work in favor of the insured.

The policy's deductibles, which usually range from $500 to $1,000, apply to the insured's chosen coverage: comprehensive, specified cause of loss, or collision. It is important to note that these deductibles will not be applied to each occurrence; instead, they will be applied to each covered auto that is listed.

For instance, if a car dealership has one hundred covered autos, each covered auto maintains its own deductible. In the case of a catastrophic event, such as a flood that causes losses to all one hundred autos parked in the car dealership, the car dealership would be handling one hundred deductibles, which could require them to pay up to $100,000 in deductibles for that one flood.

Most causes of garage physical damage are identical to those found in the BAP "Physical Damage Coverage" section; however, there are five exclusions for garage physical damage that are not identical to those found in the business auto "Physical Damage" coverage section:

- The **auto leased or rented to others** exclusion states that, if physical damage occurs while a covered auto is being leased or rented to others, coverage will not apply.
- The **false pretense** exclusion (i.e., the trick and device exclusion) exists to protect businesses tricked into parting with one or more covered autos.
- The **expected profits** exclusion states that car dealerships will only be reimbursed on a wholesale basis for covered autos.
- The **other locations** exclusion applies to loss or damage to covered autos, which are at locations not shown on the declarations page, so long as the event occurs forty-five days after the insured began using the other location.
- The **transporting autos** exclusion exists for car dealerships. It excludes damage to autos that occurs while being transported or driven from the point of purchase to a final destination. In some instances, additional premiums can be added to void this exclusion and obtain coverage.

Quick Review Questions

23) What does Symbol 31 designate on the Garage Coverage Form?

24) How many exclusions exist in garage physical damage coverage?

25) Which of the following exclusions is NOT listed in Section IV of the Garage Coverage Form: other locations, transporting auto, expected profits, or radar?

26) How many days can pass in order for the other locations exclusion to come into effect?

Garage Conditions (Section V) and Definitions (Section VI)

Most of the loss conditions and general conditions listed on the Garage Coverage Form mirror those listed on the BAP Form; nevertheless, there is one clause in which the forms differ: policy period, coverage territory.

While both forms cover the US, its territories and possessions, Puerto Rico, and Canada, and both also provide options to extend coverage to the entire globe, each form discusses these extensions differently, and the Garage Coverage Form adds additional protection for products sold and transported overseas.

The major difference between the accidents and losses coverages concerning garage operations—other than the "Covered Autos Coverage" section and the "Garage Conditions" section of the Garage Coverage Form—is that the former focuses on *physical* damage losses and physical damage coverages, while the latter focuses on *liability* losses and coverages.

Table 11.5. illustrates the ways in which definitions on the Garage Coverage Form can be compared to those listed on the Business Auto Policy Form.

Table 11.5. Similarities between the Definitions on BAP and Garage Liability Policy Forms
Identical Wording
• accident • auto • bodily Injury • covered pollution cost or expense • diminution • employee • insured • leased worker • pollutants • property damage • suit • temporary worker • trailer
Similar Wording
• insured contract • loss

Table 11.5. Similarities between the Definitions on BAP and Garage Liability Policy Forms
Not Defined Under the BAP
• customer's auto • garage operations • products • work
Not Defined in the Garage Liability Form
• mobile equipment

As Table 11.5. illustrates, most definitions are the same on both the BAP Form and the Garage Coverage Form; however, four terms are not defined on the BAP Form but are defined on the Garage Coverage Form:

- customer's auto
- garage operations, products, and work

Did You Know?

In a garage-keepers policy, anything produced, including repairs or customizations, is considered the product of the business; however, according to this form, advice or warnings about the vehicle are also considered to be a product.

Quick Review Questions

27) Which of the following coverage territories is listed automatically on both the BAP and Garage Coverage Forms: Panama, the Bahamas, Canada, or Mexico?

28) What are the two definitions of products on the Garage Coverage Form?

29) Which of the following definitions is the same on BOTH the BAP and Garage Coverage Forms: work, garage operations, products, or bodily injury?

Chapter Review

Table 11.6. Chapter 11 Review: Business Auto Policies	
Commercial Auto	
Coverage	covers all commercial auto, except garages, trucking companies, and motor carriers
Section I	lists covered autos according to the standard numeric identification
Section II	liability
Section III	physical damage coverage
Section IV	policy conditions
Section V	policy definitions
Garage and Garage-Keepers Policies	
Coverage	covers businesses that regularly care for or store clients' cars
Section I	listing of covered autos
Section II	garage operations liability—protects covered and non-covered autos
Section III	garage-keepers—protects cars left in a garage-keeper's care
Section IV	physical damage to vehicles
Section V	policy conditions
Section VI	policy definitions

Answer Key

1. The five sections listed on the BAP Form are as follows: Section I (Covered Autos), Section II (Liability Coverage), Section III (Physical Damage Coverage), Section IV (Business Auto Coverage Conditions), and Section V (Business Definitions).

2. Symbol 7 is listed under Item Three on a Declarations Form. Symbol 7 is a unique designation because it refers to specifically described automobiles. This means that Symbol 7 covers only those autos that are listed in Item Three of the Declarations Form.

3. Symbol 19 is an additional coverage symbol that might be entered beside the coverage name; it applies to mobile equipment.

4. The three criteria for an insurer that coves pollution spills are as follows: 1) the accident occurred on property that was not rented or owned by the insured, 2) the waste was not directly in or a part of the covered auto, and 3) the spill occurred as a result of the maintenance or use of the covered auto.

5. Operations is a listed exclusion on Section II of the business auto policy (BAP), but the rest can be found in Section III.

6. One exception to the pollution exclusion on Section II of the Business Auto Policy (BAP) Form (BAP) is that insurers will cover fuels, lubricants, and fluids that are released or discharged as a result of faulty manufacturing parts.

7. Electrical breakdowns are excluded according to the wear and tear exclusion in Section III.

8. An insured may choose comprehensive, specified cause of loss, or collision coverage.

9. The general loss conditions in Section IV include appraisal, duties of the insured in the event of a loss, legal action against the insurer, loss payment, and transfer of the rights of recovery.

10. Yes, but only if the insured seeks added worldwide coverage, since Mexico is not listed as a territory that is automatically granted coverage.

11. All businesses that sell, store, or service covered autos are not qualified to use any ISO forms.

12. Third-party injuries would not be covered by a garage-keepers policy since these policies focus on property damage.

13. Symbols 21 through 29 on the Garage Coverage Form are the same as symbols 1 through 9 on the Business Auto Policy Form.

14. Symbol 30 is used to provide garage-keepers coverage for employees' or customers' autos that are left for safekeeping, storage, repair, or service.

15. If Symbol 27 is listed on the Garage Coverage Form, the insured will only receive coverage for newly acquired autos if she notifies the insurance company within thirty days of acquiring the new vehicle.

16. Coverage will only apply to trailers with a load capacity of 2,000 lbs. or less.

17. The Garage Coverage Form and the BAP Form share the same exact policy language for the contractual, workers' compensation, fellow employee, racing, and war exclusions.

18. Supplementary payments and out-of-state coverage extensions for garage liability coverage are the same as in the business auto policy (BAP).

19. Products recall is not found on the Business Auto Policy (BAP) Form; it is only found on the Garage Coverage Form.

20. The limits on the form are described as covering garage operations and covered autos.

21. Any loss or damage resulting from a theft or conversion committed by the insured, the insured's employees, or the insured's shareholders or members will be excluded from coverage.

22. Legal defense fees are not counted against the policy limits.

23. On the Garage Coverage Form, Symbol 31 is applied to a declarations page for physical damage coverage for autos held at car dealerships, including those autos that are consigned to certain dealerships. These types of autos are scheduled on Item Seven of the declarations page.

24. There are five exclusions in garage physical damage coverage: auto leased or rented to others, false pretense, expected profits, other locations, and transporting autos.

25. Radar is not listed on Section IV of the Garage Coverage Form, but it can be found in Section III of the Garage Coverage Form.

26. This exclusion, which applies to car dealerships, excludes coverage for loss or damage to a covered auto which is at a location not shown on the declarations page, so long as the event occurs forty-five days after the insured began using the other location.

27. Canada is listed automatically as coverage territory on both the business auto policy and Garage Coverage Forms.

28. According to the Garage Liability Form, products can be either the goods or products made or sold in a garage business or any advice or warnings made by the insured to a customer.

29. The term *bodily injury* appears on both forms; the other terms are found only on one form.

12. Business Owner Policies

Overview of the Business Owner Policy (BOP)

The **business owner policy (BOP)** provides coverage for property damage to buildings and/or business personal property, as well as liability and business interruption coverage. The BOP bundles several coverages that benefit most businesses, whereas a commercial package policy (CPP), which is designed for larger businesses, allows the owner to pick and choose coverage.

Eligible properties covered by a BOP policy include buildings (owned or rented), additions, and outdoor fixtures. With certain stipulations, the BOP also covers business-owned property or property owned by a third party but kept on the insured property and in the care, custody, and control of the business or the business owner.

Helpful Hint

A big advantage of the BOP is the cost savings of bundling the coverage versus picking individual coverages.

As stated earlier, this policy is designed for small to mid-size businesses that meet specific criteria to qualify. These vary depending on the insurance provider and may include the following:

- business type
- location
- business size
- amount of revenue

Examples can include smaller offices, restaurants, retail stores, and apartment buildings. A BOP does not provide coverage for auto insurance, workers' compensation, or health insurance. Some insurers may not offer BOP coverage for home-based businesses or businesses with more than a hundred employees.

Quick Review Questions

1) What does a BOP typically protect?

2) What is the difference between a BOP and a CPP?

3) For what does the BOP NOT provide coverage?

4) For what does the BOP provide coverage?

5) Name three examples of businesses typically covered by a BOP.

BOP Property Coverage (Section I)

Covered Property

As with most property insurance, BOP coverages apply to any buildings, structures, and/or business personal property described in the declarations page. Buildings and structures can include completed additions, fixtures, permanently installed machinery and equipment, or personal property belonging to the insured and located in apartments, rooms, or common areas furnished by the insured as a landlord. The policy also covers personal property owned by the insured that is used to maintain or service the buildings or structures on the property such as fire extinguishers, outdoor furniture, floor coverings, and certain appliances.

Covered property includes both business personal property that is located inside the insured buildings and out in the open within a certain distance. It can be the insured's property that is used in the business or property of others that is in the care, custody, and control of the insured. Depending on the policy, it can also include tenant improvements and betterments, leased personal property, and exterior building glass, all of which come with certain provisions.

> **Helpful Hint**
>
> The additional BOP coverages are similar to the same items in other types of policies in this book. In general, they cover the same losses and have the same conditions.

Just as with other property policies, certain types of property are not covered, such as aircraft, cars, motor trucks, or other types of vehicles subject to registration. Also excluded are contraband, land, outdoor fences, antennas, trees, shrubs, watercraft, and money (except as provided by optional coverage).

Additional coverages provided by the BOP include the following:

- debris removal
- the preservation of property
- fire department service charges
- collapse
- water damage
- business income
- extra expenses
- pollutant cleanup and removal
- civil authority
- business Income
- electronic data
- interruption of computer operations
- fungi, wet or dry rot

In addition to the previously mentioned causes of loss found in other policies, the BOP includes some special additional protection that business owners might need:

- **money orders and counterfeit money:** There is a $1,000 limit for this coverage, which pays for loss resulting directly from having accepted money or services in exchange for merchandise.
- **forgery or alteration:** This covers payment for up to a $2,500 loss resulting directly from the forgery or alteration of any check, draft, promissory note, or bill of exchange from the insured or their agent or someone impersonating their agent.
- **increased cost of construction:** This coverage provides additional benefits up to $10,000 if there are increased costs to bring that part of the building being repaired up to code. Insured buildings must be covered on a replacement-cost basis for this coverage to apply.
- **glass expenses:** This coverage provides extra funds to cover openings in the building while waiting for repairs to be completed.
- **fire extinguisher systems recharge:** If fire extinguishers are discharged within 100 feet of the described premises due to a covered loss, this coverage will pay up to $5,000 to recharge the extinguishers and repair or replace property that was damaged by the extinguishing chemicals.

Quick Review Questions

6) Provide an example of preservation of property coverage.

7) What is the limit for the increased cost of construction coverage?

8) Which factors might lead to an increased cost of construction?

9) What does the fire extinguisher systems recharge expense cover and not cover?

10) Which coverage protects against out-of-pocket expenses to cover or board up openings before or during the repair or replacement of damaged glass?

11) List examples of properties that are excluded under Section I (Property).

Coverage Extensions

Coverage can be broadened on the BOP by adding extensions to property that is either in or on the property described in the declarations or out in the open as long as it is within 100 feet of the described premises.

Newly acquired or constructed property coverage protects any buildings under construction on the described premises or newly purchased buildings outside of the property but intended to be used for business. This extension of coverage has a limit of $250,000.

The **business personal property** extension includes newly-acquired property located on the business premises; however, it does not include personal property that is acquired for the purpose of performing construction work on the buildings or for wholesale activities. The limit under this coverage is $100,000. This coverage ends either when the policy expires, thirty days after the property is acquired, when construction begins, or when the value is reported to the insurer.

The **personal property off-premises** coverage excludes financial documents, such as money, securities, valuable papers and records, or accounts receivable, but other property can be covered up to $10,000 while in transit or at premises not owned or leased by the insured.

Outdoor property coverage applies to fences, radio and TV antennas/satellite dishes, signs (not attached to buildings), trees, shrubs, and plants, including debris removal expenses. The loss must be caused by a covered peril, such as fire, lightning, explosion, riot or civil commotion, or aircraft. Usually, the limit is $2,500—but not more than $1,000 for any one antenna, tree, shrub, or plant.

The **personal effects** coverage protects against the loss of personal effects owned by the insured, partners, officers, staff, members, or employees up to $2,500 at each premises. As such, it does not apply to tools or equipment used in the business or for loss or damage due to theft.

The **valuable papers and records** extension covers papers and records that the insured owns or that are in his care, custody, or control and are damaged by covered perils. It also provides for the cost to research, replace, or restore the lost information for which duplicates do not exist.

Accounts receivable coverage insures payments due from customers, interest charges on loans, expenses beyond normal collection expenses, and other reasonable expenses incurred to reestablish records of accounts receivable. The limit at the described premises is $10,000 unless there is a higher limit on the declarations. For accounts receivable not at the described premises, the limit goes down to $5,000. There is also some exclusionary language to be reviewed.

Quick Review Questions

12) What does the outdoor property coverage extension include?

13) What is the limit for personal property—off premises coverage?

BOP Coverage Limits and Deductibles

The limit amounts specifically listed under coverage extensions and/or the additional coverages are in addition to the limit of insurance under Section I (Property), which means that they are amounts allowed over and above the limit listed in the declarations page. The following additional coverages are common on the BOP:

- fire department service charge
- pollutant clean-up and removal
- increased Cost of Construction
- business income from dependent properties
- electronic data
- the interruption of computer operations

Not all additional coverages have deductible amounts; however, several do. These are shown in the declarations:

- money and securities
- employee dishonesty
- outdoor signs
- forgery or alteration

> **Did You Know?**
>
> Some policies may include automatic limit increases depending on the time of year in which the loss occurs. When in doubt, it is always best to check the declarations page of the policy.

The optional coverage deductible will not increase the deductible shown in the declarations. In other words, the optional coverage deductible will satisfy whatever the policy deductible is on the declarations. The following additional coverages have no deductible applied to them:

- fire department service charge
- business income
- extra expense
- civil authority
- fire extinguisher systems recharge expense

Quick Review Questions

14) Which additional coverages have NO deductible applied to them?

15) Which coverages are considered additional amounts of insurance, over and above the policy limits listed in the declarations?

16) Which optional coverages can have deductible amounts shown separately in the declarations?

General Conditions and Loss Conditions

There are four property general conditions; they are defined as follows:

- **control of property:** Should anyone other than the insured commit a destructive act or neglect the property, it will not affect the coverage of the policy.
- **mortgage holders:** Any payments owed or made under the coverage for buildings or structures will include any named mortgage companies on the declarations page. If the insured's claim is denied due to not complying with the terms of the policy, the mortgage holder still has the right to receive loss payment.
- **no benefit to bailee:** No other person or company apart from the named insured can benefit from the insured's policy.
- **policy period, coverage territory:** The policy affords coverage under the terms as long as the loss occurs within the policy period and the territory is agreed upon with the insured. The

territory is typically anywhere in the United States, including its territories and possessions, Puerto Rico, and Canada.

Quick Review Questions

17) Which general condition states that no other person other than the insured can benefit from the insured's policy?

18) Under the "mortgage holder" general condition, can the mortgage holder receive any payment for a covered loss if the claim is denied due to the insured not complying with the policy?

19) Which general condition states that the insured's claim will not be affected if someone other than the insured commits an act or neglects the property?

20) What does the policy period, "coverage territory" general condition specify?

Optional Coverages

The BOP offers optional coverages, and they resemble the coverages in other property policies. As with all property policies, the coverage applies as it is listed in the declarations:

- **outdoor signs:** This coverage pays for direct physical loss or damage to all outdoor signs at the described premises owned by the insured or in their care, custody, or control.
- **money and securities:** This protects the insured from the loss of money and securities used in the business while at a bank or savings institution; within the insured's living quarters; while employees have the use of, custody of, or living quarters at the described premises; or during transit and resulting from theft, disappearance, or destruction.
- **employee dishonesty:** This protects against loss resulting from dishonest acts committed by employees.
- **equipment breakdown protection:** This coverage protects against losses to covered property from mechanical breakdown or electrical failure; it does not include malfunction.

Quick Review Questions

21) Which optional coverage covers loss due to an employee's dishonest act?

22) For what does the money and securities optional coverage pay?

Limitations and Exclusions to Coverage of Loss

The BOP insures against risks for direct physical loss to covered property contingent on certain limitations and exclusions discussed below. The policy will not pay for the following:

- damage to steam boilers, pipes, engines, or turbines caused by or as a result of any condition inside the equipment; exception: loss to the equipment caused by an explosion of gases or fuel within the furnace, flues, or passages through which gases of combustion pass
- hot water boilers or other heating equipment caused by a condition inside the equipment other than by explosion
- property that is missing if the only evidence leads to the cause being a shortage when taking inventory or if there is no physical evidence showing what happened to the property
- property that has been transferred to a person or place not on the described premises
- the interior of a covered building or structure if damage caused by rain, snow, sleet, ice, sand, or dust unless the building or structure itself first sustains damage by a covered peril that creates an opening to the roof or walls through which the water, sand or dust can enter

The following types of property damage will have no coverage unless caused by one of the "specific causes of loss" or building glass breakage:

- animals
- fragile property (e.g., glassware, statues, marble, china, or porcelain, if broken

This restriction does not apply to glass of that part of the building or structure, containers of property held for sale, or photographic or scientific instrument lenses.

For losses or damage by theft, the following types of property are covered only up to the following limits:

- $2,500 for furs, fur garments, and garments trimmed with fur
- $2,500 for jewelry, watches, jewels, pearls, precious and semi-precious stones, bullion, gold, silver, platinum, and other precious alloys or metals
    - exception: does not apply to watches or jewelry worth $100 or less per item
- $2,500 for patterns, dies, molds, and forms

The following perils are excluded under BOP unless they result in a covered loss:

- ordinance or law
- movement of the earth
- governmental action
- nuclear hazard
- utility services
- war and military action
- water
- certain computer-related losses
- fungus, wet/dry rot
- virus or bacteria

Helpful Hint

Like other property policies, even if the BOP excludes certain perils, the insurer will pay for any loss caused by a covered peril (e.g., fire, lightning, or wind damage).

- weather conditions
- acts or decisions made by employees
- negligent work

Unlike the previous perils, there is no coverage for loss or damage resulting from the following, which can be reviewed more in depth in the BOP:

- electrical apparatus: artificially generated electrical, magnetic, or electromagnetic energy that damages or interferes with electrical materials, devices, appliances, or systems
- consequential losses: delay, loss of use, or loss of market
- smoke, vapor gas: from agricultural smudging or industrial operations
- steam apparatus: damage from an explosion of steam boilers, pipes, engines, or turbines owned or leased by the insured or operating under their control
    - exception: If any of the above results in damage from fire, coverage may be afforded.
- frozen plumbing: water, other liquids, powder, or molten material that leaks through plumbing, heating, air conditioning, or other equipment caused by freezing; only covered if the insured maintains heat in the building or the equipment is drained and shut off if heat is not maintained
- dishonesty: dishonest or criminal acts on the part of the insured or anyone else with an interest in the property or any of the insured's partners, managers, etc. acting alone or in collusion with others, whether occurring during or after hours; does not apply to the coverage under the employee dishonesty optional coverage.
- false pretense: voluntarily parting with any property if induced to do so by fraudulent scheme, trick, or false pretense
- exposed property: rain, snow, ice, sleet to personal property damaged out in the open
- collapse: collapse, including abrupt falling or caving in, loss of structural integrity, cracking, bulging, sagging, bending, leaning, settling, expanding, or shrinking of property.
    - Certain criteria will afford coverage, such as collapse caused by "specified causes of loss," breakage of building glass, or the weight of rain or people.
- pollution: damage caused by discharge, dispersal, seepage, or the release of pollutants unless caused by a "specified cause of loss"
- neglect: if the insured neglects to use all reasonable means to save or preserve property from further damage
- errors or omissions: in programming, processing, or the storing of data, or the processing or copying of valuable papers and records
- installation, testing, and repair: errors or deficiencies in design installation, testing, maintenance, or repair of the computer system, including data, unless the loss is directly attributed to fire or explosion
- electrical disturbance: magnetic injury, disturbance, or the erasure of electronic data, unless directly caused by lightning

- continuous or repeated seepage or leakage of water: or the presence of condensation of humidity, moisture, or vapor that occurs for fourteen days or more

Additional exclusions apply. If the excluded cause of loss results in a covered cause of loss, the BOP will pay for damage caused by that covered cause of loss.

Quick Review Questions

23) While the owner was away on a skiing vacation, the low temperatures caused a plumbing pipe to crack and leak water all over the interior of his showroom floor. Is there coverage for the carpet?

24) Which types of water losses are EXCLUDED from coverage in the BOP?

25) What does movement of the earth EXCLUDE?

26) Under what condition will the BOP NOT provide coverage for loss or damage from pollution?

27) How many continuous days must water be present for the continuous or repeated seepage or leakage of water exclusion to apply?

28) Seizure or destruction due to an order by a governmental authority is excluded unless it occurs in which situation?

BOP Liability Coverage (Section II)

Coverages

While a commercial general liability (CGL) policy only covers liability losses, a BOP covers both liability and property damage. The "Liability" section of the BOP protects against claims for bodily injury, property damage, and personal and advertising injury; this includes legal defense costs should the insured be pursued for damages by a third party.

The limits for damages are stated in paragraph D under the “Liability and Medical Expense Limits of Insurance” portion of Section II of the policy. As with other professional policies, the insurer’s right and duty to defend ends when the limits of insurance have been exhausted.

The BOP will pay for medical expenses for bodily injury caused by accidents on the premises that the insured owns or rents, on streets next to premises the insured owns or rents, or accidents due to the insured’s business operations. Any accidents must take place both within the coverage territory and the policy period, and damages must be incurred and reported to the insurer within one year of the accident date. The injured person must agree to submit to an examination—at the insurer's expense and by physicians of the insurer's choice—as often as reasonably required.

The payments will be made under this coverage regardless of fault and will not exceed the limits of insurance of Section II (Liability). Expenses include first aid administered at the time of the accident, necessary medical, surgical, X-ray, and dental services, and necessary ambulance, hospital, professional nursing, and funeral services.

Quick Review Questions

29) Name one type of expense covered in the Section II (Liability) portion of the BOP.

30) Which types of medical expenses are included under the medical expenses coverage?

Who is Covered and Coverage Limits

As with other business policies, the idea of who exactly is considered an insured includes more than the organization specifically listed on the declarations. For each type of business, the covered insured includes the people listed Table 12.1.

Table 12.1. Types of Business and Entities Covered on a BOP

Business Type	**Entities Covered**
Sole ownerships	• named insured and spouse/domestic partner
Partnerships or joint ventures	• business partners and their spouses/domestic partners • members
LLCs	• members • managers
Businesses other than partnership, joint venture, or LLC	• executive officers • directors • stockholders
Trusts	• trustees

As with all policies, the limits for Section II (Liability) are listed in the declarations, and they are the most the BOP will pay regardless of the number of insureds, claims made, or suits brought to court. The BOP generally includes the following limits:

- when all bodily injury and property damage included in the products-completed operations hazard is twice the liability and medical expenses limit
- when all bodily injury and property damage, including medical expenses and personal and advertising injuries not included in the products-completed operations hazard, is twice the liability and medical expenses limit

Helpful Hint

Other folks (e.g., volunteer workers, employees, or managers) are also considered insureds, but there are restrictions as to what is covered for each type of employee (e.g., bodily injury or personal and advertising injuries). Each BOP must therefore be reviewed on an individual basis.

- when the "damage to the premises rented to you" limit is the most the BOP will pay for damages to property damage to any one premises while rented to the insured

Quick Review Questions

31) Who is considered an insured under the BOP if the business is designated in the declarations as a partnership or joint venture?

32) How are the insured's executive officers and directors covered?

33) Does the liability and medical expenses limit shown in the declarations cover damage to premises rented to the insured?

General Conditions

The BOP includes general conditions that work the same way as others commonly found in business coverage:

- control of property
- mortgage holders
- no benefit to bailee
- policy period, coverage territory
- duties in the event of an occurrence, offense, claim, or suit
- legal action against us
- separation of insureds

However, there is one condition that does not appear in all business policies, and that is bankruptcy. According to the BOP policy, bankruptcy or insolvency of the insured or their estate does not relieve the insurer's obligation under the policy.

Quick Review Questions

34) What does the "legal action against us" condition specify?

35) If a company declares bankruptcy, will the insurer still provide benefits payments for covered perils?

Exclusions

The following exclusions apply to business liability coverage:

- expected or intended injury or property damage
- liquor liability
- workers' compensation

- employer's liability
- pollution
- aircraft, auto, or watercraft
- mobile equipment
- war
- professional services
- damage to property
- damage to your product
- damage to your work
- damage to impaired property or property not physically injured
- recall of products, work, or impaired property
- personal or advertising injury
- electronic data
- criminal acts
- the recording and distribution of material of information in violation of law

Some of the exclusions do not apply to damage by fire to premises while rented to the insured or temporarily occupied by the insured with permission from the owner. There is a separate coverage that applies to these.

With regard to medical expenses, the BOP will not pay expenses for bodily injury to the following:

- any insured, except volunteer workers
- a person hired to do work for or on behalf of the insured or an insured's tenant
- a person injured on the part of the premises the insured owns or rents that the person normally occupies
- a person, whether or not an employee of the insured, if the benefits for the bodily injury are payable or must be provided under workers' compensation or disability benefits
- a person injured while practicing, instructing, or participating in physical exercises or games, sports, or athletic contests
- those included within the products-completed operations hazard

> **Helpful Hint**
>
> Most of the perils excluded above would be covered under different additional policies (e.g., workers' compensation and employers' liability are covered under workers' compensation policies; professional services coverage can be purchased as a stand-alone policy).

The nuclear energy liability exclusion applies to both business liability coverage and medical expense coverage. This exclusion typically eliminates any coverage for loss or damage from a nuclear reaction or nuclear radiation or contamination; however, there may be coverage for ensuing fire damage. There are a few points to consider about this section of the policy:

- There may be a coverage issue if the insured is also insured under a nuclear energy liability policy.
- There may be a coverage issue if the nuclear material is at any nuclear facility owned or operated by the insured.
- There may be a coverage issue if the nuclear material is contained in spent fuel or waste and at any time handled, used, processed or stored by an insured or on behalf of an insured.

Quick Review Questions

36) What does the liquor liability exclusion mean?

37) Will the BOP pay for injuries to a third party contractor brought in to work at the business?

38) Can the insured's employee claim expenses under the medical expenses coverage?

39) What does the personal or advertising injury exclusion state?

40) Provide an example of when the aircraft, auto, or watercraft exclusion would NOT apply.

41) Name a reason for which the nuclear energy liability exclusion would NOT apply.

BOP Common Policy Conditions (Section III)

Conditions Common to a BOP

The following familiar conditions apply to Section I (Property) and Section II (Liability):

- cancellation
- changes
- concealment, misrepresentation, or fraud
- examination of your books and records
- inspections and surveys
- insurance under two or more coverages
- other insurance
- premiums
- the transfer of rights of recovery against others to us

There are a few conditions that differ from those common to other policies:

- **premium audit:** The policy can be audited if a premium is designated in advance on the declarations page. The final premium will be computed when the insurer determines the actual exposures. The insured must provide the insurer with any records or information needed during the premium computation.

- **transfer of your rights and duties under this policy:** The insured's rights and duties under the policy cannot be transferred without the insurer's consent except in the case of the insured's death. In the event of the insured's passing, the insured's rights and duties will be transferred to his legal representative—but only while acting within the scope of the duties as the insured's legal representative.
- **liberalization:** If the insurer adopts any revisions to the policy which would broaden the coverage under the policy, there is no added premium, and it is done within forty-five days before or during the policy period, the broadened coverage will apply to the policy.

Quick Review Questions

42) What does the "concealment, misrepresentation, or fraud" condition state?

43) Which condition states that if the insurer adopts a revision to the policy which broadens the coverage under the policy, and there is no added premium for that broader coverage, the insured will benefit from the broader coverage?

44) Can an insurer audit a policy?

45) What does the "transfer of your rights and duties under this policy" condition mean?

46) Who can cancel a BOP policy?

47) What happens if a loss is covered by two different coverages under the policy?

Selected Endorsements

The BOP also has some very useful endorsements that can be purchased separately. The **protective safeguards endorsement** provides the insured with credit for having an alarm system, sprinkler system, security service company, or special protective equipment (e.g., hood and duct extinguishing systems in restaurants); however, the insured must maintain whichever protective safeguards are listed in the schedule.

The following two endorsements are available to cover any potential loss suffered by the insured that is not covered by the policy due to the utility services exclusion.

- **Utility services—direct damage** coverage protects property from damage or loss resulting from an interruption by the utility services named in the policy. For example, the loss of refrigerated products due to loss of power off the premises would be covered.
- In contrast, **utility services—time element** covers additional expenses cause by the power loss. In the same example as above, if the restaurant loses power, and it cannot open until the food is replaced, the policy will help to offset the loss of income and extra expenses until it can operate again.

The BOP does not specifically mention the cause of loss of terrorism. The sections covering war and military action do not discuss terrorism either. Before September 11, 2001, commercial policies excluded damage from terrorism. The passage of the **Terrorism Risk Insurance Act (TRIA)** of 2002 voided any exclusions then in force on commercial properties and led to the creation of other terrorism endorsements that provide different coverage options from which the insured can select. The US Department of the Treasury defines an act of terrorism as "a violent act driven by the desire of an individual or individuals to coerce US civilians or the government."

Quick Review Questions

48) Lightning hits a transformer off premises, causing the insured's air conditioning to break down. The claim is denied based on the utility services exclusion. Is there an endorsement to gain coverage back?

49) A tree fell on electrical lines outside a salon, causing a blackout throughout the neighborhood that lasted two days. The claim is denied based on the utility services exclusion. Is there an endorsement that will cover the insured's loss of income?

50) What does the protective safeguards endorsement provide or exclude?

51) Is an act of terrorism covered?

Chapter Review

Table 12.2. Chapter 12 Review: Business Owner Policies	
Purpose	• for small to medium-sized businesses • prepackaged policy containing both property and liability coverages • coverage is included in a package policy that cannot be excluded by the insured
Eligible businesses	• apartments • office buildings • mercantile/processing/service establishments • contractors (certain types) • convenience stores • fast-food restaurants
Optional coverages	• *outdoor signs:* All outdoor signs owned or in the control, custody, or care of the insured can be covered. • *money and securities:* The loss of money and securities resulting from disappearance, theft, or destruction can be covered. • *employee dishonesty:* The loss to money and securities or business personal property that results from the dishonest acts of employees is covered. • *equipment breakdown protection:* This coverage protects against a direct loss or damage to covered property resulting from a mechanical breakdown or electrical failure to mechanical, pressure, or electrical equipment and machinery.

ANSWER KEY

1. The business owner policy (BOP) typically protects a business against loss or damage to property (both buildings/structures and personal property), business interruption, and liability.

2. The business owner policy (BOP) bundles several common coverages needed by smaller businesses, whereas commercial package policies (CPPs) allow owners to select the specific coverages they need to protect their businesses.

3. The BOP does NOT provide coverage for autos, workers' compensation, or health insurance.

4. The BOP provides coverage for buildings or structures (rented or owned by the insured), permanent additions, outdoor fixtures, and others' property when in possession of the business.

5. Businesses typically covered by a BOP include restaurants, travel agencies, and hair salons.

6. Preservation of property coverage allows the insured to temporarily move his property to a different location to protect it if it is in the path of a covered peril, such as a fire. If the fire changes paths unexpectedly and causes damage to the temporary location, the insured can claim the damage to the property.

7. The limit for the increased cost of construction coverage is $10,000 per building. This limit is above and beyond the policy limit for structures listed on the declarations page.

8. Increased costs of construction often occur when a building must be repaired and requires additional construction to bring it up to a new code.

9. The fire extinguisher systems recharge expense covers recharging or replacing fire extinguishers or extinguishing systems if they are discharged within 100 feet of the described premises, along with any damage to property resulting from the discharge of chemicals from the extinguishers.

10. The glass expenses coverage will pay for expenses to board up an opening until the repair or replacement of the glass is possible.

11. Contraband, land, outdoor fences, antennas, trees, shrubs, watercraft, and money (except as provided by optional coverages) are not protected under Section I (Property).

12. The outdoor property coverage extension covers fences, radio, and TV antennas/satellite dishes, signs (not attached to buildings), trees, shrubs, and plants, including debris removal expenses.

13. Personal property—off premises coverage provides for up to $10,000 in replacement costs.

14. Fire department service charges, business income, extra expenses, civil authority, and fire extinguisher systems recharge expenses coverages do not have deductibles.

15. Fire department service charges, business income, extra expenses, civil authority, and fire extinguisher systems recharge expenses are all in addition to the policy limits listed in the declarations.

16. Optional coverages that can have deductible amounts shown separately in the declarations include money and securities, employee dishonesty, outdoor signs, and forgery and alteration.

17. The "no benefit to bailee" general condition states that no other person other than the insured can benefit from the insured's policy.

18. If the insured's claim is denied due to not complying with the terms of the policy, the mortgage holder still has the right to receive loss payment.

19. The "control of property" general condition states that the insured's claim will not be affected if someone other than the insured commits an act or neglects the property.

20. The policy period, "coverage territory" general condition states that the policy will pay benefits as long as the loss or damage takes place during the policy period and within the territory agreed upon with the insured.

21. The employee dishonesty optional coverage covers loss from dishonest acts committed by an employee acting alone or in collusion with someone else other than the insured.

22. This coverage pays for the loss of money and securities used in the insured's business while at a bank or savings institution, within the insured's living quarters, or any employee having use or custody of the property at the described premises or during transit between any of the places mentioned above. The loss must result directly from theft, disappearance, or destruction.

23. There is coverage provided for property damage caused by frozen pipes as long as the insured maintains heat in the building, or if not heated, the insured has drained all plumbing or equipment.

24. Damage caused by flood, surface water, waves, tides, mudslides, backup water, sewer water, water coming from under the ground, or waterborne material are excluded from business owner policy (BOP) coverage. This type of coverage is offered through the National Flood Insurance Program (NFIP).

25. Movement of the earth excludes damage from earthquakes, landslides, mine subsidence, earth sinking, or volcanic eruption; however, if the earth's movement results in fire or explosion from any of the first four causes of loss, the BOP will pay for loss or damage caused by the fire or the explosion.

26. The business owner policy (BOP) will not provide coverage for loss or damage from pollution unless it is the result of a specified cause of loss (e.g., fire, hail, explosion, smoke, lightning, riot, or any other causes listed in the "Definitions" section of the BOP).

27. The repeated seepage or leakage of water must be ongoing for fourteen continuous days or more in order for the exclusion to apply.

28. If the governmental authority were trying to prevent the spread of a fire, it would be covered under the BOP.

29. Medical expenses for bodily injury caused by an accident on premises that the insured owns or rents, on streets next to premises owned or rented by the insured, or accidents due to the insured's business operations are all covered in the Section II (Liability) portion of the business owner policy (BOP).

30. All medical expenses and funeral services are included up to the policy limit.

31. The insured, members, partners, and spouses are all considered insureds concerning the conduct of a business.

32. If designated in the declarations as an organization other than a partnership, joint venture, or LLC, the insured's executive officers and directors are insureds with regard to their duties as officers and directors. Stockholders are also insureds concerning their liabilities as stockholders.

33. No, the most the BOP will pay for damage to premises rented to the insured is the applicable "damage to premises rented to you" limit shown in the declarations.

34. The "legal action against us" condition specifies that no insured can sue an insurer for payment of damages from the insurer's policy unless there has been compliance with all of the terms of the policy.

35. The insurer cannot refuse to pay a valid claim, even if the insured files for bankruptcy.

36. The liquor liability exclusion means that coverage for liability claims is excluded if the insured is held responsible or liable for causing or contributing to the intoxication of a person.

37. The BOP does not cover third parties who are brought in to facilities for a specific job, such as repairing the copy machine. (The contractor's employer's workers' comp coverage should pay for any injuries sustained while on the job.)

38. An employee of the insured cannot claim expenses under the medical expenses coverage if the benefits for the bodily injury are payable under workers' compensation or disability benefits.

39. The personal or advertising injury exclusion states that there is no coverage if the injury is caused by the direction of the insured, who was aware that the act would deliberately violate someone's rights.

40. The aircraft, auto, or watercraft exclusion would not apply to a watercraft while ashore on premises the insured owns or rents, if the insured does not own the watercraft, and if the watercraft is less than 51 feet long and not being used to carry persons or property for a charge.

41. The nuclear energy liability exclusion typically eliminates any coverage for loss or damage from a nuclear reaction, nuclear radiation, or nuclear contamination; however, there may be coverage for ensuing fire damage.

42. The "concealment, misrepresentation, or fraud condition" states that if the insured commits a fraudulent act or intentionally conceals or misrepresents the facts of the business, the policy does not owe for any potential losses.

43. The condition described is called the "liberalization" condition.

44. The "premium audit" condition states that the policy can be audited if a premium is designated in advance on the declarations page. The final premium will be computed when the insurer determines the actual exposures. The insured must provide the insurer with any records or information needed during the premium computation.

45. This policy condition states that the insured's rights and duties cannot be transferred to anyone without the insurer's consent unless the insured dies, in which case the insured's rights and duties will be transferred to her legal representative.

46. As with other insurance policies, according to the "cancellation" condition, the insurer and the first named insured can cancel the policy.

47. If a loss is covered by two different coverages under the policy, the "insurance under two or more coverages" condition states that if two or more of the policies' coverages apply to the same loss or damage, the insurer will not pay more than the actual amount of the loss or damage.

48. The utility services—direct damage endorsement can provide coverage.

49. The utility services—time element endorsement allows the insured to claim loss of income while the salon was closed for two days.

50. The protective safeguards endorsement states that the insured can acquire a credit on her policy premium if she has certain safety equipment or systems in place for the business; however, the insured must maintain the protective safeguards listed in the schedule for the coverage to remain in place.

51. The terrorism endorsement can be attached to a business owner policy (BOP).

Practice Test

1. When is subrogation possible on a claim?

A) when the insurance company can subrogate any payments made out on a claim when the insured is at fault for causing an accident

B) when the policy lists it as a named peril

C) when the loss does not meet the insured's deductible

D) when there is an opportunity for an insurance company to recoup the cost of a claim from a third party that is found to be liable for the loss

2. Which of the following answer options concerning the four elements of a contract is correct?

A) legal purpose: Contracts must be legally enforceable by the law. (E.g., An agreement with a drug dealer is not a legal contract because buying and selling drugs is illegal.)

B) offer of acceptance: One party to the contract makes a written promise to do something or stop doing something in the future.

C) consideration: This is the value that both parties get from the contract. (E.g., If the insured pays the insurer the deductible, the insurer will pay the insured for the repairs to the insured's vehicle.)

D) competent parties: Contract law states that only competent parties can enter into a legal contract. (E.g., Any persons under the age of twenty-five must have a cosigner.)

3. Dwelling policies would be appropriate for which of the following?

A) dwellings that are owner-occupied, tenant-occupied, or both

B) buildings with up to four residential units

C) mobile homes that are secured to the ground with a permanent foundation

D) seasonal dwellings that are vacant more than six months per year

4. Which of the following statements is true?

A) The main part of a homeowners insurance policy is the property coverage to the buildings only.

B) People live in various types of residences covered by home insurance (e.g., single-family homes, townhomes, condos, or mobile homes).

C) Tenant or renter's insurance policies (HO-4) are not considered homeowners policies due to the home not being owned by the person living in it.

D) Factors affecting homeowners insurance rates and premiums include the current economy and the tax bracket the insured is in.

5. What are the requirements for a mobile home to be eligible for a mobile home policy?

   A) It must be at a fixed location and only moved in the event of an impending emergency that threatens the dwelling.

   B) It must be designed for year-round living and have adequate systems for heating, cooling, electricity, and plumbing.

   C) It must be located in a residential trailer park.

   D) The mobile home must be a double-wide design.

6. What is the definition of the term *tort liability*?

   A) an obligation to indemnify a municipality

   B) contractual liability of the insured

   C) liabilities imposed by the law in the absence of a contract of agreement

   D) a licensing agreement that outlines specific liabilities

7. Which of the following are the parts of a CPP?

   A) the insuring agreement, declarations, and common policy conditions

   B) coverage parts, additional coverages, and coverage extensions

   C) exclusions and causes of loss

   D) A, B, and C

8. Which types of vehicles can be covered under personal auto policies?

   A) trucks, trailers, and vehicles used to service a property

   B) passenger cars, newly acquired vehicles, trucks, and vans

   C) passenger cars only

   D) trucks, vans, trailers, and commercial vehicles

9. What is the difference between scheduled and unscheduled property?

   A) Scheduled property requires an extra premium; unscheduled property does not.

   B) Scheduled property is itemized; unscheduled property is not.

   C) The business owns scheduled property; unscheduled property is the property of someone else.

   D) Scheduled property will be added at a future date; unscheduled property is not covered.

10. Which statement regarding insurance policy structure is correct?

A) "Endorsements": An endorsement amends the terms of an insurance policy, and it will state what is or is not covered and to what degree. Insurance carriers may charge extra premiums for endorsements.

B) "Conditions": Insurers place certain conditions which must be followed in order for claims to be paid. If the conditions are not met, the insured does not have to pay the premium.

C) "Declarations": This section provides a one-page summary of the information in the insured's policy, such as the expiration date, insured name(s), excluded property, premiums, and Social Security number(s).

D) "Exclusions and Policy Limits": Exclusions state what the policy will cover; policy limits refer to the minimum amount a particular coverage will pay for a loss.

11. Why must a loss be considered accidental as a condition for a risk to be insurable?

A) because it means that the insured did not deliberately cause the loss to happen

B) because if there is too much uncertainty, the risk will be considered uninsurable

C) because the amount will be small enough to make it financially worthwhile for the insurance company to want to insure it

D) because if the loss is deliberately caused by a stranger, it might not be insurable

12. How are workers' compensation premiums calculated?

A) based on the number of employees

B) through insurers applying a rating bureau classification to each $100 of an employer's payroll

C) based on the total amount of payroll

D) based on the industry classification

13. Which of the following statements is true?

A) Some forms include named perils or broad perils; other forms include open perils.

B) Certain general exclusions are common to all homeowners policy forms.

C) Homeowners policies are similar to dwelling policies in that they all offer the same named peril coverages.

D) All homeowners policies are designed to insure residences that are occupied by the owners and their family members.

14. What choices do farmowners policyholders have for causes of loss forms?

A) basic only

B) basic or broad only

C) special only

D) basic, broad, or special

15. The DP-1 basic policy does NOT include coverage for which of the following?

A) fire, smoke, and lightning

B) wind

C) movement of the earth

D) damage caused by a vehicle or aircraft

16. Which type of vehicle does a business auto policy NOT cover?

A) company-owned autos and trucks

B) vehicles leased by employees

C) vehicles the company hires or leases

D) personal vehicles owned by employees and being used for company business

17. Business owner policies are designed for which types of businesses?

A) large corporate businesses

B) small and mid-sized businesses

C) nonprofit and religious organizations

D) businesses that have representatives who travel

18. How are claims for equipment breakdown settled?

A) at actual replacement cost

B) at actual cash value

C) by the most cost-effective means to replace the equipment with a similar kind and quality

D) A and C

19. Which part of a business auto policy protects managers who assign employees to transport goods, services, or harmful substances?

A) the severability clause

B) the omnibus clause

C) limitations of liability

D) exclusions

20. An insurance contract does NOT include a provision or clause for which of the following?

 A) other insurance: This clause states which insurance policy covers what when more than one insurance policy covers a loss.

 B) proof of loss: This legal document describes the property that has been damaged or stolen and the value of that property.

 C) flooding: This is a peril that is typically excluded from policies.

 D) mortgagee rights: These grant protection to mortgage companies that have financial interests in properties and are named as additional insureds on policies.

21. Which of the following types of damage is NOT covered under "other than collision"?

 A) hitting an animal

 B) a crack in the windshield

 C) an accident in an intersection

 D) a fallen tree limb

22. Which of the following would be covered under an earthquake insurance policy?

 A) the structure of a home, its contents, and the costs of emergency repairs

 B) the structure of the home and its contents only

 C) the cost of emergency repairs only

 D) the structure only

23. Which of the following answers below BEST illustrates the law of large numbers?

 A) The Law of Large Numbers is not an accurate way for insurers to help manage risk.

 B) The more data points someone has, the more likely that person's results will be close to the average.

 C) The law of large numbers allows insurance underwriters to make predictions based on future data.

 D) Higher deductibles lessen the chance that an insured will make a claim.

24. Inland marine insurance was developed as an offshoot of which other type of insurance?

 A) cargo insurance

 B) sea insurance

 C) ocean marine insurance

 D) freight insurance

25. Which of the following corresponds with the HO-5: Comprehensive Form?

A) It is the most expensive of the forms.

B) It covers the owner of the individual unit.

C) It is used for dwellings that insurers feel are too risky to insure.

D) It covers older structures or structures with custom features.

26. Why is a DP-1 policy the least expensive?

A) because it excludes coverage on a named peril basis only

B) because the Broad Form only covers fire, lightning, or internal explosion

C) because it provides the most limited coverage

D) because it does not allow any other options

27. Which of the following statements about workers' compensation insurance is FALSE?

A) Employers in every state must cover all full- and part-time employees.

B) Certain states have set up state funds from which employers must purchase workers' compensation insurance.

C) In some states, employers do not have to purchase workers' compensation insurance for entertainers, commercial fishermen and fisherwomen, or real estate agents.

D) States can often exempt employees from having workers' compensation insurance if the employees do not work a set schedule or number of hours.

28. Which of the following types of coverage is NOT part of a business owner policy?

A) general liability

B) business property

C) business auto coverage

D) business interruption coverage

29. The loss settlement clause in the "Conditions" section of a policy does NOT describe which of the following?

A) whether it will pay the cost to repair or replace covered property

B) how insurers determine how much money they are required to pay insureds for losses

C) how certain property will be paid based on an actual cash-value basis or a replacement cost value without a deduction for depreciation

D) the coverage and limits afforded by ordinance and law

30. Which of the following is NOT a common policy condition for a commercial package policy?

A) cancellation

B) having four or more coverage forms

C) examination of books and records

D) transfer of rights and duties

31. A driver with a PAP purchased the state minimum limits of $20,000 per person and $40,000 per accident. The driver struck another car causing $25,000 damage to that car. How much would the insurer pay the other driver for the loss?

A) $25,000

B) $20,000

C) $40,000

D) $45,000

32. A garage-keepers insurance policy is designed for what purpose?

A) insuring vehicles that are in the care, custody, and control of an insured who sells, stores, or services covered autos

B) insuring vehicles against weather-related events

C) insuring vehicles against theft and vandalism

D) all of the above

33. Which description BEST characterizes a speculative risk?

A) It is covered by insurance.

B) It involves the likelihood of a future loss beyond the control of the individual or organization facing the risk.

C) Some examples of speculative risk include sickness and death.

D) It involves the possibility of a profit or a loss.

34. Which of the following is true about a watercraft policy?

A) The limit for adding a watercraft endorsement to a homeowner policy is usually high.

B) A watercraft endorsement to a homeowner policy offers more comprehensive coverage than a standalone watercraft policy.

C) A watercraft endorsement covers personal watercrafts (e.g., Jet Skis).

D) A watercraft endorsement covers liability, medical payments, and a small amount of coverage for the vessel.

35. Which of the following named peril is covered under the DP-1: Option 1 Form?

   A) vandalism and malicious mischief

   B) aircraft

   C) freezing

   D) collapse

36. Which statement regarding the underwriting process is INCORRECT?

   A) The underwriting process helps insurers assess the information they are gathering to determine whether applicants are eligible for certain types of policies.

   B) The underwriting process helps insurers assess whether applicants committed insurance fraud by having their special investigative departments identify suspicious claims as long as they are discovered before any claim payments are made.

   C) The underwriting process helps insurers assess the amounts of risks they are insuring.

   D) The underwriting process helps insurers assess whether claims should be denied for fraud, even if the application was already approved and a policy is in force.

37. Which of the following is considered a MAIN type of business insurance in a CPP?

   A) commercial property and business income insurance

   B) liability and business income insurance

   C) commercial property, business income, and liability insurance

   D) commercial auto liability and commercial property insurance

38. Who are the parties to a bond?

   A) the business owner, a vendor, and the insurance company

   B) the promisor and the promisee

   C) the obligee, the surety, and the principal

   D) the insurance company, the business owner, and the beneficiary

39. A fire broke out at a small retail store causing damage to the interior, exterior, inventory, and fixtures. Which types of property would be covered under a business owner policy?

   A) only the interior and exterior of buildings described on the declarations

   B) the interior and exterior of the building, inventory, and fixtures

   C) only the inventory

   D) the interior and exterior of the building and the inventory, but not the fixtures

40. Which of the following statements about windstorm coverage is FALSE?

    A) Loss due to a windstorm may be excluded from policies where wind damage has caused major destruction in the past.
    B) If the cause of loss of wind is excluded, homeowners cannot purchase coverage for it elsewhere.
    C) The deductible for a wind policy is usually a percentage of the dwelling coverage amount.
    D) Wind coverage may only be in force during certain conditions.

41. Which statement below is true regarding Coverage A?

    A) Coverage A includes structures attached to the dwelling unless they are construction materials not yet forming the completed building.
    B) Coverage A includes detached garages and pools if they are on the same property as the dwelling.
    C) With an HO-4 policy, there is no Coverage A because the policy only provides renter's insurance that protects the renter's possessions.
    D) Coverage A for an HO-6 policy does not cover alterations, appliances, fixtures, or improvements inside the condo unit.

42. Which provision relating to appraisal and arbitration is accurate?

    A) The appraisal clause is found in the "Conditions" section of a policy and is used as a method to determine the dollar amount of a covered loss when the insurer and the insured cannot agree.
    B) An appraisal is used to determine whether a loss is covered or excluded by a policy.
    C) Arbitration is a process of litigation by which an insured and an insurer resolve a dispute.
    D) In a binding arbitration, both parties agree that the decision made by the arbitrator can be appealed through an appraisal.

43. Inland marine policies cover which type of equipment?

    A) portable property
    B) fixed property
    C) portable and fixed property
    D) all property located on the business premises

44. Which of the following acts are NOT covered under personal injury?

    A) libel and slander
    B) copyright infringement
    C) wrongful eviction
    D) physical harm to an individual

45. Which of the following descriptions for hazards is accurate?

A) Physical hazards involve actions taken by the insured that increase the risk of damage caused by tripping, falling or breaking a leg.

B) Ethical hazards are based on moral actions taken by insureds to ensure the safety of their property and any person(s) on their property.

C) A hazard is something that could happen that would have an accompanying financial cost.

D) Moral hazards relate to the insured's buildings or grounds and might include broken floorboards or wind-blown trees.

46. Which statement below is true regarding Coverage B?

A) Buildings and other items are considered "other structures" if they are not attached to the ground but are separated by a clear space from the main dwelling.

B) Structures connected only by a fence or utility line are not covered.

C) Other structures are always some form of a building.

D) Other structures include sheds, detached gazebos, detached guest houses, and detached garages.

47. Which of the following is NOT excluded from a personal auto insurance policy?

A) vehicles designed for racing, competing, or practicing for any speed contest

B) vehicles with less than four wheels

C) a newly purchased vehicle

D) a vehicle designed for off-road use

48. Which statement regarding the DP-2 Broad Policy is true?

A) The peril of the weight of snow, sleet, or ice covers buildings, foundations, and awnings as well as contents inside a building when it is damaged by the weight of snow, sleet, or ice.

B) Lawns, trees, shrubs, and plants are covered by a list of specific named perils only, not including wind or hail, and there is a limit for the coverage of 10 percent of the Coverage A limit of $250 per any one tree, shrub, or plant.

C) The peril of freezing applies to the freezing of plumbing, HVAC, fire protective sprinkler systems, or household appliances—but only if care was used to maintain heat in the building or the water supply was shut off and drained.

D) Damage by burglars is not covered under the DP-2: broad policy.

49. If a business owner borrows a vehicle from a friend while his car is in the shop being repaired, which type of auto policy would provide the coverage?

A) the business owner's business auto policy

B) a hired, non-owned policy

C) a garage-keepers liability policy

D) the vehicle owner's policy

50. Which of the following statements about workers' compensation policies is FALSE?

A) Workers who are insured under the Federal Employers' Liability Act have a right to sue their employer if the employer is negligent.

B) In most cases, workers who are covered under a workers' compensation policy do not have the right to sue their employers.

C) Workers can choose whether they want to be covered under workers' compensation or the Federal Employers' Liability Act.

D) Workers covered under a workers' compensation policy may sue their employer if there was an incorrect assessment or if the employer acted in bad faith.

51. Which of the following duties after a loss MUST the named insured follow?

A) The insurance company must send a completed proof of loss statement to the insured within a certain time frame.

B) The condition to protect the property only applies to losses due to theft.

C) The insured must make an inventory of the damaged or lost property.

D) The insured must request an appraisal within twenty days after filing a claim.

52. An explosion occurred in a small factory that had an all-risk BOP policy with replacement cost coverage. The business owner learns that the local building codes require that the electrical system be updated to bring it up to code. How much will the business owner policy pay for the upgrade?

A) up to $10,000

B) nothing, as the increased cost of construction is not covered under a business owner policy

C) the full increased cost of construction

D) nothing, as systems used to service a building are not covered

53. A mobile home is valued at $100,000 and the deductible is $500. There is a shed adjacent to the mobile home which is valued at $8,000. If the shed caught on fire, how much would the insurer pay for the loss?

A) $7,500

B) Nothing; sheds are not covered.

C) $8,000

D) $4,000

54. A business owner experienced a cyberattack that shut down the company's computer network. Upon filing a claim for cyber liability, the business owner learns that she has coverage for repairs to hardware and software only. Which type of cyber liability did the business owner purchase?

A) first-party coverage

B) second-party coverage

C) third-party coverage

D) data breach coverage

55. Which statement below is true regarding Coverage C?

A) Personal property is often referred to as anything that can be picked up and carried out of the residence.

B) The personal property coverage on a homeowners policy only covers personal property at the address listed on the declarations page.

C) Personal property belonging to a guest or residence employee who is in a residence occupied by the insured is not covered by the HO-6.

D) Homeowners policies cover animals, birds, fish, motor vehicles and their parts, and the property of other tenants—except property belonging to relatives of the insured.

56. Which of the following can be insured under an inland marine insurance policy?

A) signage on the business premises

B) a fixed generator on the business premises

C) cash registers

D) personal computers, fine jewelry, and coins

57. Which event triggers coverage for a builder's risk policy?

A) when materials have been moved to the jobsite

B) when the owner and contractor agree it will end

C) when the project receives a certificate of occupancy

D) any of the above answers, depending on how the policy is written

58. What does the term *indemnity* mean?

A) Indemnification means that insureds are paid for covered damage to their property without any limits.

B) The insurer's indemnity is the amount of compensation owed for damage or loss to insured property, not to exceed the limit of liability on the policy.

C) Insurance companies need to limit their financial liability to remain solvent by placing limits on policies that they can exceed.

D) Any amount paid out for damage by the insured cannot exceed the insured's deductible.

59. Of the three dwelling policies, how does the DP-3: Special Policy provide the broadest coverage and have the highest premiums?

A) It covers an additional six named perils that are not listed in the DP-1 or DP-2 policies.

B) It covers all perils unless the perils are specifically excluded from the policy.

C) Premiums are based on the number of perils that are covered in each policy.

D) It provides coverage for floods, which are the costliest types of losses.

60. What is the definition of the term *subrogation*?

A) an insured who has two policies that cover the same incident

B) when the insured is required to help an insurance company recover any money paid out for a claim and the insured must hold any money received from another carrier until the case is settled and the insurance company receives its money

C) the inability of an insured to bring legal action against a carrier

D) the requirement of the carrier to provide coverage for the insured's surviving partner or legal representative

61. At what point does an insurance carrier's duty to settle or defend end?

A) when the limits of liability have been exhausted

B) when all medical bills and invoices for damage to the other parties have been paid

C) when all cars involved have been repaired

D) when the policy term ends

62. What is a binder?

A) a common term for failing to disclose information—intentionally or not—that is pertinent to the terms of the contract or would affect the other party's financial consideration to enter into the contract

B) a promise to indemnify the receiving party if a representation turns out to be false

C) a factual statement the receiving party can rely on that influences them to enter into a contract (e.g., a statement about the value of the vehicle the company will insure)

D) a temporary insurance contract that provides insurance until the permanent policy is in force

63. Why is water backup coverage EXCLUDED from a business owner policy?

A) It is too expensive.

B) The local fire department has insurance for damage caused by water.

C) It is covered by flood insurance.

D) Pollutant cleanup and removal is a separate type of coverage.

64. A company filed a claim for theft after an employee stole $500 out of a cash register. The business owner stated that the loss occurred during the policy period, so the insurance carrier paid the claim. Which type of policy does the employer have?

A) a discovery-based policy

B) a loss-sustained policy

C) an employee dishonesty/employee theft policy

D) B and C

65. A car dealership employee asked the business owner if she may borrow a car to use in a speed race, and the business owner grants permission. The employee gets into a collision during the race and the borrowed car is a total loss. How much will the business auto policy pay for the loss?

A) the actual cash value of the car

B) nothing, because the driver is not considered an insured

C) nothing, because racing cars is excluded on a business auto policy

D) the replacement cost of the car

66. Which of the following statements about the deductibles on a business owner policy is FALSE?

A) Optional coverage deductibles for additional coverages such as money/securities, outdoor signs, and employee dishonesty will be shown on the Declarations page.

B) An optional coverage deductible must be paid in addition to the policy deductible.

C) No deductible applies to recharging fire extinguisher systems.

D) No deductible applies to business income.

67. Which statement below is true regarding Coverage D?

A) The additional living expenses coverage pays for the necessary increase in living expenses the insured incurs so that the household can maintain its normal standard of living while the home is uninhabitable.

B) The policy covers costs such as eating out, doing laundry outside of the home, and expenses for extra mileage to travel to work for up to three years.

C) The fair rental value coverage protects tenants but does not cover any loss of rent for insured landlords when they are unable to have tenants due to the home being uninhabitable.

D) If a civil authority prohibits insureds from staying in their homes as a result of direct damage to a neighboring location by a peril covered in the policy, the insureds can claim the out-of-pocket expenses incurred while living away from their home for no more than six weeks.

68. Which of the following statements is TRUE about filed inland marine coverage forms?

A) The range of coverages is virtually limitless.

B) Insurance companies typically use them to market policies to their customers.

C) The policies and rates vary significantly.

D) They are reviewed and approved by state departments.

69. A builder's risk insurance policy is designed for which type of insured?

A) commercial contractors only

B) homeowners, house flippers, and contractors

C) home renovators and house flippers only

D) house flippers only

70. Which of the following is true about a first-named insured?

A) A first-named insured is as equally covered by the insurance policy as an additional insured.

B) A first-named insured is someone who is listed first on the policy and is responsible for the payments of premiums.

C) A first-named insured must perform certain duties listed in the policy, such as notifying the police on all claims regardless of how the loss occurred.

D) A first-named insured should provide the insurer with an inventory of damaged property if it is valued over $500.

71. A tax accountant was sued for giving a client bad advice that caused her to lose a significant amount of money. Which type of commercial policy would cover the loss if the tax accountant had purchased it?

A) commercial general liability

B) professional liability

C) business interruption insurance

D) business owner's policy

72. Which of the following items are NOT included under commercial property building coverage?

A) completed additions

B) commercial autos that are parked over 100 feet from the premises

C) underground pipes

D) permanently installed machinery and equipment

73. Which answer option BEST describes an insurance policy?

A) an agreement where the insurer indemnifies the insured for a financial loss as long as it meets the majority of the policy terms

B) an agreement that provides financial protection for individuals or businesses by increasing the financial risk associated with expected events

C) an agreement between two parties to provide a total financial benefit for a specified loss, injury, or illness

D) an agreement that is set out in a contract, called an insurance policy, which outlines the terms, conditions, and scope of coverage

74. Which dwelling policy covers ONLY the basic named perils?

A) All dwelling policies cover any potential hazard.

B) the DP-3

C) the DP-1

D) the Dp-2

75. An auto policy reads $100,000/$300,000/$100,000 under the "Liability" section. What does the $300,000 number refer to?

A) the policy limit for damage to the claimant's vehicle

B) the policy limit for bodily injury for all injured claimants per vehicle, per accident for care, loss of services, or death

C) the policy limit for bodily injury per person, per accident for care, loss of services, or death

D) the policy limit for uninsured motorist coverage

76. Strong winds damaged the dock door of a warehouse. The storm was accompanied by surface flooding. Waters entered the warehouse through the door, which was damaged by the wind. Would this loss be covered under a business owner policy?

A) No; flooding is not covered under any circumstances on a business owner policy.

B) Yes; although flooding is excluded, it is covered because it would not have happened if the wind damage had not occurred first.

C) No; all types of water damage are excluded on a business owner policy.

D) Yes; flooding is covered as a cause of loss on a business owner policy.

77. Which of the following coverages is NOT part of a cyber liability insurance policy?

A) libel and slander

B) the replacement or restoration of data coverage

C) cyber extortion coverage

D) website publishing liability

78. A group of visitors scheduled time to tour a factory. All visitors were required to wear steel-toed shoes before starting the tour. One visitor did not follow the rules and his foot was injured when a piece of equipment fell on it. The medical bills were limited to an ambulance ride and an emergency room visit. Would this incident be covered by the liability portion or the medical payments portion of a business owner policy?

A) It would be covered under the liability portion because all injuries fall under this coverage.

B) It would be covered under the medical payments portion because it pays for minor medical injuries, regardless of fault.

C) The emergency room bill would be covered under the liability portion, and the ambulance bills would be covered under the medical payments portion.

D) Neither portion would cover the payments because the injury was the fault of the visitor.

79. Which statement below is true regarding Coverage E - Personal Liability?

A) Personal liability coverage pays for claims against a resident for bodily injury or property damage anywhere in the world.

B) The policy will pay for damages for which the resident is legally liable up to the policy limit.

C) It is not possible to add additional umbrella coverage to the policy limit.

D) Motor vehicle, watercraft, aircraft, and hovercraft liability are all covered by homeowners policies.

80. Which of the following is true about the Fair Credit Reporting Act?

A) It was passed into law to ensure that credit reports shown by credit reporting agencies are accurate, fair, and protect the privacy of people's personal information.

B) It states that an organization can access someone's credit report without a permissible reason.

C) The law expands the way credit reporting agencies can gather, access, utilize, and share credit and personal information without regard to the protection of consumers.

D) Insurance companies can disclose personal information to third-party individuals or organizations if the request is made in writing.

81. Certain types of expenses (e.g., legal expenses, loss of earnings, court costs, and interest accrued in a suit against the insured) are considered which types of payments?

A) riders

B) endorsements

C) usual and customary payments

D) supplementary payments

82. A contractor purchased a builder's risk policy. The contractor has materials on the jobsite, in storage, and en route to the jobsite. Where does coverage apply?

A) only on the jobsite

B) only while in storage

C) on the jobsite, in transit, and while in storage

D) none of the above

83. Which of the following statements about umbrella and excess liability policies is FALSE?

A) Umbrella and excess liability policies pay before any underlying policies pay.

B) They are generally follow-form policies.

C) They pay only for third-party liability claims.

D) They only pay when the underlying policy limits have been exhausted.

84. Of the several types of property coverage in a policy, which of the following statements is INACCURATE?

A) Coverage A applies to the dwelling itself; Coverage B protects other structures on the property that are separated from the dwelling by clear space.

B) Coverage C covers contents that do not form part of the dwelling or other structures and are not permanently attached to the buildings.

C) Coverage D provides protection in case the owner or the resident has to move out of the property while repairs are being made; Coverage E pays additional expenses that the insured may encounter if the dwelling is rendered uninhabitable

D) Coverage F includes coverage for debris removal from the property regardless of the cause of loss, and the limit is 10 percent of the Coverage A limit.

85. For which of the following does Coverage F – Medical Payments to Others NOT pay reasonable fees?

A) bills to treat an injury not caused by the insured's property

B) ambulance bills

C) X-rays

D) hospital bills

86. An explosion occurs at a paint factory, causing damage to the building as well as chemical spillage. How much will the insurance carrier pay for pollutant cleanup and removal?

A) up to the maximum liability limit for the structure

B) up to $10,000

C) zero (not covered)

D) the entire cost of the cleanup

87. What is the purpose of the GLBA act?

A) It allows banks to sell insurance as long as it is their primary activity.

B) It repeals parts of the Glass-Steagall Act (1933) which allowed commercial banks to offer financial services such as insurance and investments as part of their normal operations.

C) It requires property and casualty producers to explain their practices to customers related to information sharing and to guard their personally identifiable information.

D) According to the act, property and casualty agents must share customer information with third parties.

88. Who are the THREE parties involved in an inland marine insurance policy?

A) the shipper, the carrier, and the bailee

B) the insured, the customer, and the seller

C) the carrier, the insured, and the customer

C) the shipper, the seller, and the customer

89. Select the answer option that provides accurate information.

A) Commercial insurance companies include stock insurers, mutual insurers, participating companies, and excess and surplus lines insurers.

B) Stock insurance companies are owned by their investors, who receive profits generated through premiums and investments in the stock market; they often generate less profit than traditional insurance companies.

C) The earnings from the stock insurer's assets are used to pay policy dividends in cash or stocks to their shareholders or to fund reserve requirements mandated by regulators.

D) Excess and surplus lines allow those who are unable to obtain coverage elsewhere to find a viable option by providing coverage for products that more common insurers decline to cover, such as furniture, antiques and cars.

90. Which of the following is NOT considered an uninsured motor vehicle under a personal auto policy?

A) a vehicle that does not have bodily injury liability coverage or a bodily injury liability bond at the time of the incident

B) a vehicle that has lower bodily injury limits than what is required by the state

C) a vehicle owned by, furnished by, or available for regular use by the policyholder or any family member of the policyholder

D) a vehicle that the driver insures when hit by another party who cannot be identified

91. What does the Coinsurance clause refer to?

A) Property must be insured for 80 percent of its value.

B) Property must be insured for 100 percent of its value.

C) The insured must provide an appraisal of the property.

D) Property can be insured for any value the insured chooses.

92. Which of the following are included in the three main sections of a commercial general liability policy?

A) commercial property, business income, and liability insurance

B) commercial property, bodily injury and property damage, and medical payments

C) bodily injury and property damage, personal and advertising injury, and medical payments

D) commercial property, equipment breakdown, and liability insurance

93. A farmowners policy is designed to cover all of the following types of risks EXCEPT which of the following?

A) the farmer's home

B) farming operations

C) unharvested crops

D) farming equipment

94. The homeowners policy Other Coverages section includes a coverage that allows insureds to use up to 10 percent of the limit of liability for coverage A for increased costs for the enforcement of codes or regulations related to construction, demolition, remodeling, or renovations. Which of the following coverages is being described in this question?

A) reasonable repairs

B) property removed

C) ordinance and law

D) loss assessment

95. Which of the following statements regarding the TRIA law is INCORRECT?

A) Before September 11th, 2001, insurers lacked data to estimate future terrorism losses and included terrorism coverage on commercial policies at no charge.

B) Some commercial insurers excluded terrorism coverage from their policies or began to charge very high premium rates for the coverage after the September 11, 2001, terrorist attacks.

C) The TRIA law was enacted by the government to help businesses manage the risk of terrorism; it requires insurers to offer terrorism coverage, although customers are not required to purchase it.

D) Under the TRIA law, each state's government elects whether to share financial losses with commercial property and casualty insurers when the causes of loss are due to terrorist acts.

96. A homeowner woke in the morning to find that his property, the properties on both sides of him, and the property behind him were flooded. Each parcel is one acre in size. The homeowner's home and the three adjacent properties all sustained flood damage to their structures. The homeowner and the property behind him have NFIP policies, but the properties on either side do not. Which of the property owners would be able to file a flood claim with the NFIP?

A) all four of the property owners

B) only the homeowner and the owner of the property behind him

C) none of them, since their homeowners policies would cover the losses

D) none of them since the losses do not meet the definition of flood losses.

97. Excessive rains caused several mudslides in a particular area. A homeowner in that area has a homeowners policy and a flood insurance policy. After noticing mud in the basement, the homeowner files a claim with her homeowners insurance company. Will the homeowners insurance company pay this claim?

A) Yes, because mudslides are covered losses under homeowners policies.

B) Yes, because basements have more coverage on homeowners policies than they do on flood insurance policies.

C) No, because mudslides are not covered under either policy.

D) No, because mudslides are covered under flood policies but not homeowners policies.

98. A landlord informs a tenant that the building flooded a few years back. For this reason, the landlord strongly suggests that the tenant purchase a flood insurance policy. The tenant agrees it is a good investment for the premium and buys coverage for $100,000 with a $1,000 deductible. The landlord purchases $100,000 of flood coverage on the structure with a $2,000 deductible. A flood occurs, causing $150,000 in damage to the structure and $25,000 to the tenant's contents. Who would receive a payout and for how much?

A) the landlord for $150,000 and the tenant for $100,000

B) the landlord for $148,000 and the tenant for $99,000

C) the landlord for $98,000 and the tenant for $24,000

D) the landlord for $100,000 and the tenant for $25,000

99. A homeowner purchased the full $250,000 of NFIP coverage on the building and $100,000 on the contents. The homeowner has a $5,000 deductible. A flood loss occurs. The homeowner expects to receive $345,000 for the building and contents—minus the deductible—plus another $10,000 in additional living expenses because he has to secure temporary housing while the dwelling is being repaired. What will the homeowner be entitled to under the policy?

A) payment for the building and contents up to the policy limit, minus the deductible

B) payment for the building and contents up to the policy limit after the deductible and the actual cost of additional living expenses with no deductible

C) payment for the building up to the policy limit and up to 10% of the dwelling coverage for additional living expenses, minus a $5,000 deductible

D) payment for the building and contents up to the policy limit after the deductible and the actual cost of additional living expenses with an additional $5,000 deductible

100. Commercial property owner A purchased a flood insurance policy from the NFIP. Commercial property owner B purchased a flood insurance policy from a private insurance carrier and got broader coverage and higher limits than commercial property owner A. Flooding occurred on both properties after news broke that the private insurance company had gone bankrupt. Which property owner would be compensated for damages?

A) property owners A and B

B) property owner A only

C) property owner B only

D) neither property owner

Answer Explanations

1. D: Subrogation, or the act of surrogating (i.e., substituting) a person or company, is only possible if the insured is not liable for a loss and the other party to the loss is liable. The terms of this condition can be found in the Conditions section of most policies. The insurance company can only subrogate a person or company if it has made a payment on a claim, which means that the loss amount needs to be higher than the insured's deductible.

2. A: For an offer of acceptance to apply, *both* parties must make a written promise to abide by their side of the contract. (E.g., As long as the insured abides to the policy terms, the insurer agrees to pay for any resulting damage caused by a covered peril.) "Consideration" is the value each party gets from the contract. (E.g., An insurance company offers to provide auto collision coverage, and the driver agrees to the price of the *premiums*—not the deductible.) Contract law states that only competent parties can enter into a legal contract; this means that minors under the age of eighteen—not age twenty-five—cannot enter into a legal contract as they are not considered to be competent enough to make final decisions. Persons who are over age eighteen do not need a cosigner.

3. D: Dwelling policies are appropriate for seasonal dwellings if they are vacant for three or more months per year.

4. B: The main parts of a homeowners insurance policy are the property coverage (the structure and the insured's personal property) and liability portions of the policy. Tenant or renter's insurance policies (HO-4) are considered homeowners policies even though the resident does not own the building. This policy covers the personal property of the resident and gives that person liability protection in case someone gets injured while visiting or if the tenant is personally liable for damage to the building. Factors affecting homeowners insurance rates and premiums include claim history, the neighborhood where the home is located, crime rate, the availability of building materials, coverage options, coverage amounts, and the condition of the home.

5. B: To be eligible for a mobile home policy, a mobile home must be designed for year-round living and have adequate systems for heating, cooling, electricity, and plumbing.

6. C: The term *tort liability* refers to liabilities imposed by the law in the absence of a contract of agreement.

7. D: The parts of a commercial package policy (CPP) are the insuring agreement, declarations, and common policy conditions; coverage parts, additional coverages, and coverage extensions; and exclusions and causes of loss.

8. B: Vehicles covered under personal auto policies (PAPs) typically include private passenger cars, vans, pickup trucks, trailers, newly acquired vehicles, and in certain circumstances, non-owned vehicles.

9. B: Both scheduled and unscheduled properties may appear on an inland marine policy, but only the scheduled property will be specifically described.

10. A: The "Conditions" section of a policy (option B) concerns how insurers place certain conditions on when they will act or fulfill their promises to pay claims. If the conditions are not met, the insurers do not have to pay the claims. The insured must also pay the premium in order for the policy contract to be in effect. The "Declarations" section (option C) shows the policy number, insured's name(s), effective dates, the agent's contact information, coverage limits, covered property, deductibles, and premiums—it does *not* show excluded property or Social Security numbers. The "Exclusions and Policy Limits" section (option D) shows what the policy will *not* cover, and the policy limits refer to the amount a particular coverage will pay for a loss.

11. A: For a risk to be insurable, it needs to meet three conditions:

The loss must be accidental. (If an insured deliberately causes a loss, it is not considered accidental.)

The insurance company should be able to predict that the loss can occur.

The loss should be significant enough for folks to be willing to pay the premium in exchange for protection from a loss.

12. B: There are standardized classifications for every job type, and employers must inform insurance companies what their employees do and how much they make. The rate is based on the employee's classification and each $100 of the employee's pay.

13. A: Certain general exclusions are common to all homeowners policy forms; these include neglect, nuclear hazard, governmental action, and movement of the earth. Theft, falling objects, and freezing are named perils and not excluded. Homeowners policies are different than dwelling policies in that dwelling policies are designed in three tiers, with the lowest tier having the least coverage and the highest tier having the most coverage. Homeowners policies are designed according to the type of residence they insure, and all homeowners policies—except HO-4—are designed to insure residences that are occupied by the owners and their family members. The HO-4 insures the tenant's property.

14. D: Farmowners insurance policyholders have three options when it comes to causes of loss forms: basic, broad, or special.

15. C: Movement of the earth is typically excluded in a basic dwelling or property policy.

16. B: The person who leases a vehicle is responsible for insuring it. A business auto policy will cover vehicles owned by the company and personal vehicles being used for company business as well as any vehicles the company hires or leases.

17. B: Business owner policies are designed for small and mid-sized businesses; large companies are better served by commercial package policies.

18. D: The Equipment Breakdown Form requires the insurer to pay for the cost of repairing the equipment or replacing it at the actual replacement cost without considering depreciation. The form allows insurance companies to base payments on the most cost-effective means to replace the equipment; however, the replacement must be of a similar kind and quality as the damaged equipment. Insurers may opt to replace damaged equipment with generic equipment or equipment that has used or reconditioned parts.

19. B: An easy way to remember this is that an omnibus is a bus that transports people and goods. An omnibus clause, therefore, protects company managers when they ask employees to transport goods.

20. C: Flooding is a peril that is typically listed in the "Exclusions and Policy Limits" section of a policy and is not considered a provision or a clause. Flood coverage is usually purchased separately from the Federal Emergency Management Agency (FEMA).

21. C: An accident in an intersection would be considered a collision and fall under that coverage category; the other answer options are all examples of damage caused by something considered "other than collision" in insurance terms.

22. A: In the insurance industry, earthquakes are considered catastrophes since they can damage a home's structure and the contents inside the home; for this reason, earthquake coverage is not typically part of standard homeowner insurance and must be purchased as an add-on or a standalone policy. When in place, earthquake coverage covers the cost of repairs to a home's structure, the costs of emergency repairs, and the cost of the contents inside the home.

23. B: The law of large numbers is used by insurers to predict the likelihood that a hazard will occur. This means that the more a certain action is tested, the more likely it is that there will be an average result. For example, if someone throws a dart at a dartboard five times, that person is more likely to miss the inside center ring than hit it; however, if the person throws the dart a hundred times, chances are that person will end up hitting the inside center ring around the same number of times as the person hits the outside of the ring. Underwriters use a large pool that contains data from past losses, which helps them predict what the outcome will be, making it an accurate way to help insurers manage risk.

24. C: Long ago, goods were typically shipped overseas, so ocean marine coverage was devised to insure goods on ships. As trading expanded inland, inland marine policies were developed to insure goods while in transit across land.

25. A: The HO-6: Condominium Form covers the owner of the individual unit (option B). The HO-2: Broad Form is used for dwellings that insurers feel are too risky to insure (option C). The HO-8: Historic or Special Building Form covers older structures or structures with custom features (option D).

26. C: The DP-1 policy provides coverage on a named peril basis only.

27. A: Workers' compensation insurance is regulated at the state level, and each state has its own rules about which types of companies must provide workers' compensation policies and the types of employees for which those companies must provide workers' compensation coverage. The rules vary from one state to another.

28. C: A business owner policy covers small business owners for general liability, business property, and business interruption, but a business auto policy is necessary for insuring company vehicles.

29. D: Ordinance and law coverage is described in the "Additional Coverages" section of the policy—not in the loss settlement portion of the "Conditions" section; however, loss settlement stipulates that the cost to repair or replace the property does not include the increased costs to comply with any ordinance or law applying to specific repairs unless it is already provided for in the ordinance and law portion of the "Additional Coverages" section.

30. B: Common policy conditions in a commercial package policy (CPP) include rules about cancellation, coverage changes, audits, premiums, inspections, and assignment of the policy; there is no condition that includes having a certain number of coverage forms.

31. B: If a driver with a personal auto policy (PAP) of $20,000 per person and $40,000 per accident causes an accident resulting in $25,000 damage to the other vehicle, the insurer would have to pay the other driver $20,000—the maximum per-person limit on the policy.

32. D: Garage-keepers insurance was designed for businesses such as car dealers and car storage services. The purpose of this type of insurance is to protect customers' vehicles while they are in the care and custody of the business owner.

33. D: Speculative risk is not covered by insurance because it can involve a profit or a loss, such as investing in stocks or developing real estate. Pure risk, on the other hand, involves the possibility of a loss only, and one that is beyond the control of the insured, such as a fire, theft, or accidental death.

34. D: The watercraft endorsement to a homeowner policy covers liability for damages caused while operating a boat or damages to a boat that is docked; it also covers liability and medical payments for injuries caused by the insured while operating a boat. The limit for coverage for a watercraft endorsement on a homeowner policy is usually very low—typically around $1,000.

35. B: Vandalism and malicious mischief are covered under the DP-1: Option 2 Form. Freezing and collapse are covered named perils under the DP-2 and DP-3 policies, with certain stipulations.

36. B: If an insurance company paid a claim and later discovered that the policyholder misrepresented information on the application or during the claim investigation, the insurance company could file a lawsuit to recoup their payment.

37. C: Commercial property, business income, and liability insurance are considered the main types of business insurance in a commercial package policy (CPP).

38. C: The obligee is the party that requires assurance that another party will satisfy its obligations. The principal is the party that provides the goods or services, and the surety is the party that provides a bond to take responsibility for ensuring that the goods are delivered or that the services are performed.

39. B: A business owner policy covers buildings inside and out and any fixtures or built-ins; it also covers inventory and other property of the insured.

40. B: Homeowners may be able to purchase wind coverage either from the state or from an insurance company.

41. C: Coverage A includes structures attached to the dwelling (option A); however, it also provides coverage for materials on or adjacent to the residence premises that are used to construct, repair, or alter the dwelling or other structures on the premises where the residence is located. Option B is incorrect since detached garages and pools are included under Coverage B. Coverage A for an HO-6 policy *does* cover improvements inside the condo unit, including alterations, appliances, and fixtures; therefore option D is incorrect.

42. A: An appraisal is used as a method to determine the dollar amount or value of covered damage and cannot be used to determine whether there is coverage or not for a certain loss. Arbitration is typically preferred by insurers as a method of dispute resolution over litigation. In a binding arbitration, both parties agree that the decision made by the arbitrator cannot be appealed and stands as decided by the arbitrator.

43. A: Portable property is covered by an inland marine policy; fixed equipment is insured under a commercial property policy.

44. D: Physical harm to an individual is considered "bodily injury" and is therefore not covered under personal injury in commercial general liability insurance policies.

45. C: A physical hazard relates to the insured's buildings or grounds and can include injuries from a broken floorboard or damage to a home from a fallen tree due to a windstorm. A moral hazard is based on an action or inaction taken by an insured that could have possibly avoided the hazard. For example, the insured could have failed to check the home for broken floorboards or failed to repair a floor that was known to have broken floorboards. Another example would be an insured allowing trees to grow in a place where they could damage the insured's home or knowing the trees are in poor condition and not cutting them down.

46. D: Buildings and other items are considered "other structures" if they are permanently attached to the ground and separated by a clear space from the main dwelling. Structures connected only by a fence or utility line are also covered. Other structures are not always buildings; they can include pools, mailboxes, and fences.

47. C: Newly purchased vehicles fall under the definition of "your covered auto" in a personal auto policy (PAP) and are therefore included in the policy.

48. C: Buildings and contents inside buildings are covered when they are damaged by the weight of snow, sleet, or ice; however, coverage is not included for losses to awnings, fences, patios, pavements, pools, foundations, retaining walls, bulkheads, piers, wharfs, or docks. Coverage for lawns, trees, shrubs, and plants is limited to 5 percent of the Coverage A limit or $500 per any one tree, shrub, or plant. Damage by burglars is covered under the DP-2: Broad Policy.

49. D: Generally, auto insurance policies follow the car, so the car would be insured under the owner of the car's insurance policy and would have no bearing on the business.

50. C: The Federal Employers' Liability Act is only available to railroad workers who are injured on the job. Most everyone else is covered under a workers' compensation policy. Workers who are covered under a workers' compensation policy may not sue their employers unless there was a mistake or the employer acted in good faith, whereas a railroad worker can sue their employer over negligence.

51. C: The insured must send the proof of loss statement to the insurance company within a certain time frame. One of the duties after a loss indicates that the insured must protect the property from further damage or loss. The policy even includes coverage for reasonable or temporary repairs to protect the property and excludes coverage for repairs if the cause of loss is due to neglect. While the appraisal provision can be found in the "Conditions" section of the policy, it does not form part of the "Duties After Loss" portion of the policy.

52. A: Under the "Increased Cost of Construction" section on a business owner policy, the most an insurer will pay for the increased cost of construction is $10,000.

53. A: "Other structures" (i.e., not the dwelling itself) are covered for 10 percent of the dwelling amount, which, in this case, is $10,000. After paying the $500 deductible, the payment for the shed would be $7,500.

54. A: First-party cyber liability insurance covers hardware and software repair following a cyberattack; third-party cyber liability insurance covers the costs of regulatory fines and lawsuits.

55. A: Most things in the building that are not permanently attached would be covered as personal property.

56. D: Signs, fixed generators, and cash registers stay on the property and would therefore be covered under a commercial property policy. Personal computers, fine jewelry, coins, and other objects that are portable and may have a higher value than the actual cash value are insured under an inland marine insurance policy.

57. D: While the trigger that starts builder's risk policy coverage is generally when the materials are moved to the jobsite, the policy may describe some other trigger, so it is important for policyholders to thoroughly understand the terms of the policy.

58. Insurance companies need to limit their financial liability to remain solvent by placing limits on policies that they CANNOT exceed. The limits of liability define the maximum dollar amount an insurer will pay out for covered damage. While the amount paid out by the insured for covered damage should not exceed the insured's deductible, it has nothing to do with the insurer's responsibility for payment or indemnification. The process of indemnification on the part of the insurer should not exceed the limit of liability on the policy.

59. B: The DP-3: Special Policy does not have named perils listed for Coverage A since all perils are covered. To finalize coverage on a peril, one must instead review the list of excluded perils. The number of named perils on a policy does not dictate how much a premium will be since there are several other factors involved in determining the premium amount. Flood is not covered by a DP-3: Special Policy.

60. B: The term *subrogation* means that the insured has the obligation to help the insurer recover any money paid out for a claim; if the individual receives any money from another company, it will be held in trust until the case is settled and the insurance company receives its money. Insurers have the right to subrogation.

61. A: An insurance carrier's duty to settle or defend ends once the limits of liability of the policy have been exhausted.

62. D: The term *concealment* concerns failing to disclose information (intentionally or not) that is pertinent to the terms of the contract or would affect the other party's financial consideration to enter into the contract (option A). A warranty is a promise to indemnify the receiving party if the representation turns out to be false and the insurance company warrants that an insurance contract is legally enforceable (option B). Representation is a factual statement the receiving party can rely on that influences them to enter into a contract (option C).

63. A: Nearly all personal and commercial property insurance policies exclude damage by water that backs up by sewers and drains because of the vast expenses involved in cleaning it up and renovating. Fire departments do not have any responsibility for the damage that water backups can cause, and flood insurance only covers surface water claims. Pollutant cleanup and removal is covered separately.

64. D: In this case, it is a loss-sustained policy because the loss occurred during the policy period. It is also a claim that would be covered under an employee dishonesty policy, which covers dishonest acts committed by employees.

65. C: While the employee had the owner's permission to use the car for racing, coverage would be excluded for this purpose on a business auto policy. In order to have coverage for this type of loss, the car owner or person borrowing the car would need to purchase specialty auto insurance that covers the peril of racing.

66. B: Certain coverages may have an optional deductible; if so, the business owner only has to pay the optional deductible for that particular coverage. Other deductibles, including the policy deductible, do not apply.

67. A: The policy does cover costs, such as eating out, doing laundry outside of the home, and expenses for extra mileage to travel to work (option B); however, coverage usually lasts for the shortest time required to repair or replace the dwelling or within a specific time frame—usually twenty-four months. The fair rental value coverage *does* cover any loss of rent for insured landlords when they are unable to have tenants due to the home being uninhabitable; it does *not* offer protection for tenants (option C). If a civil authority prohibits insureds from staying in their homes as a result of direct damage to a neighboring location by a peril covered in the policy, insureds can the claim out-of-pocket expenses incurred while living away from the home (option D); however, this coverage is typically only available for two weeks—not six.

68. D: Insurers commonly offer unfiled policies, for which they can establish their own rules. Only filed policies have been reviewed and approved by state departments.

69. B: Builder's risk insurance policies protect buildings during the course of construction and are designed for homeowners, contractors, and people who flip houses.

70. B: Any person or business meeting the definition of an additional insured is entitled to receive only certain benefits and some amount of coverage under the policy. The police only need to be notified if a crime was committed or the claim involves criminal activity. The first-named insured has a duty to provide the insurer with an inventory of all damaged property, regardless of its value.

71. B: Commercial property and general liability policies do not cover losses when a professional gives advice that negatively impacts a client. Only professional liability insurance covers errors, omissions, mistakes, and personal injuries.

72. C: Pipes, flues, or drains that are underground are not included under commercial property building coverage.

73. D: The insured must meet all of the terms of the policy; the policy reduces or eliminates the financial risk of an unexpected event that causes damage. The financial benefit the insurer provides the insured has a predetermined amount, called a policy limit.

74. C: The DP-1 covers the named basic perils of fire and lightning, internal and external explosions, windstorm, hail, riots, smoke, aircrafts, vehicles, and volcanic explosions. The DP-2 adds the following to those coverages: cracking or bulging, freezing pipes, vandalism, the weight of snow, electrical damage, glass breakage, collapse, and water or steam. The DP-3 covers all perils except those specifically listed, such as flood damage, which is purchased separately from FEMA.

75. B: In an auto policy, the first number represents the policy limit for bodily injury per person, per accident for care, loss of services or death. The second number represents the policy limit for bodily injury for all injured claimants per vehicle, per accident for care, loss of services, or death (in this case, $300,000). The third number represents the policy limit for damage to the claimant's vehicle per accident.

76. B: Flood damage may be covered by a policy if a covered cause of loss occurs first and the flood damage is a consequence of the covered cause of loss. Flooding is not covered under a business owner policy, but if a covered loss causes flooding, the carrier will cover it.

77. A: Although each cyber liability policy is a bit different, these policies generally cover cyber extortion, website publishing liability, and the replacement or restoration of data. Libel and slander claims would fall under a professional liability policy.

78. B: Liability coverage is intended to cover large claims where there may be court involvement. Medical payments provide payments regardless of fault (i.e., no-fault coverage). This type of coverage is intended to prevent large lawsuits and settlements.

79. B: The insurer's indemnification is determined by the policy limits in place.

80. A: The Fair Credit Reporting Act states that no person or organization can access someone's credit report without a permissible reason, such as offering credit, issuing an insurance policy, or renting a dwelling. The law restricts the ways in which credit reporting agencies can gather, access, utilize, and share credit and personal information to protect consumers. Insurance companies are not allowed to disclose personal information to nonaffiliated, third-party individuals or organizations unless they have a permissible purpose (e.g., underwriting), obtain the consumer's permission to get medical information, or provide notice if they increase rates or deny or terminate a policy based on a consumer report.

81. D: Supplementary payments are typically included in a business auto policy and would be listed under the section that discusses supplementary payments. This coverage does not have to be added by a rider or endorsement.

82. C: A builder's risk policy covers the policyholder's construction materials while they are on the jobsite, in storage, and while they are being transported to the jobsite.

83. A: An umbrella policy is a form of excess liability insurance. In both cases, the underlying policies would pay before the excess policy. Excess policies typically follow the underlying forms; however, they may also include additional coverages, and they only pay for third-party claims.

84. D: Coverage F - Other Coverages includes coverage for debris removal from the property as long as the debris is the result of insured cause of loss. The limit for this coverage depends on which coverage is being utilized for that particular portion of the loss. For example, if the estimate is written to replace the roof of the dwelling, the debris removal of the original roof materials would be paid under the limit for Coverage A.

85. A: The medical payments coverage applies if an occurrence arises due to a condition on the insured location or an area that adjoins it, is caused by the activities of an insured, is caused by a residence employee while on the job, or is caused by an animal for which the insured is caring.

86. B: Additional coverages for building and business personal property policies include pollutant cleanup and removal costs of up to $10,000 to extract pollutants from land or water.

87. C: The Gramm-Leach-Bliley Act allows banks to sell insurance as long as it is NOT their primary activity.

The Gramm-Leach-Bliley Act repeals parts of the Glass-Steagall Act (1933) which prevented commercial banks from offering financial services such as insurance and investments as part of their normal operations.

According to the act, property and casualty agents must explain privacy practices to their customers, give them a chance to opt out of having any of their information shared, restrict information they share with third parties and ensure personal identifiable information is secure.

88. A: The shipper arranges for the shipment of goods, the carrier transports the goods, and the bailee receives the goods.

89. C: Mutual insurers are noncommercial insurers. Stock insurers typically generate more profit than traditional insurance companies. Excess and surplus lines provide coverage for products that other insurers would normally decline, such as hazardous materials, art, or classic cars.

90. C: In a personal auto policy, an uninsured vehicle does not include any vehicle or equipment that meets the following criteria: owned by, furnished, or available for the regular use of the policyholder or any family member; owned or operated by a self-insurer unless the self-insurer is or becomes insolvent; owned by any governmental unit or agency; operated on rails (trains) or crawler treads (continuous track—e.g., a military tank); designed for use mainly off public roads; located for use as a residence or premises.

91. A: The 80 percent coinsurance clause applies to coverage extensions. This means the property must be insured to 80 percent of its value.

92. C: The three main sections of a commercial general liability insurance policy include bodily injury and property damage, personal and advertising injury, and medical payments.

93. C: Farmowners policies cover family homes and everything in them, personal liability for farmers and their families, farming equipment, livestock, and farming products. These policies typically exclude coverage for unharvested crops. Farmers can get coverage for harvested crops up to the limit stated in the policy.

94. C: Coverage for reasonable repairs (option A) will pay reasonable costs for insureds to take necessary measures to protect their properties from further damage due to covered losses. Coverage for property removed (option B) pays for covered property from a direct loss of any kind while someone moves it away from the premises to get it out of danger. Coverage for loss assessment (option D) pays up to $1,000 for the insured's share of a loss assessment fee by a corporation or property owners' association.

95. D: Under the Terrorism Risk Insurance Act (TRIA), the federal government—not state—shares in financial losses with commercial property and casualty insurers when terrorism is the cause of the loss.

96. B: The National Flood Insurance Program (NFIP) defines flooding as "a general and temporary condition of a partial or complete inundation of two or more acres of normally dry land area of two or more properties." In this scenario, there are four, one-acre parcels that are flooded, which meets the first half of the definition. Two or more properties are also affected, so the second half of the definition is also met. Only the properties that have NFIP policies would be compensated.

97. D: Mudslides are covered losses under flood policies but would not be covered under homeowners policies. While it is true that homeowners policies cover more for basement damage than flood insurance policies do, a mudslide as the cause of loss would negate coverage on a homeowners policy. Mudslides are specifically listed on flood insurance policies as covered causes of loss.

98. C: The landlord insured the structure for $100,000. After subtracting the $2,000 deductible, the landlord would receive $98,000. Unfortunately, in this case, the landlord would have to pay out of pocket for any repairs the claim does not cover. The tenant would be insured for the full $25,000 for her contents, minus the $1,000 deductible, and would receive a payment of $24,000.

99. A: The homeowner can expect a maximum payment of $250,000 for the building and a maximum payment of $100,000 on the contents for a total of $350,000 minus the $5,000 deductible. There would be no payment for the additional living expenses since there is no coverage for these on a National Flood Insurance Program (NFIP) policy. A homeowner who opts for a flood policy through a private insurance carrier may be able to get coverage for additional living expenses.

100. B: National Flood Insurance Program (NFIP) policies are backed by the federal government; private flood insurance policies are not. Therefore, while commercial property owner B had the benefit of having comprehensive coverage, she did not have the security of knowing her policy was backed by any other entity, which poses a risk if an insurer goes bankrupt. By contrast, commercial property owner A had the benefit of knowing that his policy was secured by government funds.

Made in the USA
Coppell, TX
26 February 2024